Group Dynamics:
Spatiality, Technology and Positive Disintegration

CLIVE HAZELL
DIANA SEMMELHACK
BRADFORD CZOCHARA

authorHOUSE

AuthorHouse™
1663 Liberty Drive
Bloomington, IN 47403
www.authorhouse.com
Phone: 833-262-8899

Published by AuthorHouse 07/14/2021

ISBN: 978-1-6655-3144-3 (sc)
ISBN: 978-1-6655-3143-6 (e)

Library of Congress Control Number: 2021914063

Print information available on the last page.

*Any people depicted in stock imagery provided by Getty Images are models,
and such images are being used for illustrative purposes only.
Certain stock imagery © Getty Images.*

This book is printed on acid-free paper.

Contents

Introduction: Psychodynamics of Social Systems

1: Purpose

The aim in this study is to bring together several domains of thought in order to gain some understanding of individuals, groups, organizations and society. Toward this end, the following theories will be conjoined; the psychodynamics of social systems, theories of socio-technical systems, Dabrowski's theory of positive disintegration and theories of spatial organization. An outline of a theory of socio-technical systems will be offered. We will then add to this theory an additional dimension of psychodynamic operations and we will examine how these complex systems play out geographically. These ideas will be further amplified through the integration of Dabrowski's five-level scheme of emotional development and Heidegger's thoughts concerning technology. The Venn diagram below pictorializes this. The central area, where there is overlap of the four theoretical domains shall be our area of operation.

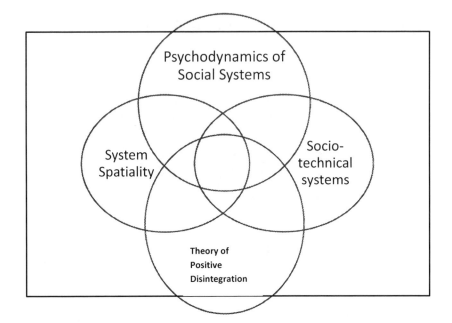

Figure xxx: Socio-technical systems, Psychodynamics and Spatiality

2: Prologue: Model of the Mind

Before we embark on the project of integrating psychodynamics, technics, positive disintegration and spatiality, it will be necessary to outline in broad form the model of the individual mind that meshes with, creates and is affected by these larger systems. Individual psychology is replete with examples of such models. Each of the major paradigms (humanistic, behavioral, cognitive, psychodynamic, developmental etc.) presents its own version and within each paradigm, we find a multiplicity of more specific models. Strolling past this array, here, we will commit to a broadly conceived version of *object relations theory*, a theory included within the psychodynamic paradigm, as an adequate model of the mind, the essentials of which mesh quite neatly with the theories of group, positive disintegration, technics and spatiality that will follow.

Object Relations Theory

Again, within the domain of object relations theory, we discover another array of models of the mind—Klein (1975), Fairbairn (1952), Guntrip (1992)Kohut (1971,1977), Winnicott (1965), Tustin (1972) and Balint (1979), for example. Furthermore, if we press the definition of object relations theory we are lead to include Stern (2000), Bowlby (1952), Ainsworth (2015), Spitz (1963), Sullivan (1953), Mahler (1975), Greenacre (1971), Berne (1996) and Jourard (1965,1971), to name but a few. We might even be led to include theories emanating from other paradigms. Freud's superego can be easily conceived of as an internal object.

Given this panoply, this embarrassment of riches, we seek some common fundamental assumptions. Namely, features that can be found in each of these theories, once assembled, would deliver an abstract, generic object relations theory broad enough to include all of these theories but not so abstract as to be of no practical use.

Fundamental Assumptions of an Object Relations Theory

1. It is a psychodynamic theory in that it assumes there is a mind of which a goodly portion is unconscious.
2. Much behavior is driven by the dynamics of this unconscious part of the mind.
3. When humans have significant relationships they internalize a representation of this relationship. This internalization, called an **"Object Relations Unit,"** operates as a template to help govern the person in that and other relationships not only with humans but also with all other aspects of the world. The template is "internalized and generalized" (Stern, 2000)

4. The most powerfully charged templates are those laid down in the earlier months and years of life, since it is at that time that one's existence is most dependent upon the smooth functioning of these relationships.

5. These internalized relationships are structured in the form of **"Self," "Other,"** and the **"Links Connecting Self and Other."**

6. The links connecting self and other take on many forms—emotional, cognitive, physiological, sensorial, imaginational, psychomotoric and so on.

7. Most of these object relations units are unconscious, held there by various means depending on the nature of the internalization. If the relationship was traumatic the means of holding the object representation in the unconscious is through the use of a "primitive" defense mechanism, such as those described by Vaillant (1998) and Fairbairn (1952). If the relationship was benign the object representation is not so violently and anxiously maintained in the unconscious and is more amenable to memory. These internalized relationships can be recalled and consciously relived. They can thus be updated with experience. Object relations units internalized under traumatic conditions will be introjected (Fairbairn, 1952; Guntrip, 1992) and will not be as available to modification through experience. They will, however, continue to exert influences, usually disruptive, on behavior.

8. Internalized object relations units exert influence over other internalized object relations units. In this way the mind may be viewed profitably, as Ogden suggests (1993) as a group of semi-autonomous sub-personalities. To this we would add that sometimes these sub-personalities are almost completely autonomous, operating as isolated elements in "the matrix of the mind."

9. Recall that most of these internalized object relations units are operating in the unconscious. They are, therefore,

following traditional psychodynamic thinking, operating not according to secondary process thinking, but according to primary process thinking. Thus they are prone to all the features pointed out by Freud in, "The Interpretation of Dreams" (1900)—condensation, displacement, reversal and all of the other features of infantile, juvenile thinking we find described by other developmental theorists—Piaget's sensori-motor, preoperational and concrete operational thinking (1969) and Sullivan's Prototaxic and Parataxic modes, for example (1953). The modes of rationality we apply to conscious relating will not apply as easily when we start to think about the unconscious group existing in the human mind. People can switch places in a trice. "A" can be "A" and "not A" at the same time and no contradiction is experienced. Such thinking is described vividly by Matte-Blanco (1981). Simply touching something, or imitating someone can turn you into the object, person or animal, much in the way described by Fraser in his renditions of "contact magic" and "imitation magic" (1958). The interactions in the unconscious object world, the "inner world" referred to by Kernberg (1994) that so powerfully dominates and shapes our relations to "external reality" are perhaps best captured by animations themselves. When we look at the phantasmagoria of "Ren and Stimpy" (1991-1995) or the sadistic exploits of "Itchy and Scratchy" (The Simpsons; 1989-present) we can visualize how objects can expand, flatten, contract, distort and morph, die and be reborn in a domain where the rules of secondary process do not apply—it is the "haptic" domain, captured by surrealists, by Dali, Munch and van Gogh, for example. In order to relate to this domain, the practitioner needs must slip into a binocular vision--through one eyepiece she can see everyday reality; through the other, the inner world of objects and their ever-changing relationships.

10. We may thus view the inner realm as a network of objects, connected by links. This situation is depicted simplistically in Figure 1. In it we can see the circles representing internalized representations of self and other. Some are large to signify that they are important figures in the internal world. Some are small, representing what might be called "minority figures" in the internal group. The links are most numerous between pairs of object relations units, but links exist between units. We thus have an inner network, an internalized social network and much of this network is subject to primary process thinking. In addition, elements in this network that cause pain can be ejected into other people, places and things via the defense mechanism of projective identification. This network displays many of the dynamics of a group of bodies and personalities in relation. We see that some object relations units are in the conscious, some are in the preconscious, meaning that they are relatively easily admitted to consciousness and some are in the unconscious. And are thus "unthought" and, as such, are more likely to be "acted out."

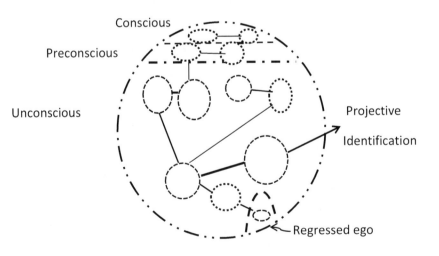

Figure 1: Diagrammatic representation of the inner object matrix.

11. This inner world of objects can be regarded as a system, that is, as a set of objects with attributes, connected by a network of links with flows along these links. It can also be seen as obeying all the other rules of systems. (Bertallanfy, 1969; Hazell, 2006) These would include concepts such as dynamic equilibrium, step functions, openness, closedness, interrelatedness, dispersal of causality, entropy and so on.

12. The pool of internalized objects operate with a good degree of autonomy. At any time one can exert considerable influence over consciousness, only to be replaced a moment later by another which has perhaps been triggered by an event. These triggerings obey, much of the time, the rules of behavioristic, stimulus-response, psychology. The sequencing of the dominance of the object relations units in the internal group and over the consciousness create shifts in mood, emotion, perception, cognition, bodily sense and sense of self and others. Sometimes two object relations units or a subgroup will occupy consciousness and this will result in the individual experiencing and evincing a conflicted state of mind.

    Corvo-Lopez (1999) elaborating on Kleinian ideas, demonstrates with great utility the concept of "self-envy" where one object might enviously spoil the libidinal exploits of another object, thus sabotaging the individual's relationship with the world, much in the same way that someone might "rain on someone's parade" or jealously destroy their successful strivings.

    Just as the possibilities of permutation and combination of the relationships in a group are enormous, so are the possibilities for permutation and combination amongst the internal objects. Such matrices are available for all sorts of computations.

13. Various theories have categorized the array of internal objects, such as:

a) Klein (1975), where there is a categorization of "good breast" and "bad breast" being processed under the two rubrics of "paranoid-schizoid position" and "depressive position", or

b) Fairbairn(1952), whose "endopsychic model" gives six categories—"central ego," "ideal object," "antilibidinal ego," antilibidinal object," "libidinal ego" and "exciting object", or

c) Kohut (1971,1977), with the concepts of "selfobject," "grandiose self," "empty depleted self" or

d) Guntrip (1992), who makes the terrifically valuable contribution of the idea of the "regressed ego" this being especially useful in cases of deep trauma such as found in victims of torture. In this, the individual takes the most pained part of themselves and the most terrifying aspect of the other and secretes them in an "oubliette" in the darkest corners of the deep unconscious, often, in a part of the body.

These categories are all extremely useful in charting this underworld group and its often chaotic and pained dynamics. They provide useful templates to the goings on in the internal matrix. However, the situation is so dynamic that it is an error to cling to one map and one map only. Just as it is not wise if one wishes to understand the geography of a region that one would simply focus on a road map, -- one should also consult maps of various sorts— vegetation, hydrology, geology, climate, weather, relief, topography, location, and hundreds of other distributions. By extension, one ought to consult a vast array of mappings of the internal object relational matrix, bearing in mind that it, too, is a dynamic system, subject to constant change as it accommodates and assimilates inputs and exportations of information of many kinds.

14. An important dimension of the inner world of subjects and objects, of self and other representations, is its cohesion. As mentioned previously, the inner object relations units are bonded together by multiple links. These links, however, can be placed into at least three broader categories. Following Bion (1978), they are Love (L), Knowledge (K) and Hate (H) links. Expanding on Bion's hypothesis, we argue that these links are different in bonding strength. The strongest links are the Love (L) links; next in strength are the Knowledge (K) links and weakest of all in strength are the Hate (H) links. Bion posits Negative K links (-K) and we here hypothesize negative H links (-H). When these values are inserted into the internal network of interconnected object relations units and summed, we end up with a measure of the internal cohesion of the personality. For example, an individual with a preponderance of L links will have a cohesive inner world. It is unlikely to split into parts and is unlikely to projectively identify elements into other people, places and things. On the other hand, an individual who has a preponderance of the relatively weaker H links and, in addition, both -K and −H links, will be much more likely to split off and projectively identify elements of the self into other people, places and things. This will be done in order to preserve the integrity of the islands of cohesion and coherence in the inner object world. In this reasoning, we follow Klein. The world, both inner and outer, is held together (as the Beatles and others suggest) by love. In the psychodynamic paradigm it would be said that the internal world and external reality is held together by a preponderance of good internalized objects over hateful ones. The same tendencies toward or away from cohesion can be noted at all levels of organization, from individual through group through organization and so on.

  Thus, just as certain objects (rocks for example) are fissiparous, that is, liable to split, crumble, fragment or be fissile under shock, strain or stress and others are durable, so the internal object world can be held together (by L links) or rendered friable (by H, -K and –H Links). It is interesting to speculate on how this could be mathematized using matrix algebra.

15. The inner world of objects is prone, especially when under stress, to the primitive defense mechanisms of splitting and projective identification. Grotstein (1977) has done an exemplary job of describing these and the reader is referred there to explore further. For our purposes, a cursory survey will suffice sans an examination of the history of the concepts.

Splitting is a "primitive" defense mechanism, meaning it is an unconscious psychological manouevre aimed at reducing psychological pain that is used from the earliest weeks and months of life and operates at considerable cost to the individual's contact with reality. In it, the person, in the imaginary and symbolic register, splits off an unwanted part of the self—an unwanted thought, feeling, idea, impulse or experience and sequesters it in such a way that it does not have contact with other parts of the personality. It is more "primitive" than repression, for example, insofar as with repression the unwanted impressions still may be accessed, albeit with some resistance, by other parts of the personality. On a large scale, we see examples of splitting in the fictional character of Dr. Jekyll and Mr. Hyde (Stevenson, 1886) and in individual and systemic "dissociative identity disorder."

Projective Identification is a defense mechanism that frequently accompanies splitting since often the split off part of the personality is "sent" somewhere else—into other people, places and things. In this defense mechanism, which can also be classified as "primitive", that is, as occurring very early in the life of the person and as being extremely costly in terms of contact with reality. An unwanted element in the person (or group) is sent, often with great force and through various techniques and channels, into the other where it resides. The sender of the unwanted elements now stands in a paradoxical relation to the container of the protectively identified entity. On the one hand, the other is abhorred because it now contains a despised or feared element. On the other hand it is held on to, perhaps even treasured, insofar as it now contains elements of the self. The subject feels as though the projected element is at one and the same time part of me and not part of me and that they must keep a close watch on it because it is potentially dangerous and also because "there go I!" This ambivalence helps explain the confused, entangled relationships that defy superficial rational explanation. A vivid and prescient illustration of this dynamic is given in Kafka's, "The Truth about Sancho Panza" (1971).

These two defense mechanisms, so often working in tandem, help unravel and explain the unconscious dynamics of the individual and the social system. They were developed by Klein (1975) and her followers (Bion, 1978; Meltzer,1973; Rosenfeld, 1985,1987) but they may also be applied to other object relations theorists such as Kohut (1971,1977), Fairbairn (1952), Guntrip (1992) and Winnicott (1965). Each of these theorize different elements of the personality ("grandiose self" (Kohut), "internal saboteur" (Fairbairn), "regressed self" (Guntrip) and "going on being" (Winnicott) and these may be split off and projectively identified into others.

16. The internalized objects can thus, with greater or lesser ease, depending on the strength of the links in the internal object relations network, be projectively identified out of the mind and into other people, places and things. The people might be individuals or groups which are unconsciously called upon to contain the split off and unwanted parts of the personality. Places will include locations, neighborhoods, regions, settlements, countries, even continents that will, in the imaginary and ultimately,

the symbolic register be seen as containing unwanted elements of the individual or group mentality. The types of "things" that will serve as containers for unwanted parts of the individual and ultimately the group mind form a large category, including everyday objects, fetish items, airplanes, artifacts, memorabilia, and monuments as well as metaphysical things, ideas that have been hypostasized or "thingified" such as -- ideals, narratives, concepts and so on.

In addition, these split off elements of the personality can be seen as forming what Hazell (2005) refers to as "imaginary groups" where the split off elements coalesce in the unconscious of the group mentality and there form an imaginary group. This group may remain submerged, unconscious in the group mentality and may not manifest until the historical situation arises that enables and calls for its emergence, where an idea, a person, technology and a situation come together in such a way as to enable the emergence of the previously submerged imaginary group in the form of a "movement," which may be large, as in the great historical movements such as the emergence of Protestantism or smaller movements, such as a call for a rearrangement of office spaces in a business or the creation of a new group or department. This movement will be heralded by the emergence of a leader or subgroup of leaders who act as the spokespersons for the imaginary group arising from the depths of the group mentality.

17. Ambivalence in relationships: The deployment of the above dynamics helps explain many features we see in human relationships at all levels—individual, group, institution, nation and civilization. Especially clarified are the bizarre relationships where participants seem entwined in an excruciating love/hate embrace. Each hates the other since it contains the split off, feared and unwanted elements of

the other and because the other has willfully forced these elements into them. And yet there is this obsessive mutual fascination. The fascination derives from the fact that the other now contains elements of the self, for not only has projection occurred, resulting in and from a distortion of perceptions, but also, elements of their personalities now, in the realm of imagination, reside in the other. They are identified with the other. "Where they go so goes a part of me". This can result in the psychoticlike desire to kill the other who contains these "evil" parts and yet also a tacit recognition that one must sustain the existence of the other such that those selfsame parts (which are part of oneself) have a place to live. This dynamic, by the way, may help explain some murders that are followed by the suicide of the perpetrator. The murderer commits the error of thinking that if they kill the "evil other" then the evil that has been projectively identified will be gone forever. Upon the commission of the act, however, they realize their catastrophic error. The psychic fact remains intact and unchanged. The repository of their unwanted parts is now dead and with this so died their containing function. Now the projectively identified elements return in full force, amplified by fantasies of vengeance and the perpetrator, in catastrophic despair, seeks to end the torment of it all by killing themselves.

Feuerbach (2013), many decades before the disquisitions on these dynamics by the psychoanalysts of the twentieth century, pointed out a similar dynamic between humans and God where humans projectively identified potentially troublesome elements of their personalities into the concept of God. This makeshift defense (which is a social as well as an individual defense) resulting, as defenses so often do, in an impoverishment of the personality.

On a far smaller scale, we see these dynamics operating in the conflicted family where, for example, a parent, uncomfortable with their own sexual drives or the regressive elements of their personality, becomes over-involved in the life of their child in such a way that the child is unconsciously encouraged to act out, becoming a chronic problem for the family system, while expressing the unconscious conflicts of it, especially in the leadership of the family. Family systems theory, especially as laid out by Minuchin (1978) elaborates on these themes.

Conclusion: The ground is now set for an explanatory theory linking object relations theory to the psychodynamics of social systems, socio-technical systems and spatiality. Using the notions of splitting, projective identification at the level of the individual and then again at the level of the group in all its manifestations, we can explain how people, places, things, and ideas become swollen with excess meaning, how this process then feeds on itself leading to relationships that are confused and ambivalent at best and, at worst, psychotically deranged and horrendously destructive. Often, all that is needed to set the process going is a nudge from the Real—resulting from such factors as distribution of natural resources, locational advantage or disadvantage, natural disasters, climate change. Often the nudge is delivered by a technological innovation that alters all elements in the socio-technical system and reveals elements in the group mentalities that were hitherto occluded. Once this nudge or shove or blow has been delivered to the socio-technical system it activates the defense mechanisms, both individual and social. Potent among these are the powerful primitive defense mechanisms of projective identification and splitting and these deepen the rift between individuals and groups while at the same time entangling them in what all too often is a death grip—a Mobius strip-like serpentine embrace that only painful self-examination can unwind. These defense mechanisms are unconscious. Thus the world careens along at an ever-increasing pace, with the "numbing sense of reality" (Bion, 1978) attempting to solve global problems with a vision that is, at best, cyclopean. This text, attempts to introduce "binocular vision" (Bion, 1978) in that it asserts that in order to address the pressing problems humanity now faces, not only the manifest, but also the hidden must be examined. True, the hidden is hidden, much as the Earth's core is hidden, but we may form hypotheses as to the underlying structures and processes, evaluate the predictions that emanate from these different constructions and, when we are lucky enough, hit upon a viable hypothesis and then act upon it. This text, for example, hypothesizes the existence of imaginary groups in the group mentality, the unconscious of groups. This hypothetical construct, when linked with ideas about technology and spatiality, may help explain much of what goes on in socio-technical systems. In geology, we find the concepts of the Sima, Sial, the Moho and Gutenberg layers. These explain much of what occurs in our planet. Similar constructs regarding the deepest layers of the human unconscious, individual and social, may assist in explaining much of our social life.

3: Psychodynamics of Social Systems

Introduction

Having laid out a generic object relations model of the individual and anticipated some of the ways in which this model might articulate with a model of group, intergroup and inter-organizational functioning, we now proceed to flesh out the model at the level of the group.

The Basic Group Model

Most of the time, behavior is explained as if its causes emanated from within the individual. This model is founded on the individualistic assumptions that are emphasized in "western" culture and economic systems and forms the basis of what constitutes the prevailing diagnostic system in the United States Mental Health system. Thus, for example, "depression," "anxiety," "bipolar disorder" are seen as diseases that need a cure that is aimed at the individual who needs a different set of cognitions or a different "chemistry" so that they might function better. This approach is mirrored in popular culture where, for example, violence is explained by dynamics that exist within the perpetrator. Only rarely are these phenomena seen as resulting from social forces and even when that is the case, the social forces brought into play are usually of a more conscious type. Thus, for example, the behavior of an individual might be attributed to poverty, racism, bullying or some other form of social dislocation. These latter attempts move closer to the approach being forwarded here and in other texts, but still lack the full explanatory power of a full-fledged "group-as-a-whole" or "psychodynamic systems" approach.

Also closer to the approach here is the acknowledgment of trauma in the etiology of the above-mentioned problematic behaviors. For when we introduce trauma into the causal matrix, we, of necessity, introduce social and historical factors which, again, move a step closer to the psychodynamic systems approach being forwarded here. In addition, trauma studies clearly demonstrate that unconscious factors play a pivotal role in the causation of behavioral and psychological difficulties. This is especially the case if we introduce notions of inter-generational, secondary, tertiary and quaternary trauma (van der Kolk, 2015). However, despite a renewed interest in trauma-based psychotherapies, the DSM 5 still adheres to the more individualistic "medical disease model" of diagnosis that ignores the psychodynamic systems approach being outlined here.

Also notably absent from prevalent diagnostic codes are models of causation that are based on interpersonal patterns of interaction where emotional difficulties are explained as resulting from interactions between people. One does find ideas of couples having interactional problems and "factitious disorder by proxy," it is true, but by and large the explanatory template is one lifted from the medical world where people have diseases, like Parkinson's or Type 1 Diabetes. However, even if we press this so-called medical model too far, it also succumbs to the same critique that I am leveling at the prevalent mental health model. A moment's reflection informs us that the distribution and epidemiology of many diseases—Type 1 Diabetes, Tuberculosis, AIDS—are driven by powerful social forces—social forces that are not only conscious but also unconscious. The examination of unconscious social system dynamics (USSD's) will offer many keys to problems in the medical field. We may argue, for example, that USSD's play a vital but overlooked role in the "opioid epidemic" and "the war on drugs" along with the many impacts of social factors on the immune system as delineated in the field of psychoneuroimmunology (Daruna, 2004).

Outline of the Model.

Wells (1985) provides an extremely useful avenue into the group-as-a-whole approach. Figure 2 provides an illustration to help guide the way.

Figure 2: Levels of Behavioral Explanation (From Wells, 1985)

1.   **Intrapersonal causality**: The cause of the behavior lies within the individual.

2.   **Interpersonal causality:** The cause of the behavior results from the relationship between two or more people.

3.   **Group-as-a-whole causality:** The cause of the behavior is seen as emanating from the "group mentality."

4.   **Intergroup causality:** The behavior is seen as resulting from tensions between groups.

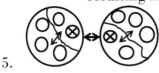

5.   **Inter-organizational causality:** Behavior results from tensions between organizations.

Explanation and examples of the five levels of behavioral causality

A simple story might help demonstrate how the same set of behaviors gets a radically different explanation and, consequently, a radically different intervention when it is explained at each of the levels of Wells' scheme.

Timmy, the class clown: A Fable at five levels...

We may imagine a fifth grade classroom. Ms. McGillicuddy is the teacher of the thirty-five pupils. Timmy, sitting at the back is being particularly boisterous this morning. At the moment he is making farting noises by placing his hand under his armpit and vigorously moving his arm down so as to create a rapid expulsion of air. This is causing considerable amusement among his classmates. Mrs. McGillicuddy, a patient woman, at first simply asks if Timmy would cease his activities, but he persists and the class is becoming more and more distracted...

This vignette offers us an opportunity to put each of the explanatory models to work.

Level One: Intrapsychic explanation: At this level the phenomena might be explained as follows. Timmy has a problem. The origin of his problem lies within him. We might, if this has been an ongoing issue, be tempted to "diagnose" him—perhaps with some sort of "conduct disorder" or a disorder of attention or "hyperactivity." To resolve this problem we would operate at the level of the individual for it is Timmy who needs to be acted upon. Perhaps he will be referred for individual counseling, be disciplined or given medications.

Level Two: Interpersonal explanation: At this level we might look to dynamics operating between Timmy and those around him. We might notice that Timmy only behaves this way when he is near Nigel Pipkin and Robin Flowerdew who might be "egging him on.". Our intervention might then be at the interpersonal level. We might counsel all three boys and separate them in the classroom. Or, we might discover that Timmy only behaves this way in Ms. McGillicuddy's class, in which case we might posit that his behavior has something to do with their relationship. If this is the case, then we might work on the relationship between teacher and pupil to clear up whatever might be causing such disruptions. We cannot, at this point, rule out that it is entirely possible for two or more levels of explanation to be fitting at the same time for the same phenomena. In fact, this is probably usually the case—behaviors are driven by forces at all five levels concurrently. Thus in order for them to be dealt with, an analysis at all five levels is usually required when attempting to explain and come up with interventions for problematic behaviors.

Level Three: Group-as-a-whole explanation: At this level the framework of analysis jumps up another level to include the idea that an individual might be expressing something that is "on the mind" of the entire group. One imagines the group-as-a-whole, including teacher and pupils to be a sort of "organism" with a "group mentality" and asks what events might have impacted that "group-mind" in such a way that, in this case, Timmy, was unwittingly enlisted to act it out. In a way one imagines that the group is under stress and that Timmy has become the "symptom" of that stress and, as with any symptom, is comprised of a compromise formation, a complex, densely encoded communication about that very stress. All we need to do now is identify the stress, decode the symptom and intervene at the group-as-a-whole level.

This always means we need more data. In this case, let us say Ms. McGillicuddy, using level three analysis, asks herself what stresses her class may have been under recently. She recalls that she gave a quiz yesterday. It was on Chapter 5 of the Social Studies text but somehow all the children had studied for Chapter 4. Consequently there was a massive experience of failure in the room. Gasps of shock and dismay resounded as Mrs. McGillicuddy handed back the grades. Two students, who were dedicated to high achievement, started crying. Others sulked, some tried to make light of it. Then there was fire drill and recess. When they re-assembled for class Mrs. McGillicuddy carried on without addressing the feeling about the "unfair" test results.

Using this data, we may now explain events this way. Everybody in the room was upset about the test. These feelings were denied, repressed, split off or otherwise defended against. However, the truth will out somehow. Timmy unconsciously picked up on these covert rebellious feelings and gave expression to them as if they were entirely his own. In all likelihood, he was not aware of his resentment over the test and is certainly not aware that he is being used as a sort of proxy by the rest of the class to express their pent up feelings of resentment, frustration and rebelliousness. Why is Timmy the one who is unconsciously selected as the repository for these disavowed feelings? Perhaps he has had practice in playing this role in other groups elsewhere; he is a "role specialist." Perhaps he is "one of a kind," the only person from a socio-demographic group. Perhaps he is low in status, for these individuals are often unconsciously selected to carry troublesome feelings in the group or society. Perhaps he is "on the boundary," peripheral—he maybe just joined the class, or is a visitor from another class or is soon to leave. All of these factors and more can predispose an individual to become an unconscious scapegoat and to be looked down upon and at the same time needed by the group as the one who contains frightening feelings and thoughts for them.

The intervention, when we analyze at this level, is at the level of the group. We identify the stressor (the unfair test) and "unpack" it, that is, process, talk about the reactions. We then problem-solve in a way that copes with the feelings as best we can. Finally we might consult to the group and to Timmy as to what has just been going on, that is, that the group was using Timmy as a repository for its feelings and that Timmy was falling for that role. Usually this leads to some critical evaluation of the utility of such a dynamic. In this last phase, the group is becoming much more savvy as to its dynamics and individuals are gaining more insight into their predispositions to play certain roles for this and other groups—and the costs and benefits of playing such roles. In Bion's terms, the group is becoming more sophisticated. It is becoming a "working group." It is also a much safer place to be since one is less likely to be used by the group as a dumping ground for their unwanted feelings.

Again, explaining at this level does not invalidate explanations at any of the other levels. However, as Wells (1985) argues convincingly, it is a good place to start since there is less likelihood of injurious scapegoating. In addition, taking this view does not imply a sloughing off of individual responsibility. If anything, the horizons of responsibility are expanded in that one is called upon to examine how one might be colluding with the unconscious wishes of others to act out their split-off thoughts, feelings and impulses. Moreover, one finds oneself, in a sophisticated group, examining how one might be enlisting others to perform acts, think thoughts and otherwise behave on your behalf as they live out split off parts of yourself. This latter can be very difficult to do since it of necessity involves a reclamation of that which has been split off and projectively identified into others. This reclamation involves experiencing the stresses and strains of the depressive position described by Klein (1975).

Level 4: Intergroup explanation: At this level Ms. McGillicuddy would think of the groups that comprise her class and think about the ways in which tensions between these and issues of membership and representation might serve to explain Timmy's behavior. It turns out that Ms. McGillicuddy, as a means of improving classroom behavior, had divided the class into two groups, the Sunflowers and the Bluebirds. Each team could score points for desirable behavior. These were tallied on a bulletin board in the classroom and the winning team would get a reward from a grab bag of gifts at the end of each week. Timmy was a member of the Bluebird group and this group had been losing for several weeks in a row. In addition, things did not look good this week. The day that Timmy's behavior was noticed was a Friday, about an hour before the results were to be announced and the children of the opposing team, the Sunflowers, were to line up and, one by one pick out a prize from the grab bag in front of the class. Despite the remonstrances of Ms. McGillicuddy, this had devolved into an emotionally charged situation with some taunting and teasing going on between the two groups.

Viewed from this perspective, Timmy's behavior can be seen as a manifestation of intergroup tensions. He was unconsciously acting on behalf of the defeated Bluebirds, defiantly expressing their anger and disgust at the situation they found themselves in.

Once again, to the extent this intergroup explanation accounts for the behavior, the intervention itself should be at the intergroup level. Perhaps Ms. McGillicuddy should review the costs and benefits of the "Bluebirds versus Sunflowers" competition she has installed and examine this with the students themselves, since it does present a life-learning situation.

Level 5: Inter-organizational explanation: When we shift perspective to this level, we think of what inter-organizational tensions might be channeling through Timmy. Again, we cast our net wider as we think of the broader context of the classroom. When we do this we find that Timmy is the son of the President of the Parent School Council (PSC) and that this organization has been very active since his tenure in this role. It has been active in petitioning for the removal of the principal, who it deems incompetent, and it has also been applying pressure on several of the teachers who they think are sub-par. Feelings have been running high in PSC meetings. The principal has felt under siege and the teachers have become anxious and torn in their loyalties. Most of the students are unaware of these dynamics, but Timmy hears about it every day as his father is incensed and on a mission to improve the school. Timmy carries these impressions into the classroom and they perhaps inform some of his behavior.

When we add these layers of data, we perhaps can see Timmy's behavior as encapsulated in a set of "Russian Dolls," only these dolls all interact with one another in very complex ways. We are led to have some sympathy for the players in this scene, beset, as they are, with multiple layers of interpretation. We especially have sympathy for the manager of the situation, Ms. McGillicuddy, who, while dealing with all of the conscious complexities of the classroom and its challenging tasks, must also diagnose this situation and act in a useful way in quite a short period of time. Viewed from this perspective, the task of managing a classroom is enormously complex and should be highly respected and handsomely rewarded.

Theoretically, there is no reason to stop our analysis at the inter-organizational level. Ms. McGillicuddy would be well advised to inquire as to any events that had occurred in the school, in the community in which the school is embedded. Even influences from further afield--in the town, region, nation and even the globe should be scanned for possible explanatory vectors. Events like 9/11, assassinations, nuclear threats, plant closings, natural disasters, mass shootings reverberate through the group mind at all scales and will be picked up by individuals who for some reason are sensitized to these events. We might note that these stresses, strains and traumata might be acute and sudden, as suggested in the foregoing list, or cumulative and chronic as with chronic unemployment, oppression and risk. Also to be included are transgenerational, secondary and tertiary trauma. Each level of analysis calls for a different set of interventions. Usually, since behavior is determined by forces emanating from multiple levels, the intervention will have to address multiple levels also.

The same set of principles and explanatory procedures can be applied to any other group or institutional setting: families, businesses, departments, neighborhoods, communities, regions, even globally. In applying such a multi-level set of explanations one is more likely to identify underlying causes and therefore to enact more effective solutions.

Now that we have at least a rudimentary idea of what is involved in the world of inner objects and the various levels of understanding behavior, we may proceed to the "cauldron model," a psychodynamic description of the dynamics of the underworld of groups and social systems in general.

The Cauldron Model

The dynamics of the group-as-a-whole can be best explained and described if we take the "pizza pie" image of level three behavioral explanation above, turn it on its side and draw it in three dimensions. The "cauldron model" below is an attempt at this.

The disk of level three (group-as-a-whole) explanation has been turned on its side in this diagram. We see the five members of the group, each with a small, semi-permeable bubble on top to represent their conscious mind which is, to a greater or lesser extent, involved in the achievement of the conscious task of the group. Beneath each individual hangs an individual unconscious mind, itself semi-permeable and suspended in the group mentality, which we may imagine as the group mind, as a sort of mini collective unconscious that forms with collectivities of individuals under certain circumstances such that they become emotionally connected. When the collection of individuals is not connected emotionally, this group mentality is not present and it would be called, following Sartre, (2004) a "series." Such a group is found in a waiting room or on a bus, if there is no particular stressor involved. However, the group mentality can spring into being quite quickly, especially if the group is subjected to some stressor that evokes an emotional response.

Figure 3: The Cauldron Model of the Group

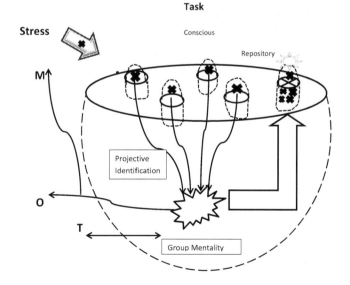

The group mentality is unconscious and itself has semi-permeable boundaries as it is in contact unconsciously with neighboring group mentalities and is nested in larger group mentalities. The arrows M, T and O represent three types of transactions that can take place across this boundary. These will be described shortly.

The task itself will create stresses for members of the group insofar as it resides in reality which is fraught with frustrations, challenges, difficulties and pains. In addition, we see that in this diagram an additional stress has been visited upon the group. This is represented by the arrow in the top left corner. The stress can take many forms—threats of layoffs, new tasks, new members, changes in roles, new technologies, new ideas and so on. A stress can come from outside the boundaries of the group, as is the case, say, in a change in the physical environment or a political, technological, economic or social change. The stress could also come from what might be construed as the internal environment of the group, as is the case when a member has a sudden change in health or behavior, or when that which is repressed or suppressed surfaces into the consciousness of one or more group members. This latter might include changes in health or employment status of a member. It might also include the revelation of secrets or, at a deeper level, the return of the repressed. These stresses evoke emotional responses in the members of the group. These emotional reactions are designated in the diagram with a bold **x.** Let us assume, as is often the case, that this "**x**," is difficult to cope with. It is therefore placed, through some defense mechanism or other, into the unconscious of each member. However, when the individual is connected to a group mentality, another line of defense is available, one that enables the placement of the unwanted, thought, feeling or impulse even further from their consciousness, for they are able, via the defense mechanism of projective identification to split the feeling off and send it into the group mentality. It is almost as if the human being comes equipped with a trapdoor at the bottom of their personal unconscious through which they can vigorously expel unwanted mental contents into the group mentality, which operates as a sort of psychic dumping ground. Whether this occurs in the "real" or not is moot. It is an imaginary function that will soon re-occupy the life of the group in symbolic form.

It is this defensive function that is available to us when we are in a group that contributes to the human necessity of being a member of a group. If we are not in a group, this line of defense is not available to us and we are left holding in our own mind all these unwanted thoughts, feelings and desires. This is what can make solitary confinement so very painful, at least for the unanalyzed individual. This line of defense is also what makes groups potentially dangerous places to be, since these unwanted ideas, feelings and impulses might well end up being projectively identified into us. We could then be scapegoated and terrible things could happen to us. This is the psychodynamics of why we are group animals at war with our own groupishness. We need groups not just for our material well-being; we need them for our psychological equilibrium but this exposes us to the risk of being scapegoated. The way we join, participate in and leave groups and the roles we take up in them represent our ways of resolving this existential dilemma.

Through this mechanism of projective identification, we may visualize the group mentality becoming charged up with the thoughts, feelings, ideas and impulses which have been split off and forced into it. This charged "force field" may now travel in several different directions.

One direction is pathway "O" (for Other) on the diagram where that which is unwanted is "sent" via projective identification into another group—perhaps another department, team, company, race, class, nation, religion. This group now becomes the container for these unwanted feelings, impulses, ideas and thoughts. They are therefore disparaged. At the same time, this other group is desperately needed, for without it the originator group might have to repossess the split-off and denied feelings and experience the original terrible anxiety. The situation is now the classic paranoid-schizoid position. As far as the participants are concerned the underlying unconscious dynamics are just that, unconscious, so the hatred, fear, suspicion and mistrust is taken in stride, with the "numbing sense of reality" and its irrationality passes unnoticed for the most part.

The second direction is designated by pathway M (for Malaise) on the diagram. In this mechanism, that which is split off is sent into the "group atmosphere" and becomes part of general a feeling of the group which can be varied—it might be "creepy," depressed, forlorn, listless, jumpy, maniacal and so on. Sometimes this atmosphere is so thick that people might say, "You could cut the air with a knife." This can be taken as an indication that the disowned parts of the group members have not been metabolized and worked through, have not been sent into another group (or at least not adequately so as to relieve the pressure) nor have they gone through the third pathway which is into one of the group members who is unconsciously (like Timmy in the above fable) called upon to act as a container for the split off and projectively identified parts of the members' minds.

It is the third pathway, where an individual (like, say, a Falstaff or an Iago), or sometimes a pair (as in Romeo and Juliet, or Lord and Lady Macbeth or Othello and Desdemona) or sometimes a subgroup (as in any one of a plethora of exiled, subjugated and persecuted minorities) is elected unconsciously to carry and contain unwanted parts of the group's experience. These individuals can then be understood as representing the return of the repressed, as symptoms that manifest in an encoded fashion that which is on the group's mind that the group doesn't really want to look at but cannot fully deny or eradicate. In this, the scapegoat presents a pathway to the truth. As Tony Montana says, in "Scarface" (1983), "Say hello to the bad guy...even when I lie, I tell the truth... You need me!"

What makes individuals prone to scapegoating? Several factors seem to emerge again and again as predisposing individuals, subgroups, regions or communities to becoming repositories or "dumping grounds" for unwanted thoughts, feelings, fantasies and ideas. They are:

1. Being a singleton, or being, "one of a kind." This includes occupying the extreme point of a socio-demographic dimension in the group, for example, being the oldest, youngest, best educated, wealthiest, poorest etc. etc.

    The singleton is frequently targeted as a repository for whatever contents are ascribed to his or her group in the most stereotypical way. Thus, the old white male in the group might be seen as rigid and unaware of their privilege, while the young black male might be seen as embodying the stereotype of "angry black man." These ascriptions are very powerful, subtle and usually very difficult for the individual to overcome. The repository will often be acted upon to behave in the group in ways that are consistent with the projected stereotype, thus cementing the original perception and creating "role lock." Even small expressions, verbally or behaviorally, that are consistent with the longed-for projection will be eagerly seized upon and used as evidence to bolster the claims. It is thus a good idea, when one is in a group, to do a socio-demographic head count—how many persons of color? How many males and females? What is the age range? Who is a singleton? Where do I and others stand in all this?

2. Being located at the boundary of a system, at its intake or export boundaries, or being about to leave or newly-arrived sets a person or sub-group up to be a repository. In addition, the individual, or subgroup that belongs to two overlapping or interacting groups is vulnerable to becoming a repository. Thus, the stepchild, who belongs to two nuclear families and often shuttles between them will be vulnerable and may end up as a container of whatever tensions, conscious or unconscious, are residing in either group or the multi-family system as a whole. The stepchild,

and other individuals in similar structural positions are frequently used as message carriers, and this role carries with it an additional risk of becoming a repository. One is reminded of the old saying, "Don't kill the messenger!" When we examine the underlying dynamics of groups, this edict takes on an extra layer of meaning.

The person located at the boundary or who has the role of often crossing the boundary, for example a "liaison" or "ombudsperson," is likely to become a repository since they will become the target of magical thinking. The unconscious is likely to think that these individuals, since they have come into contact with "the others" have somehow become infested with this otherness. Since the other is often invested with the projective identifications of the group, they are at risk of becoming seen as "like them" in some way. For these reasons, it is often a good idea to have a team or a pair of individuals, "work the boundary" of a social system, since they may create a microculture that can help ameliorate the impact of these projective identifications. This does not solve the problem entirely, however.

3. Having low status in the formal or informal, conscious or unconscious hierarchy of the system is a factor that renders the person or subgroup vulnerable to scapegoating. Projective identifications tend to "roll downhill." Thus, people who occupy positions with less authority, for whatever reason, are more liable to become filled up with whatever is roiling in the group mentality. Just as a receptionist in a professional office might find his or her desk and work space, occupied by and used as storage by those in power, so they might also find themselves being used as the unconscious repository of whatever is "on the mind" of the organization. Just as they might not have the authority to say, "Please do not leave your bags on my desk." They do not have the authority to patrol and enforce their

psychological boundaries and say, "Please repossess at least some of the thoughts, feelings, fantasies and impulses you have projectively identified into me." They are thus more prone to becoming filled with whatever thoughts, feelings and ideas that are being experienced and then split off and placed into the group mentality. We might also note that the receptionist is located at the boundary and is thus in double jeopardy. If they are also a singleton in a significant socio-demographic fashion, or even in a minority, they are in triple jeopardy. This "filling" of the individual might manifest itself in a number of forms. They might become emotionally, cognitively or physically distressed. They might become prone, in everyday speech, to "meltdowns". They might develop an "attitude problem". They might become forgetful, or manifest "irrational thinking." They might also develop physical symptoms, perhaps stress related, perhaps more metaphorical in nature, such as an "angry rash," vomiting ("sick of it all"), constipation ("full of shit"), leg cramps ("unable to take a stand") and so on. In this way the individual repository, whatever the causal chain, becomes the "group symptom," encapsulating in the compressed coding of the symptomatic formation, the underlying conflicts and issues of the group-as-a-whole. The ways in which individuals might somatize unconscious conflicts existing in the group is discussed, with further examples, in Hazell and Perez (2011).

Some isolated communities reputedly employ the services of a "sin eater." This is a marginal person, who lives at the outskirts of the community. People in the community, wishing to rid themselves of their wrongdoings will place a symbolic crust of bread in a bag hanging outside the village at a pre-appointed place. The sin eater collects the bag, eats the crusts deposited in it and thereby helps alleviate the villagers of the pressure exerted upon them by their consciences. In this structure we see what is enacted informally and unacknowledged every day in all the groups we live in.

Looking at groups in this way, we garner some helpful hints for leaders, managers and any participant who wishes to understand the group they inhabit. Namely, that it is a good idea to listen to those who are vulnerable to repository—the singletons, those at the boundary, those having low status-for they are manifesting, unconsciously, that which is preoccupying the group. They are valuable source of data. The trick is the kind of listening one does—it is a "listening with the third ear" (Reik, 1948)

4. Having personality features that predispose one to being a satisfactory container of the unwanted parts can create a vulnerability to being used as a scapegoat. This personality feature frequently comes from having had a history in previous systems; often back into childhood, of playing such a role. One has become a "role specialist." Thus, for example, a person, who in childhood was the sibling who stood up to an autocratic parent, might become the "leader of the rebellion," in the group. Similarly, an individual who become a caretaker in the family might take over that role in the group. The list of possible roles is indeed long—the "identified patient" in the family is at risk of falling into the role of "troublemaker" or "difficult person" in the group. These roles, it should be noted, are not automatically enacted. It is as if these individuals, or more accurately, parts of individuals are recruited when they are needed in the life and current struggles of the group. When they are not needed, then the parts or sometimes the entire person becomes "unemployed" in the group. Thus, for example, the counterdependent role specialist might be quite active during the "storming" stage of the group (Tuckman, 1965) but relatively quiescent during "tamer" periods of the group such as "norming."

In addition, the manner in which people introduce themselves to a group can "set them up" for the performance of certain roles at different points in the history of the group. Thus, the nurse, social worker, policeman might find that they have been called upon, unconsciously, to perform their respective duties in the group—caring for the afflicted, helping people cope, keeping order—and so on.

In this fashion, the scapegoat, or repository becomes a central person in the group, a sort of leader of an imaginary group, perhaps of the sort described in Hazell (2005). Leaders themselves are singletons and will serve repository functions for the group. The emotional strain of taking up these projective identifications and metabolizing them is a frequently overlooked part of the leadership function. In turn, the leader is often placed into the leadership position him or herself as a sort of symptom for the underlying dynamics of the group. Thus a group under duress is likely to promote and install a "fight-flight" leader; a group suffering from despair will seek the succor and hope provided by the pairing leader and a group that has "lost its way" will seek and find a dependency group leader.

What is projectively Identified?

The short, technical answer to this would be "objects". By this we do not mean actual physical objects but inner representations. To touch on philosophy for those interested in exploring further, these would be akin to objects as construed by Husserl (2014). These objects can be seen as inner representations of ideas, thoughts, feelings, emotions, fantasies and the mind can be seen as a jostling interacting matrix of these entities. Sometimes they become troublesome to the individual mind and then they are projectively identified, extruded and banished, sent out into otherness—other people, places, objects, things, groups and so-on. There is a cluster of object relations theories that help provide some beginning organization to these objects and their nature.

For Melanie Klein, the inner objects, especially in the paranoid-schizoid position are split into good objects, that are perfection itself, and bad objects that evoke paranoid terror. These two categories of objects can come in many guises—warm full breasts overflowing with milk, gnashing teeth that rip and tear, dangerous, invasive phalluses, angels, saviours, and so on. Thus, beneath the polite surface of a group's conversation we might find magical thinking imbued with such exciting and terrifying imagery. Clues as to the nature of these unconscious dynamics might be gathered through the application of analytic listening procedures.

For Kohut, the objects have more to do with self-esteem—narcissism. In this map of the unconscious world of objects we find a "grandiose self," inflated defensively with its own specialness and entitlement, expecting admiration and applause, turning vengeful and spiteful, perhaps even disintegrating when the admiration is not forthcoming. We also find the other extreme—the empty, enfeebled self, lacking self-worth, ambition or self-love, finding it hard to get a purchase on life. Thus these objects might get located in an individual, subgroup, or entire group as the group as a whole attempts to cope with issues of social self-esteem.

Fairbairn's world of internal objects is perhaps the most complex, with the largest cast of characters. There is a libidinal ego that strives to make loving positive contact with the world. There is an internal saboteur that attempts to thwart the expansive attempts of the libidinal ego in an attempt to protect it from re-traumatization. There is also the "exciting object" which is the entity that tempts, taunts and teases the libidinal object but never comes through with the "real thing," namely, a satisfying relationship. Finally there is the more conscious object pair of the "central ego" and its object which is adapted to reality and is energized to a greater or lesser extent by the access it might have to the libidinal ego. This, of course depends, to a great extent on the activity of the internal saboteur. Again, we might see these objects (almost imaginary sub-personalities) being projectively identified throughout the group and organization as it attempts to cope with stresses and strains of its internal and external environment.

Guntrip appends an element to Fairbairn's theory that is of use in understanding the schizoidal situation. In this scenario, the individual, under extreme duress, splits off part of the libidinal ego and secretes it in a sort of "oubliette" in a far-removed chamber of the unconscious, for safe keeping. It is rather analogous to the storm cellars found in certain regions of the Midwestern United States, or a "safe room" of popular culture. This internal manoeuvre enables the psychic survival of the individual but at the cost of liveliness and contact with the world. It is as if they have become a "cold fish" or one of the "walking dead"—alive but not quite. In fact, we posit that the cultural fascination with zombies and the like is a manifestation, at the group and cultural level of a vast underlying schizoidal adaptation in society—a response to massive societal, intergenerational trauma in the form of what can be taken as a social dream. At the level of the small group, we might see certain individuals, who, by virtue of their role, location in the group's organization or by their predispositions and other features, becomes a repository of the deep trauma in the group by enacting these schizoidal defensive manoeuvres so aptly delineated by Guntrip.

We may thus imagine group dynamics as an assemblage of several persons each containing multiple "semi-autonomous sub-personalities" to employ the felicitous term of Ogden (1993). In this we are seeing the person as comprised by subpersonalities that might get activated by various social situations, stresses and strains. What is being added in this formulation is that these semi-autonomous sub-personalities can be projectively identified into members of the group, sub-groups, other groups, people, places, things, ideas and objects in the broadest Husserlian sense (Husserl, 2014). Whether or not these projectively identified elements form "imaginary groups" as formulated by Hazell (2005) is to be taken up or not as a matter of explanatory convenience.

While the list of potential internal objects provided by Klein,

Fairbairn, Kohut, Guntrip and others (e.g. Meltzer, Balint, Tustin, Winnicott) are indeed useful in understanding what is "flying about" the room or the institution or even region or planet, The list is not an exhaustive one. The unconscious is infinitely creative and will generate as yet unencountered objects.

Leaders as Symptoms (Sinthomes) of the Psychodynamic Socio-Technical System

Following the theory of imaginary groups as described by Hazell (2005) we may view a leader, whether they are formally or informally instituted as emerging from the resultant forces of a constellation of imaginary groups formed in the group mentality or the collective unconscious of the group.

Hazell's theory posits that when a group is formed the individuals in the group split off unwanted elements in their personalities and projectively identify them into the group mentality. Once there, we may imagine that these split off part objects assemble to form imaginary groups occupying an imaginary space in the group mentality. They interact in the form of intergroup meetings with all the complexity that entails. The observation of an intergroup event at any tavistock or group relations conference will quickly convince almost anyone that this is indeed a situation fraught with tensions of all kinds. These imaginary groups can reside more or less "peacefully" in the group mentality or, if stimulated, may realize themselves in various ways. They might be projectively identified into neighboring or other distant groups and evoke group as-a-whole fantasies of varied sorts—persecutory, salvational, fusional, for example. They might be projectively identified into the group consciousness so that the group becomes affected by an "atmosphere," a miasma, a vague inchoate feeling—perhaps dismal, frightening, dreadful or perhaps hopeful, giddy, hypnotic, surreal.

Commonly the imaginary group will find a spokesperson who will act as a leader of sorts, a representative as it were for the underlying group composed of split-off part-objects. This is the traditional role of the repository. The addition here to traditional theory, however, is that the repository is seen as a leader of an unconscious ensemble of unwanted bits and pieces of the entire group. Thus formulated, one can see how the repository is regarded with awe, needfulness and suspicion, for they speak for treasured yet unwanted parts of the group--parts of the group that are unthinkable. Much of the time this representational role or leadership role is informal. The fate of many repositories is not a happy one which is understandable once we acknowledge that they contain treasured and unwanted pieces at the same time. Such tensions can tear one to shreds, both literally and figuratively. The repository is also found in the formally appointed leader. Even though this leader may have been appointed through overtly rational means—selection committees, voting procedures, platforms, debate, interviews, background vetting and so on, the unconscious, in its enormous power, will have its way in the end. The formally appointed leader will express, in his or her own way, the "will" of the ensemble of imaginary groups active in the group mentality.

Turning to Bion's basic assumptions, which are equivalent to imaginary groups, we may end up with a fight-flight leader during times of warfare. Winston Churchill would be a good example of such a type. Once the war was over, Churchill was voted out and he was replaced by Clement Attlee whose socialist policies might be more in keeping with a basic assumption dependency leader. The widespread fascination over the royal family and whom they are to marry or fall in love with can be seen as a pre-occupation with pairing. Somewhere in the group mentality there lives an imaginary group fascinated with mummy and daddy and making babies. Some of these thoughts are unbearable, so let us institute a structure to synthesize and perform these concerns in some ritualized, contained way. That way we can acknowledge and deny our interests at the same time.

The leader is thus representative of a compromise formation

in several ways. First there is a compromise between the wish to know and the wish to not know. Curiosity killed the cat. We do not want to suffer the fate of Oedipus who asked and answered too many questions. On the other hand, these groups' constituencies demand expression, require a voice in some form or another. The leadership position can enshrine this voice while at the same time muting it or encoding it so that only a few can see.

Macchiavelli (2015) wrote, in the sixteenth century, guidelines as to how to be a good prince. Perhaps one thing he left off of his impressive list is paying attention to the unconscious of the people, listening to it with the third ear, decoding it and anticipating its cues.

Since Bion, several other basic assumptions have been forwarded (much as several different types and categories of internal object relations units have been posited). For example Hopper (2003) posits basic assumption massification and basic assumption aggregation. These are said to be active in groups where trauma is found. One might also, building on Tustin (1972), posit basic assumption fusion or "floppiness," where the group fuses into one amorphous blob and individual differences are eradicated, and "encapsulation" where the group retreats into a hardened, protective shell.

In addition, we may add several other possible imaginary groups. Edelson (1970) posits four functions in organization that serve the functions of Motivation, Integration, Consummation and Adaptation, these corresponding to the ego ideal, the superego, the id and the ego respectively. We posit that it is possible for these elements in the personality to be split off and projectively identified into the group mentality where they form imaginary groups corresponding to Edelson's functions.

We may also mobilize Nancy's concepts of the Political, Managerial and Community elements of a group. These too can be seen as unconscious imaginary groups.

We may continue in this fashion until we have a "bank" of imaginary groups residing in the group mentality, each highly energized but awaiting the focal situation that will potentiate their emergence. This situation will require elements from the four part model mentioned later, namely—person, situation, technology and idea. When these combine in a synergistic, mutually facilitating manner then the imaginary group will have been called upon by:

a *situation* (say a stressor from within or outside the groups boundaries—such as a war, an historical concatenation or a developmental process taking place or a setback of some sort)

a *person or sub-group* that is set up to contain, express and in some manner "lead" the expression of the imaginary group. (Erikson in his studies of Hitler, Luther and Ghandi (1993a, 1993b, 1993c) provides excellent examples of how historical situation and the person can come together so "fatefully."

a *technology or technological ensemble* that enables, facilitates or, in Heideggerian terms, "enframes" the idea or ideas contained in the imaginary group or groups. For example, television performed such a function for a host of groups that were previously hidden—African American struggles for civil rights, the close up view of war in Vietnam and so on.

an *idea or set of ideas* contained in the imaginary group or groups—for example the idea of individualism promoted by the advent of the moveable type printing press, the idea of "spaceship earth" enabled by photographs of planet earth taken from deep space.

Edelson's motivational group may surface through the *person* of an inspiring leader who shares their *ideas* and uplifting goals at a time when the *situation* of the group especially needs such encouragement and when available *technologies* enable the dispersal of these messages. Analogous confluences of person, situation, technology and idea can help explain the emergence of leaders who are more managerial, more monitoring, more adaptational, more political, more communitarian or celebratory and consummatory.

Many intervening variables will complicate the picture. For instance not every individual "elected" as the leader of such imaginary groups will be competent in the performance of their role. They might also not receive adequate authorization or resources to carry out their function. The utility of the model still stands, however, since it perhaps provides some means of reading the underlying tensions, aspirations and anxieties operating in the group. One would keep a close watch on the emergence of leaders of all types in a wide array of sub-groups, and hypothesize that they have a constituency that lies in the group mentality and that this constituency is seeking a voice.

We are close here to Erikson (1993) in his comparative analysis of the child-rearing and management of infant care in the Lakota Sioux and the Yurok. In the management of the feeding schedules of the infant Lakota, he posits that frustration is deliberately, if unconsciously introduced into the infant's life so that it develops attitudes that will be adapted to the prevailing socio-technical system of long, lonely, demanding hunts on the high plains. The activation of this attitude, which is more prominent for boys can be regarded, in this system, as the activation of an imaginary group, one that approximates the "fight-flight" group of Bion. Perhaps this groups is linked with another which we might call the "perseverance under conditions of extreme pain and deprivation group." This group, following Erikson's observations and analysis, shows up in many forms of the tribe's culture—in the pains of the sun dance for example.

A similar train of thought is found in his depiction of the Yurok, where special attention is paid to toilet training in the rearing of children. This is then related to the observance of cleanliness required in relation to the fishing upon which the tribe depends.

It is as if groups unconsciously pick up on which imaginary groups are going to be of particular use in adapting to the environment, even given the innovations in the socio-technical sphere, and then mobilize early developmental experiences to achieve some sort of adjustment to this regimen. As we can see in the examples given so far—the Lakota Sioux, the Yurok, and those to be addressed later, such as suburban USA and the Maya— these expressions all have a powerful spatial expression. Thus the leader is evoked by combination of socio-technical forces that may be conceptualized as an engine of history, a schematic device we will soon proceed to outline.

Working with the part-objects: Reverie, Metabolism

Given that these dynamics can create tremendous suffering and chronic unsolved problems, we are inevitably led to the question, "How might we ameliorate the impact of these processes?" We find a clue in the work of Klein and Bion in their descriptions of mother-infant relationships. We may take their descriptions of the earliest months of human relationships between mother and infant and apply it to the manner in which human groups might "manage," "metabolize," "handle" or "process" these powerful emotions, fantasies and impulses.

In the earliest months of life the predominant way in which the infant communicates to its caretaker is through projective identification. It expels the unwanted feeling into the mother and makes the mother feel what he or she is feeling. The mother, if she is receptive enough (Bion calls this being in a state of "reverie") will take in the projective identification and metabolize it through her stronger ego and communicate the ensuing understanding back to the infant in words, tones and gestures that the infant can manage. The analogy might be to food. The mother might chew a lump of food until it is paste and then give it to the child in a form the infant can swallow and easily digest. (Desmond Morris (1999) argues that since this was probably done in deep antiquity and involved mouth to mouth contact, that it is the origin of kissing.)

This metabolism might take everyday forms of lullabies or soothing talk or play that gives the baby the secure feeling that its impulses and feelings are manageable and can be yoked in the human relationship. The result is a feeling of deep security, probably related to Erikson's "basic trust" (1993). This mother is what Bion would call a "continent mother". It results in a contented child, other things being equal. Unfortunately, some mothers, perhaps by virtue of their having been traumatized or because they are stressed and feel unsupported, simply react explosively and expulsively or with withdrawal when they find themselves containing the split of parts of their infant. Instead of metabolizing the feelings and impulses through their stronger ego they might retaliate and send it back to the infant. This has the effect of creating an overwhelmed and lonely infant, afraid of its impulses and feelings, adrift and cut off from others by virtue of them. Most groups, most of the time, are left in this situation. Thus, if one were to attach to the group a mechanism that acted much like the continent mother, one would diminish the power exerted by the projective identifications, reduce scapegoating at all levels of groups and increase the capacity to collaborate in rational problem solving. While there are social mechanisms for this processing, for example, art, we shall see, this is not always so easy. This is not to imply that the process of reverie is easy. Many times the mother, or analyst, or consultant, or person, or group is the recipient of the unthinkable and it is unthinkable not because of the simple benign lack of cognitive structure. It is unthinkable because it is a dreadful, terrible thought—one that is too much to bear. In these instances the resources of the container are strained to the max and the likelihood of acting out (of migrating to Bion's A6 cell (1978) as depicted in his organizing grid as seen in Figure 3.) is great. This latter will, unfortunately only amplify the original problem. In such cases of overwhelmedness, the contents are perhaps best dealt with by a group, the collective mentality of which might be up to the task of metabolizing the awful ideas. The group of course, would have to be a "sophisticated one" (Bion, 1961). Unfortunately, at the time of writing, these are very rare.

The term "metabolize" when used in reference to psychology is roughly equivalent to the term "process" as in, "I will need some time to process this experience." It has a variety of meanings but perhaps can be explained or described in systems language. We metabolize an experience when one or more of our "coding systems"({and here the reference is to Piaget (1969) and Lazslo

(1969)) has experienced inputs that are not easily assimilated, that is, not consistent with the pre-existing codes. In systems parlance this is called "positive feedback." In Piagetian terms it is called accommodation. The term positive feedback seems to imply a good thing, but too much positive feedback, in systems parlance, causes the individual to experience disquiet, anxiety or in extreme case shock and trauma, for positive feedback is input that calls upon the system to change, sometimes radically, sometimes in the form of a "step function" (Bertallanffy,(1969). On the other hand, too much information that is consistent with one's pre-existing templates or codes, which is called, in systems parlance, "negative feedback," or, in Piagetian terms, assimilation, can be boring. We experience habituation. We seek, as Czikszentsmihalyi (2008) suggests, a "flow," a sweet spot between too much new information and too little new information. I hypothesize this constitutes a triumvirate of "drives"—we seek new information, we seek familiar information, all in a never-ending attempt to achieve Piaget's "dynamic equilibrium"—an ever-shifting balance between accommodation and assimilation. Lest it be seen that I am here proposing a bare cognitive model, I remind the reader that Piaget took pains to connect thought and feeling, as did Tompkins (1962, 1963, 2000).

Unfortunately, such systems parlance has been cast, it seems, in an intellectual frame and has not been sufficiently applied, in my opinion, to other realms. Laszlo (1969) shows how this information processing model might be applied not only to cognitive frames, but also to emotional, political, religious, interpersonal, aesthetic frames, to name but a few. In addition, input into one frame of analysis, say emotional, will redound to and affect all the other frames of analysis, say, political and cognitive. The frames of analysis are only semi-autonomous and there is a drive for some consistency across and between frames—that is, a quest for some integration at the inter-paradigmatic level. We find this idea forwarded in a respectable manner by Quine (1970). Piaget took pains to point out that thought, action and emotion, for example, were all interrelated, a change in one subsystem called for changes in all the other subsystems. Stern (2000) uses a systems based approach to describing object relations as templates, using the concept of "relationships that have been internalized and generalized." Bowlby (1952) goes to great lengths to use systems theory to explain and describe emotionally charged patterns of infant attachment.

Thus, from this information-processing perspective, we may understand metabolism as the time the "biocomputer" (Lilly, 1968) and its half dozen or so sub-biocomputers—the enteric nervous system, the autonomic nervous system, the limbic system, and the several divisions of the neocortex—take to "process," to categorize, file, differentiate and integrate new information that can take on numerous different forms—kinesthetic, sensory, emotional, spatial, interpersonal, aesthetic, social—and so on. The task of metabolism can be considered completed, for the time being at least—when some sort of dynamic equilibrium has been achieved within and between the systems. Following Piaget, we would see a period of play, "assimilation in action" following the achievement of this new level of complexity, this increased level of differentiation and integration, as the new schemas are tried out in the world, reinforced and fine-tuned, perhaps shared with others.

What this means for teachers, parents, psychotherapists, friends and group consultants is that an environment ought to be provided that facilitates the dual processes of accommodation (adjusting to the new) and assimilation (affirming the old) while maintaining some dynamic equilibrium. This is like riding a bike—one is always losing balance and then regaining it on a moment-to-moment basis.

In this way the systems of understanding (emotional, cognitive, kinesthetic, sensual, aesthetic, political, ethical, spiritual, psychomotor, imaginational, symbolic, intrapsychic, interpersonal, social etc. etc.) stabilize through reaching a dynamic equilibrium. This stabilization occurs within each semi-autonomous subsystem and between subsystems. (One might strive, for example, for a consistency between the codings for, say, the spiritual and ethical realms and the political realm.) Individuals, groups and societies may be more or less open to new inputs. One way of conceptualizing this openness is to observe the obverse of openness which is the array of defense mechanisms, the manoeuvres individuals, groups and entire societies (and, one might plausibly argue, the entire species of humans) deploy to reduce anxiety and depression. Karl Popper, in "The Open Society" (2013) addresses these issues.

The processing or metabolism can take place through the utilization of multiple languages—written, spoken, visual, body language, gesture, the various aesthetic languages (the visual arts, poetry, dance, music etc.), the various logics we find in mathematics, probabilities, fuzzy logic and the languages of philosophical schools of thought such as phenomenology or hermeneutics. These attempts to re-code experience in other languages serve multiple functions. They help "reduce" the experience into different components—elements that are more easily assimilated into pre-existing schemas. They help one gain a sense of mastery insofar as what was previously experienced to be an inchoate, perhaps overwhelming experience becomes one that can be expressed or contained in a language. One perhaps shifts from an experience having hold of me to one where I have hold of an experience. Thirdly, languages are by their very nature communal. When we encode an experience into a language it automatically becomes shareable if not shared. Others may not understand it completely. It may come across like "Finnegan's Wake (Joyce, 1999) or Lucky's speech in "Waiting for Godot" (Beckett, 1982) but at the very least, something must be picked up by the "witnessing other" and a step is taken out of what can be the terrifying isolation of the overwhelming experience. Metabolism is akin to Bion's notion of "taming wild thoughts" (1997). It helps calm, provide a sense of control and a sense of interpersonal connectedness. In this, there is some hope. Given the amount of trauma in the world at all levels of society-- primary, secondary, tertiary, quaternary and intergenerational--there would seem to be plenty of material in need of metabolism. There also appears to be a dearth of social mechanisms for this vital psycho-social process. Not only that, there are considerable cultural forces that resist, much as the individual might resist, examining their individual trauma, the examination of group, institutional and social trauma.

Patrick de Mare (2011) shows how this metabolic process might be engaged in median groups, that is, groups of between 12 and 40 persons. In his depiction he shows how, once the underlying "hatred" has been worked through, a sense of community, *koinonia* or of "impersonal fellowship" may be achieved. I would argue that in these groups the working through process involves the metabolism of the projective identifications. Bion's Northfield experiments may be understood in the same way insofar as the interest groups that emerged served as sublimations for the underlying urges in the members of the community. Sublimation stands in inverse relation to projective identification. Vaillant (1998) points out that it is one of the "mature" defense mechanisms while projection and its conjoined twin, projective identification are among the group of primitive defense mechanisms, namely, defenses that are extremely costly in terms of the ability of the individual to maintain contact with reality. Sublimations include hobbies, activities, art, games, sports, crafts, science and problem solving. Thus Bion's and Rickman's "interest groups" can be seen as providing avenues for sublimations at the individual and group level, these sublimations being powered by a "fight-flight" assumption mobilized against "neurosis." As Adorno, in "Minima Moralia (2006) points out, "Every work of art is an unexecuted (*abgedungene)* crime." Once mobilized, these sublimations replace the paranoid-schizoid dynamics of projective identification that prevent the development of *esprit de corps* so essential for military and any other forms of morale.

Hazell and Kiel (2016) describe several other methods for providing for this metabolism of unconscious group dynamics. As Bion's experiments show, the installation of such procedures and organizational structures and processes is fairly straightforward. However, the resistances to such procedures can be considerable, for, just as individuals often find it difficult to process their uncomfortable feelings and resist, so will groups put up many superficially "rational" resistances to such metabolic innovations.

As the metabolizing function takes hold in an individual, group, organization or society so it takes on the role of a "calming object." As it is internalized, so it becomes an ***inner calming object*** helping to modulate the many self-states to which humans are heir.

Along one dimension, the metabolizing function relates to Bion's theory of thinking (1978) insofar as the capacity to metabolize may be construed as the capacity to think. In Bion's theory, this is equivalent to moving both down and across the axes of his grid. That is, metabolization involves the transformation of beta bits into alpha elements and from these into dreams and myths. These then are modified through the process of conception--the "mating" of preconcept with concept to form ideas which may then be joined into formations such as theories which then may be mathematized. Along the horizontal axis, the metabolization first involves forming definitory hypotheses—namely, notions of how certain impressions join together in "constant conjunctions" (i.e. they are always found together). The next step involves overcoming the *psi* barrier which constitutes a resistance to linking, thinking, curiosity, open-mindedness or putting things together. If this resistance is overcome then the next step is the notation, the "noting down" of an experience. This is followed by attention to the phenomena which is followed by inquiry, or curiosity. Finally, there is action, something is done in regard to the thought. This action may be well thought out or thought through ((i.e. highly metabolized as in the cells in the lower right hand corner of the grid (Figure 3)) or it may be more akin to acting out—a rapid reaction to a sensory impression—a beta bit—without notation, attention or inquiry. This latter is roughly equivalent to what happens in unmetabolized projective identification—a person picks something up from their internal or external world and just does something with it—acts upon impulse or projectively identifies it somewhere else. When asked about their intentions, they are genuinely at a loss for, essentially, there was hardly any thinking at all. In addition we might notice an obdurate *psi* barrier—a strong resistance to do any thinking, or, in Bion's terms, an unwillingness to have ones cogitations float with relative freedom across the cells of the grid.

Bion's Grid								
		Defin atory Hypo theses	Psi	Nota tion	Atten tion	Inquiry	Action	...n,
A	beta elements	A1	A2				A6	
B	alpha elements	B1	B2	B3	B4	B5	B6	...Bn
C	Dream Thoughts	C1	C2	C3	C4	C5	C6	...Cn
D	Pre conception	D1	D2	D3	D4	D5	D6	...Dn
E	Conception	E1	E2	E3	E4	E5	E6	...En
F	Concept	F1	F2	F3	F4	F5	F6	...Fn
G	Scientific Deductive System		G2					
H	Algebraic Calculus							

Figure 3: Bion's Grid: A Theory of Thinking.

The necessity of willfully building such metabolic functions into organizations has increased recently and will continue to increase because of the powerful impact of technology on society. In chapter II we outline what may be naively called the "engine of history". In this model, the mutative and (to employ Heidegger's felicitous formulation) the revelatory function of technology is emphasized. Technology impacts society in all ways imaginable. Each "wave' of technology (Toffler, 1984) brings about enormous, sometimes cataclysmic effects that redound through the centuries. On a global level, for example, humans are still adapting to the advent of the moveable type printing press. The Gutenberg galaxy has not yet been fully supplanted by the Global Village (McLuhan 1994, 2001, 2011) and this impacts every aspect of human existence. The pace of technological change is increasing, such that a radical change is introduced within the span of a generation, or even a decade rather than the millennia it took in prehistoric times, in what Bowlby terms out "environment of adaptation" (1952,1976,1982,1983). These changes not only affect the conscious realm of behavior, culture and organizational boundary management, they also function in the way of traumata—traumata that require processing in an ever-increasing amount. The model of Emery and Trist (1965) is especially useful in charting these changes. We have clearly moved away from the "earlier' environmental textures they posit (Placid Random and Placid Clustered) and might find it hard to find a spot on earth that had their third texture, namely, the Dynamic Reactive. Far more common is the Turbulent Field environment with much of the planet moving towards the Vortical environmental texture. Humans' "environment of adaptation" is a very stable socio-technical one. Witness the millennia between the invention and utilization of fire, the invention of writing and the advent of agriculture. Each of these had enormous social-psychological impacts that reverberated around the planet and, one could argue, are still, in some isolated areas, still being integrated into social systems in the 21st century. However, recently, humans are radically altering their socio-technical environments several times within the period of a lifetime. Without the institutionally-provided means to think through and feel through these changes, humans will act more and more like victims of PTSD, and this will be in addition to the vast amount of trauma already left unrecognized and unprocessed. The situation is thus ripe for symptom-formation. Technology clearly, "makes things better", but we also see that things tend not to improve as much as we thought and that we inherit many unforeseen problems. Many of these have to do with the massive impacts of technology in its socially mutative and revelatory functions not being "worked through". Structures and processes that are being suggested here would provide one avenue for working through these impacts on all levels of social organization.

Thus one may see that the pressure to think things through in a "Bionian" fashion has been increased by the changes unleashed by technology. These pressures are in addition to the usual level of pressure experienced by humans, plus the challenges of working through the multiple types of trauma, trauma that has been accumulating throughout the ages and which is revealed and amplified, in turn, by new technologies.

We now turn to the description of a generic model of the socio technical system, first examining its more overt dynamics (which nevertheless are still usually not noted) and then moving on to describe the more covert dynamics.

II

Socio-Technical Systems

1: The Socio-Technical System

In this section we will describe the functioning of what might be regarded as an engine of history. Figure 4 delineates the properties of the socio-technical system. It is based on the ideas of McGinn (1990). The basic assumption of the model is that a society, being a group of individuals gathered together upon a piece of land to achieve an end, is comprised (for the sake of exposition) of nine components; political, cultural, religious, economic, ideational, material, aesthetic, individual, behavioral and social. These nine interacting elements (let us call them the 'PIBSCREAM') also have sub-components. They also intersect with the physical environment in which the society is situated. The PIBSCREAM both shapes and is shaped by the physical environment.

Out of this intersection of the society and physical environment emerges an *invention*. This then *diffuses*, is *used* and *adapted* to different functions and encounters *resistance*. Ultimately the technology impacts both the physical environment and the PIBSCREAM. The process is cyclic. Historically, the speed of the cycling process and consequent social change, has increased exponentially such that very few people live nowadays in a stable socio-technical environment. This places considerable demands on human beings who have spent most of their evolutionary history in a relatively stable socio-technical environment.

In the very center of this system sits the individual. This individual is located inside a family, a social network and probably a number of groups and institutions. These, to a greater or lesser extent, may help the individual articulate their personality with the larger socio-technical system. This will be done with a varying degree of success depending on multiple factors. For example, some individuals by virtue of their developmental history may find it extremely difficult to decode the ever changing socio technical system they inhabit. This process becomes ever more challenging as the speed of technological development and the ensuing social change speeds up. Additionally, some families might operate more as closed systems, thus depriving the growing child and adolescent with a broad range of contacts with the evolving socio-technical system. As a further example, some regions, as a result of a complex of geographical, historical and psycho-geographical factors, may find themselves in a rather insulated situation, shut off from socio-technical changes sweeping through neighboring regions or other parts of the world. Through this dynamic, inter-regional tensions are created.

At the level of the individual we may apply a Piagetian-systems model. The individual, placed in the center of this system, is engaged in processes of accommodation to and assimilation of new information from all aspects of the socio-technical system, maintaining, one would hope, a dynamic equilibrium. Mental health issues can thus be understood as resulting from the relative success of the individual in developing, generating, maintaining and testing out new codes having to do with the socio-technical system. These variations in adaptation will have a spatial expression. In deep history the rate of change was slow, so the demands placed on the cognitive systems (broadly defined) of individuals was not as great. One could rely on tradition or one might safely be instructed by one's parents or forebears. More recently, especially since the industrial revolution and at an ever-increasing rate in the twentieth and twenty-first centuries, the "clock speed" of the "socio-technical engine" has increased enormously, placing hitherto unseen pressures on the individual and her ensconcing institutions to re-program and create new mental maps of the socio-technical sphere. One could further argue that as we venture further into the twenty-first century, the socio-technical environment has become, in Emery and Trist's (1969) parlance, "vortical", thus requiring a cognitive map that itself can contain such fluidity if it is to be well-adapted. At the same time, very little in the way of study or support is offered in this realm. Much of history is written as if it is a chronicle of personalities, ideas and power, rather than as a story driven, in large part, by technological changes and the ubiquitous change wrought by this.

Figure 4: <u>THE SOCIO-TECHNICAL SYSTEM</u>

This operates as a system, i.e. all parts are inter-related and affect one another in a never-ending process of self-equilibration.

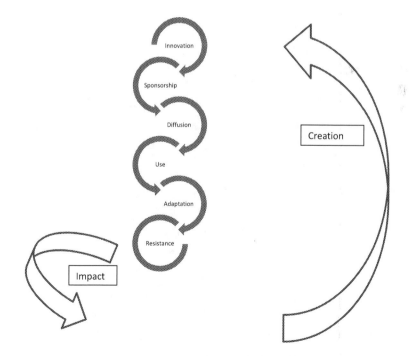

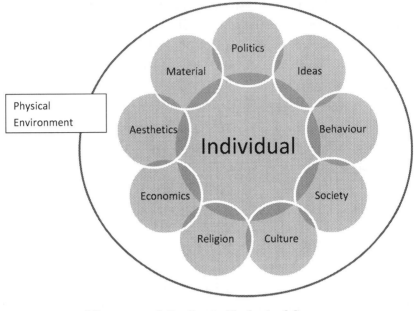

<u>Elements of the Socio-Technical System</u>

<u>The Process</u>

<u>Invention</u>

This is the process whereby a technology is invented, is brought into existence and, like all the other elements in the model, is a complex system in and of itself. Following are some of the questions to be asked in this domain: who invents? How are things invented? What happens to inventors? Is technology invented by individuals, teams or in vast collaborative enterprises such as the Manhattan project and its development of the atom bomb? Why do inventors invent? What is the relationship of education to invention, does it always help? What political or religious systems promote invention? How important are patent and other laws to the invention process? What is the attitude towards invention? What is the inventor's relationship to his or her parents? How are inventions related to one another (the bicycle to the airplane, the refrigerator to the rocket)?

The answers to these questions and others will determine the overall inventiveness of a society. Some will see invention as a positive thing and support it in many ways, while others may have resistances to innovation for various reasons. In the former case, one will expect to see a society that changes in multiple ways, while in the latter case the society will tend to be (*ceteris paribus*) more stable.

Diffusion

This has to do with the way in which and especially the speed at which technology spreads. In some societies, for example, there is very little "spread" of technologies. For example, television very soon saturated the USA and Europe but took much longer in many other countries. A similar pattern can be found with personal computers. These differences in the rate of adoption can be explained by a host of variables. The wealth of the population is one. If people are poor, they simply cannot afford the device. Infrastructure is another reason. If there is no electricity in one's village then electrical devices make no sense. People also have to know about a technology before they can adopt it. Therefore the informational structure and process of a society will affect the rate of spread. In the U.S., for example, information spreads far and wide through multiple media. There is also a high level of motivation, economically and culturally driven, to share and promulgate technological information.

Finally, the rate of diffusion is affected by resistances — resistances that range from geographical factors — long distances, mountain barriers, lack of transportation — but also include cultural resistances, taboos, values, social norms and political and religious factors. Examples of these will be given when we get to the topic of 'resistance.' One can already see here how all of the elements in this system interact. The rate of diffusion is affected by resistance, by the process of invention, by patterns of use, by possibilities for adaptation and on and on in an extremely complex fashion.

Use

This concept refers to the typical patterns of use of a given technology. A classic example is that of the steam engine, invented by Hero of Alexandria some 2000 years B.P. (Before Present). The Roman Empire, however, only used it as a toy or a decoration. Arguably they had slaves to do heavy work and thus had no use for steam power as is interestingly amplified in the novel by William Golding, (1972). Similarly the Chinese develop gun powder but use it for fireworks. Europeans, encountering gun powder centuries later, use it for weapons, perhaps because they are in a very unstable, competitive political environment.

Sometimes, a technology is developed and, while amazing, serves little use. The early Wright Flyers were mostly carnival attractions. Boole's Boolean algebra sat in a library relatively unnoticed for about a century before its application to digital electronics was realized.

These stories alert us to the importance of storage systems – means of storing ideas and designs for technologies that seem to have no current use. The establishment and maintenance of such social memory systems rests upon ideas regarding the utility of knowledge and the value of knowledge for its own sake.

Sometimes, for want of a use, technologies founder because they can find no sponsor. Marconi, with his ideas on radio, was rejected by the Italian government, but accepted by the British, because they saw in it a use for administering their enormous empire.

Sometimes uses emerge for a technology over a long period of time. For example, the laser has a decades-long history of new uses being developed for it. New uses are still being developed for it. An early use was the 'welding' of the retina at the back of the eye to help individuals retain their eyesight. Later on lasers are used in seismology, sighting, reading bar codes, light shows, and pointers. Probably many more uses await us in the future.

Sponsorship

Integral to the use and spread of a technology is the extent to which the technology is sponsored by influential individuals, groups or constituencies.

As previously mentioned, Guglielmo Marconi, when he first approached the Italian government with his ideas on radio, was rejected. His wealthy mother, however, had connections in England and the British government was willing to sponsor him because they saw the technology as very helpful in their maritime ventures and in their efforts to run an empire. Once Marconi had such a powerful and wealthy sponsor, he was able to develop his technology.

As a negative example, we may note that J.P. Morgan was unwilling to sponsor Nikola Tesla's Wardenclyffe project – a project that could ostensibly provide wireless electricity for the entire planet. Morgan could not see how to turn a profit from it. "If anyone can use it, where do I put the meter?" was his famous question.

An inventor, to be successful, must not only possess the intellectual and technical gifts, he must also have connections, or at least, know how to generate them. Such connections will be a function of the social networks operating in the social system.

Adaptation

Individuals and groups typically alter technologies to meet their individual and local needs. Automobiles designed and built in Detroit may be stripped and rebuilt when they are used in a rural village or may be "tricked out" with hydraulics and tinted windows to express aesthetic taste or cultural values.

One way of developing ideas for new products is to observe

how people alter technology to meet their needs and then to manufacture and sell the altered product. For example, in the late 1960's college students would go through long and involved processes to make their new blue jeans look "faded" – soaking them in cold water over night and rubbing them with house bricks. It did not take very long before manufacturers recognized there was a market for "stone washed" jeans.

The very complex issues of "technology transfer" (where a technology is moved from one culture to another one) are very much related to this topic. Just because a technology works well in one place, doesn't mean it will work well in another place. Adaptations will have to be made. For example, Stephen Lansing (2007) the anthropologist, describes how, when the "Green Revolution" introduced new strains of super productive rice into Bali, rather than engendering increased yields, it brought about reduced yields and infestations of pests. For the first time farmers had to use pesticides. Lansing goes on to explain that this was a result of the new crops not being adapted to the local cropping patterns and water management. These techniques had been developed over centuries and were managed by the water Temples and the high priest. Lansing and his colleagues developed a computer model that took these ecological factors into consideration. Interestingly, the model confirmed the recommendations made by the water priests and brought on increased yields. This case is also instructive in that it shows that the usual trope of an inevitable conflict between "technology and religion" is limited in its applicability for in this case the technological algorithm supported the ancient wisdom of the water temple priests.

Clearly, technology, before it is introduced to a new environment must be carefully evaluated and perhaps altered in its basic nature or in its deployment so as to obtain benefit or at best do no harm.

E.F. Schumacher (1973) in "Small is Beautiful" shows how many "large" technologies while perhaps well adapted in some ways to highly industrialized settings may not be well adapted to agricultural economies where smaller versions might be beautifully effective.

Resistance

Although the story of technology usually emphasizes its benefits, any new technology usually harms some individual or group in some way. This individual or group will then attempt to resist the new technology. There are many reasons for resistance to technology and examples are rife. The Luddites were groups that would break into factories in the early phases of the industrial revolution and break the machinery. They resented the way the new textile mills had broken up the cottage industry mode of textile manufacturing.

The so-called "morning after" pill, RU-486 that induces abortions in pregnant women, while accepted in Europe, took many years before it became accepted in the U.S.A., where it was regarded as unethical. Even when it was finally accepted by the F.D.A. companies were reluctant to manufacture and distribute it because they feared a boycott by consumers of their other products.

Sometimes a new and useful technology is resisted because it is seen to harm business interests. The British cable companies resisted Marconi's radio innovations and Thomas Edison fought against Nikola Tesla's A/C system of electricity.

In other instances, the resistance can be ideational. Even after the Wright brothers' first powered flight at Kitty Hawk in 1903, many people refused to believe that humans had flown; it was not regarded as a possibility.

Further, technology or groups of technologies can be resisted because they are seen as endangering a whole way of life. There are certain sects of Amish who reject most technologies of the industrial era, fearing that it will harm their religion, community, families and culture.

Resistance to technology can thus come from many quarters, under many guises and with many means at its disposal. New technology often brings about new deployments of power often because new dispersals of information are enabled; for this reason it will often be stalled or outright squashed by those already in positions of power and privilege.

We can regard the preceding domains as operating as a sort of filtration system for the socio-technical system, regulating the flow of new technologies into the social system. We now turn to describe each of the elements of the social system with a brief example to show how it might be affected by a technological introduction.

The PIBSCREAM

Any society can be (arbitrarily) said to be comprised of the following nine interacting elements:

Politics
Ideas
Behavior of individuals
Social features
Culture
Religion
Economics
Aesthetics
Material Culture

For simplicity, I call this the "PIBSCREAM". Clearly these categories overlap. Some could be combined or new ones could be added. For example, societies have ethical systems that interact with all of their nine sub-sections. In addition, societies have information storage and retrieval systems and institutional systems such as the military, universities, and policing systems. For the present, I believe this simplified "PIBSCREAM." Set-up serves as a useful organizing device.

Next we will examine each of the elements of this

"PIBSCREAM" with an example of how it might affect of be affected by technology.

Politics

This has to do with the manner in which power and decision-making is managed in a society. The relationship between politics and technology is double-edged. New technologies cause changes in gradients of power. The internet in China creates possibilities for dissent, assembly and information gathering that could weaken the grip of the central government. The Chinese central government has responded with measures to control and monitor its citizens' internet communications.

Similarly the photocopier in the former USSR presented possibilities of citizens copying and distributing banned books. Access to photocopies thus had to be controlled.

One can see these examples how, in the interests of maintaining political power, a government might sacrifice operational efficiencies offered by new technologies and thus reduce the productivity of the economy. This, in turn can ultimately weaken their power. On the other hand, technology can increase wealth and well-being while also offering protection. To these ends, governments may sponsor technologies and technological efforts. Sometimes technologies serve to enhance the status of the state. For this reason countries will often sponsor or underwrite military technologies or a fleet of nationally-named jetliners to ensure that they appear modern. When the USSR launched Sputnik, the USA was not only militarily threatened and taken by surprise, it also suffered a loss of self-esteem. It responded with a massive funding of science, technology and the space program.

Technology has also obviously changed the practice of politics in many ways. It is amusing to imagine Abraham Lincoln delivering his address at Gettysburg in the context of 21st century communications technology. It is likely he would have been advised to cut it short and tailor it for a "sound bite" on the six o'clock news. The value of "speechifying" in politics has been reduced, as has the value of debating; perhaps also the complexity of political thought carried out in public has declined. Perhaps, with the advent of film and television, appearance has increased in importance. The Nixon-Kennedy debates are a well-known case in point. They were the first presidential debates to be televised. Kennedy wore make-up and looked good. Nixon did not and looked unwell. It has often been argued that this contributed to Kennedy's victory. Politicians in the post-industrial era must be media-friendly.

Tomes could be filled on the theme of politics and technology; all that is intended here is to give some indications of the manifold complexities of this domain.

Ideas

This element refers to the concepts, thoughts, notions available for thought in a society. It has to do with the way we think. The very thoughts we have are affected dramatically by technology.

Examples of these are ubiquitous. On December 7th, 1972, the first photograph of the planet earth, a beautiful sphere of blue, white, green and brown hanging in the black, was published. It became a famous poster and it changed how people thought. People saw that the earth was beautiful and finite, perhaps even vulnerable. An awareness seemed to set in that earth was like a spaceship and that it was "whole," integrated. About this time Buckminster Fuller's book "Operating Manual for Spaceship Earth" (2008/1968) and "The Whole Earth Catalog" (Brand, 1971) were published. Many people seemed to believe that it was important to care for this "spaceship" and its passengers. The environmental movement gained momentum; the study of ecology gained pace and used this image of the whole earth in a variety of contexts.

Ideas of possibilities change as new technologies are developed. Before the Wright flier it was not widely believed that humans could fly. But if humans could fly, what else might they be able to do?

The notion of individuality and that the individual being is important is a modern concept, a concept in many ways potentiated by various technologies. Robert Romanyshin in "Technology as Symptom and Dream" (1989) argues that the development of the perspective drawing technique by Alberti and Bruneleschi in the fifteenth century had the effect of enabling humans to pry themselves loose from their visual field, to get some distance from the object to gain perspective and to start to experience themselves as a separate entity.

Similarly, the deployment of the moveable type printing press, at roughly the same time as the development of perspectival art, and the associated increase in printing of Bibles in several languages (often against violent resistance) enabled the notion of the individual having an individual unmediated relationship with God. These ideas of individuality, we believe, ultimately evolved into strengthening ideas regarding human rights and thus, democracy. – ideas vigorously at play in the world today.

Technologies can enhance sensation and perception and thus change ideas. The telescope contributed to notions of a heliocentric planetary system and the idea that humans were not center of the universe. The electron microscope contributed to the construction of the double helix model of the gene.

Technologies can expand horizons and put new thoughts in our heads on a very personal level. A very beautiful movie that illustrates this is "Endurance" (1999) in which we see a young Haile Gebrselassie, the son of peasant farmers in Ethiopia, get the idea that he will be a runner after listening on a battery-powered transistor radio (a device which readily spread to areas without an electricity grid) to Miruts Yifter win the Moscow Olympics 10,000 meter race. He was inspired. His horizons were broadened and his life was changed. He also affected global culture as he became a famous, record-breaking marathoner.

Behavior

This domain has to do with the ways in which individual behavior is affected by technology. It, of all the categories, most clearly overlaps with and interacts with other domains and examples are infinite. I will just give a few to illustrate the possibilities here.

The famous time and motion studies of Taylorism (2016/1911) where workers movements were timed to second and shaped so as to achieve maximum efficiency mark the way in which individual behavior became increasingly mechanized throughout the industrial revolution. Chaplin's prophetic movie "Modern Times" (1936) captures and indeed anticipates many of these behavioral changes wrought by the hegemony of the new socio-technical system: psychosomatic problems, nervous breakdowns, fast food, substance abuse, tics, alienation. At one point, Chaplin is even eaten alive by the machine.

Before the advent of the telephone, people who could write wrote letters, using pen and paper. Nowadays, if we wish to write a biography of a famous 19th century personage, say, Sigmund Freud, we may consult his thousands of letters: letters he wrote to Jung, Fleiss, and Martha, his wife.

Letter writing, as a behavior, faded as the telephone took over during the 20th century. Interestingly, at the close of the 20th century the internet and email perhaps reversed the situation – people are communicating more frequently in a textual form that can easily be saved. Future historians and biographers will perhaps have this additional data to pore over.

In the early days of television people would complain that it was killing "the art of conversation;" people were forgetting how to talk to one another, perhaps forgetting how to entertain each other, how to tell stories, how to soothe and calm each other and themselves.

Thousands of studies have been carried out with the net effect of demonstrating that exposure to television does raise levels of aggression and lower creativity and reading scores in children. These results perhaps have more to do with what is shown on television than on the simple fact of watching television. This latter is explicated very ably by McLuhan (1994, 2001, 2011) who argues that the advent of the television has wrought upon us an utter change in our sensoria such that we have become immediate participants in a "global village", this accompanied by a shift from "hot" (mostly print) media to "cool" media—television.

The list of examples of behavior-modifying technologies is endless. Pondering the following list of technologies and how they have impacted individual behavior will quickly generate a long list: The microwave, VCR, remote control, ball point pen, refrigerator, cell telephone-- on and on until our very being has perhaps been invaded by technology, leading a thinker such as Ellul (1967) to posit technological autonomy, the notion that technology, far from being under human control, lives its own life, independent of us and yet wreaking enormous impacts upon us.

Social

This is an enormous grab-bag of a category. It has to do with the groups from which a society is composed, their structure and the processes that go on within and between them: social classes, race relationships, family structure, kinship, social mobility, caste systems, class, "ocracies" of all kinds (meritocracies, bureaucracies, aristocracies, etc.) and general trends in society, changes in values, attitudes and orientation.

Societies can be turned upside down and inside out by technologies. The Skolt of Lappland, for example lived in a symbiotic relationship with reindeer of the Arctic tundra (McGinn, 1990) . It took a while to learn the ways of the reindeer and thus gaining in age implied a gain in useful knowledge, and thus, power. This society was also quite self-sufficient. Introduce, however, a snowmobile and the social system changes. A young man on a snowmobile can find and herd reindeer without having to rely on decades of experience. Thus, young men gain in social influence while the old suffer a relative decline in power. In addition the society becomes reliant on gasoline supply and, thus, cash. It does not take much to think of the manifold social consequences of such a change. Anthropological literature is full of examples of such as these.

Technological advances in health care and other fields have greatly increased average longevity in industrial and post-industrial societies. These societies have thus been changed in many ways. Declines in infant mortality help reduce the number of children women have, especially when combined with the technologies of birth control. The demographics of these populations change. They have an increased proportion of old people in their midst. These factors and others reverberate through these societies; fewer children, smaller families, more retirees all create far-reaching social changes.

It is not frequently pointed out that by increasing the average life span of a population, one is in effect increasing the average length of time humans have to gather experience and solve the problems of life on earth. While some problems can be solved in the first few decades of a life, many require many decades of study before new insights can be offered. By increasing longevity we are increasing human problem-solving time, thus increasing the likelihood that long-standing human problems (especially problems involving "wisdom") might be better solved. This is a point of hope, if societies can build structures to profit from it.

Television altered race relations in the United States of America and in the world. When the police fire-hosed and loosed attack dogs on marchers in Selma, Alabama on May 3rd, 1963, and when protestors of apartheid were shot at and killed in Sharpeville, South Africa, on the 21st of March 1960, they were seen on television by a very large number of people. Protests had obviously been made before and been met with violent reprisals. However, prior to television, they were more likely to remain local events, unexposed to the broader array of public opinion and cultures. In many ways one could argue that the civil rights movements of the 1960's and the dismantling of apartheid were potentiated by a cluster of technologies; important among them was television.

A similarly structured argument could be made about the protests against the Vietnam war, which was the first (and, so far, last) extensively televised war. Seeing Buddhist monks immolate themselves, and young men wounded on a screen in one's living room really brought home the realities of the war. Significantly, television has not been so close to the action in military engagements since.

Technology is also used as a means of expressing social status and values. The type of technology one uses and the uses it is put to can serve as a signaling device as to one's standing in society. Bourdieu (1994) and Veblen (2009) provide systematic expositions of these ideas. Thus, for example, the punk rock culture in some ways expressed, through its usage of used clothing, a rejection of the acquisitive society in which they found themselves embedded. Similarly, one might find those who are at ease with a consumption oriented society flaunt their high-end, cutting edge usage of technologies.

Culture

This has to do with the set of ideas and beliefs about behavior that are learned and shared by a group. It is the system of norms (rules), beliefs, customs (that are largely taken for granted, as being "real") that govern behavior in a society or a social group.

Television arguably has a very strong influence on culture. Narratives on televisions shape values on sexuality, families, politics, values; the list goes on. Television is saturated with commercials that are themselves loaded with cultural messages about consumption, clothing, behavior, body shape and odor amongst a litany of other variables.

From a different angle, persons located in isolated cultures might find themselves exposed to different cultural ideas. Women in a very patriarchal culture might get "feminist" ideas from watching "western" television.

As a young English boy I was very affected by the "relaxed American" portrayed in cowboy and military movies from the USA. I wanted to be casual and laid back like them not stiff and starchy as many of the English heroes of the "silver screen" seemed to be. I wanted to drink root beer and drawl like an American. At a tender age, my culture was being affected. The mass media can have powerful impacts on the many dimensions of culture, but culture can also be affected by other features of the socio-technical system.

When we look at the culture of the inhabitants of Bali (Lansing, 2007), we find a calm, friendly, emotionally low-key way of life. Perhaps this attributable to the prevailing socio-technical system traditionally found on the island of Bali. Coordinated irrigation is vital to their way of life. Escalating conflict or overt competition would be disastrous since everyone depends on everyone else for their sustained well-being. This contrasts markedly with the culture of industrialized capitalism with its emphasis on individualism, competition and autonomy. As the island becomes a destination for mass tourism (this itself potentiated and enabled by a set of technologies) we will likely see the culture change. In addition, the changes in culture will express themselves differently in different regions of the island.

The book, "Family Systems Activity Book" (Hazell, 2006) delineates thirty dimensions of culture. Each one of these can be powerfully affected by technology.

Religion

This is the component of society that has to do with the systems of belief that are established to provide answers to empirically unverifiable questions regarding life, death, ultimate meaning and purpose.

Prime examples of the interaction of technology and religion can be found in the idea that the moveable type printing press contributed to the creation of Protestantism in 16th century Europe and, further, Galileo's run in with the church over the place of the planet Earth in the relation to the Sun.

More recently tensions between technology and religion have focused on issues around birth and death: suicide machines, birth control and abortion, for example. Usually the relationship between religion and technology is portrayed as competitive. Some Amish communities are suspicious of what modern technology will do to their religious agrarian way of life. The Taliban of Afghanistan were suspicious of several post-modern technologies (computers, television, the internet) arguably insofar as they posed a threat to their traditional religious and social values. On the other hand, modern weaponry was not so regarded.

The relationship is not always competitive, however. For example, as was noted in the previously mentioned study of irrigation on the island of Bali, a computer model was generated to help optimize decisions regarding cropping patterns and the timing of irrigation. Very interestingly, it was discovered that the derived model gave results very close to those generated by the age old technologies of the water temple priests who communed with Dewi Danu, the water goddess. The priests had been routinely ignored by the planning authorities, but with the advent of the computer and its predictions, it became clear that the religious leaders had been on to something and a bridge between governmental officials and the religious leaders was built.

Technology also affects religions in its means of distribution. Religion was powerfully affected by television, bringing with it the advent of televangelism and the possibility of religion as a big business. This also created the potential for religious advocates to impact the political sphere.

We see currently strong interactions between the political sphere and religion, captured tellingly in the fictional "Handmaids Tale" (Atwood, 1989). Such conflict and resultant splitting is in many ways, potentiated by technological advances and how they are expressed spatially.

Economics

This has to do with the way in which wealth, goods, services, resources, money are stored, flow, distributed and exchanged in a society.

Technology almost always affects this domain. In fact it is to bring about changes in this domain, that technology is often developed in the first place. Technology is often developed to increase wealth, to ensure its continued generation or to protect wealth. For this reason, examples of technology affecting economics are easy to summon.

Televisions were in almost every household in the USA by the 1960's. This technology carried into every household hours and hours of commercials. Not only did these advertisements stimulate demand, but also created a burgeoning of the advertising industry.

Technologies such as television, microcomputers, and telephones and internet not only stimulate the economy by creating entire new industries (and harming others), they also can be used to stimulate demand for certain goods and services.

Computers and the internet have changed the nature of the marketplace. Trading in stock exchanges is done nowadays by or with computers or computer assistance. In fact "Black Monday" when the stock market nose-dived on October 19th, 1987 was held by some analysts to be the results of computers trading within computerized parameters that were poorly designed.

Those who trade in futures of pork, oil and other products note that their job changed dramatically with the advent of computer trading. The market moves so much more quickly that errors in judgment can prove very costly in a matter of seconds.

Countries that fail to invest in time to burgeoning technologies can find themselves following behind economically. On the heels of this follow political instability, social tensions, cultural disorientation. Making the right technological strategic decisions is difficult but crucial.

For example the USA has decided (at the time of this writing) to pursue stem cell research in a measured way. It has done this following moral precepts regarding the sanctity of life. Other countries have taken a much more pragmatic approach and are pursuing stem cell research more energetically. Could it be that in 20 to 50 years' time the United States will find itself lagging behind economically because of these decisions, paying a high economic price for its moral rectitude?

Sometimes the network of causality is very long and complex. Global warming, potentiated over decades by the burning of fossil, fuels, will (if even modest predictions turn out to be true) change land values, cropping patterns and perhaps result in entire cities being abandoned. Low-lying islands and real estate will be submerged or vast sums will have to be spent to rescue them from rising waters. In addition, these economic changes will impact all other elements of the "PIBSCREAM." Multiple examples of these types of changes are documented in "Collapse" (Diamond, 2011)

The Marxist view (1993) that technology is a weapon used by the bourgeoisie to reduce the value of the labor of the craftsperson by automating it and thus rendering skilled labor unnecessary and easily replaced by lower paid semi and unskilled labor is a provocative one that illustrates the intimate inter-relationship between technology, class, culture, ethics and politics.

Aesthetics

Philosophers, artists, critics and thinkers of many sorts have wrestled with the definition of aesthetics for centuries. Here, we adopt the following definition. It is the means whereby a society creates objects or systems of beauty, including plays, music, poetry, sculpture, narrative, paintings, and dance. Some societies are extremely aesthetically expressive and rich. Others are less productive in this domain. Either way, technology is intertwined in a reciprocal relationship with aesthetics just as it is with every other element of the socio-technical system.

Sometimes a new technology brings about a new art form. The still camera initiates artistic photography; the movie camera, the film; the radio, the radio play. These then impact the rest of the socio-technical system. Sometimes a new technology amplifies both literally and figuratively an existing art form. The electric guitar was perfected throughout the 1950's and '60's. This brought on the era of rock and roll and many of the socio-cultural changes associated with this.

Early in this century a computer program has been developed that can analyze a song's structure and predict its likelihood of becoming a hit (Economist, June, 2006). Developments like these seem to substantiate Adorno's claims (1983) that we have entered the era of the "cultural industry," an era of mass produced culture.

Art can also affect technology. There are many movies, novels, poems and songs that voice opinions, explicit or implicit, about technology. "Silkwood" (1983), "The China Syndrome" (1979) and "2001, A Space Odyssey" (1968), "Chernobyl" (2019) are examples of movies that give their own "takes" on attitudes to technology. "1984," (Orwell, 1950) "Brave New World," (Huxley,2006) are examples of novels pointing out dangers of possible future technological developments. "Blade Runner" (1982) and "Gattaca" (1997) along with much of the writings of Dick (2009) are fine examples of movies delineating ethical issues emanating from deployments of technology.

John Masefield's, "Dirty British Coaster" (1944), John Betjeman's "Slough", (1937) William Blake's "Jerusalem" (1997) and much of John Clare's work (2003) provide us with examples of poetry that comments on the dehumanizing of potential of technology. In a similar vein, the poets of the first World War, notably Wilfred Owen (2018) can be understood as commenting on the charged nature of war with mass slaughter resulting from the use of poison gas, armored tanks and the machine gun.

Sometimes the linkages between art technology and society can be extremely subtle and powerful. In the previously mentioned instance, Romanyshin (1989) argues that the development of the artistic technique of perspective by Alberti and Brunelleschi in about 1500, changed peoples' mentalities in such a way that they were able, as it were, to stand back and gain some distance from the object. This "stepping back" can then be connected with some other ideas such as the scientific method (as expressed in "Novum Organum" by Francis Bacon (2000) and the moveable type of printing press to potentiate the historical flood tide of the renaissance and later, the enlightenment.

Volumes could be (and have been) written on this topic. I believe these few lines serve to show that the interactions here are potentially very powerful.

Material

Once again, this is a big "grab bag" concept. Here it is defined as the system of knowledge, attitudes and beliefs regarding the material world in general and with regard to specific materials. Examples are rife in the history of technology. Petroleum, prior to the advent of the internal combustion engine was not particularly valued. Dog faeces, prior to the invention of modern techniques of tanning were regarded as useful in the tanning of high quality leather. There was even a profession, the "pure gatherer", one who collected dog excrement for the purpose of leather-manufacture. Cow dung might be regarded as smelly waste or as a potential source of methane which itself might be harnessed to power turbines to create electricity. In its early days, plastic was regarded with some apprehension and disdain. In the sixties, it was used as an epithet to describe someone or something as a phoney, as an imitation. Nowadays, with the advent of many different types of plastic, types that rival the original material in attractiveness, durability or efficiency, this attitude seems to have altered somewhat. Still, some materials retain their cachet, often for seemingly irrational reasons—gold, platinum, diamonds, exotic woods, various animal parts and so on. At times fantasies about materials and the things they are taken to symbolize might place them off bounds for use for certain tasks. These attitudes towards the material can also be thought through very deeply, as in say, the case of modern physics and chemistry or they might be thought about in a very "everyday" sense where the material is treated with relative negligence and taken for granted. The material might be taken as inexhaustible or rare and these attitudes also may change as the socio-technical system unfolds. Water, or the oceans, once considered limitless in certain regions of the world, are now seen as more precious commodities, worthy of conservation.

The Physical Environment

The physical environment is the complex of the natural ensemble of ecosystems in which the society is located. The effect of this on the society is no way deterministic. However, the influence is extremely powerful. Deserts, mountains, rivers, climate, geology, soils, ocean currents and location are but a few of the variables that will impact the form and dynamics of the PIBSCREAM. While modern technologies seem to erode the impact of space in many ways, some impacts still remain. This force of spatiality is being recognized more in several disciplines as we see documented by Diamond (2011), Tally (2013), Marshall (2015), Kaplan (2012) and Bachmann-Medick (2016). As argued here, this trend might be profitably taken up in the study of group dynamics.

The Individual

Finally, enmeshed in this now dynamic, now vertical assemblage, lays the individual, for whom we might have some compassion, as they attempt unceasingly to articulate themselves with an ever-changing socio-technical context.

To the extent they yoke their identity to this surround and its institutions, they will have to continually update their mental maps of their situation, context and meaning. For some this will be an enjoyable demand, something of an adventure. For others it will prove baffling, overwhelming and too much to bear. This differentiation in responses will depend upon a host of variables— among them the cohesion and coherence of the inner world of objects and the dynamics of the groups in which the individual is ensconced. Additionally, as we shall see, geographic-spatial and developmental factors have a determining influence.

At the Winter Sea Ice Camp

In this video by Quentin Brown (1967) we see a day in the life of the Netsilik Inuit as they build their igloo, hunt, share food, socialize and pass the time in the depths of an Arctic winter. It is very moving and beautiful. In the movie we see a social system displaying all of the elements of the PIBSCREAM in a manner adapted to the physical surround. Briefly, we see:

Politics: In the way in which the food (the dead seal) is distributed. This follows traditional pathways. The hunters are assigned a partner at birth and the relatives take turns in the selection of seal parts in pre-designated order.

Ideas: We see the manifestation of ideas in the trapezoidal shape of the snow used to form the curved surface of the igloo. In the conversations during the food sharing.

Behavior: We see an amazing range of behavior—co-operation in the building of the igloo, playing with babies, the dour perseverance of the frozen hunters, mutual enjoyment of the company of others.

Social: We note that it is the men who go out on the long arduous hunts, that the young participate in building the igloo, that the atmosphere in the igloo is warm and calm.

Cultural: The intensity of the culture seems low key and relaxed. The elders seem to be treated with respect. The babies are close to the mothers and there seems to be a good deal of playing of games for amusement. Between the men, the games have to do with physical strength. Amongst the young, they have to do with skills that are useful to hunter-gatherers.

Religion: No visible sign of religion in this vignette. This in and of itself is perhaps significant. In some cultures religion is found in the interstices of everyday life.

Economic: No sign of cash or barter in this vignette. The wealth is in materials, food and resources used by the group. In addition, in this vignette, no sign of economic conflict as traditional rules govern the use of materials, tools and the sharing of food.

Aesthetics: There is a charming incident where an elder tells a story to the young, and they listen entranced. Several games are played that have an aesthetic quality.

Material: There is a wide array of materials at hand—bone knives, sealskin boots, a slab of frozen lake-ice for an igloo window, seal-oil lamps, soapstone containers, snow dwelling, caribou coats all deftly fashioned to purpose.

Physical Environment: Is out on the sea ice in the depths of Arctic winter. Little sun shines, no soil, no wood and brutally cold. Inside the igloo, which is surprisingly spacious, it seems quite warm.

Individual: The film does not offer insight directly into the individuals but one can but imagine what kind of personality it would take to be adjusted to this socio-technical world. One would very likely have to be as tough as nails, calm, patient, forbearing, respectful of others and of nature, willing to share and also able to enjoy long months of close interpersonal contact.

Examining groups in differing socio-technical situations throws light on so many features of group dynamics. This study is the domain of anthropology. Sadly, the amount of inter-disciplinary work in this domain is parlously small.

Conclusion

There are thus more than a dozen elements to the model of the socio-technical system outlined above. It emphasizes the more "sociological", that is, observable, aspects of the technological process as it is generated and returns to impact the multifaceted and interacting complex elements that go to make a society. The model is a generic one that can be applied to all levels of social organization. When we integrate it with object relations theory and group relations theory, as we shall demonstrate, further explanatory pathways are opened up. We see, for example that interpersonal relationships are altered. In addition we see the task and boundaries of institutions are often dramatically and traumatically redrawn. Insofar as individuals rely upon stable internal *institutional object relations,* further demands are made to the individual's capacities to self-regulate. Since there is a direct relationship between object relations and the group mentality, the nature of group dynamics and institutional life is impacted by the advent of technologies. These dramatic alterations occur not only at the manifest level described in the socio-technical model but also at the latent, unconscious level as delineated by object relations and group-as-a-whole theory. In addition, the applications of Heidegger's ideas on the "enframing" function of technology, when taken into account further amplify the momentous impact of a new technology or technological ensemble.

We now move on to explore some of the potential ramifications of these theoretical integrations. Later, we will attempt to integrate this with Dabrowski's theory of emotional development to see what other illuminations might be forthcoming.

2: A Model of History

As intimated above, the viewing of history with an emphasis on the contribution of technology leads to a different interpretation of historical events; this history to be delineated at all levels of scale, from the individual (how the narrative of an individual life is impacted by technology) through the family, small group, institution, nation and civilization. We thus take here a short divagation to offer such a model, this to stand as a counterweight to notions of history that employ ideas, individuals, movements and events as major explanatory devices.

Collingwood (2014) demonstrates quite convincingly that the very idea of history—its structure, function, meaning and purpose undergoes historical development, thus expanding the very notion of historiography. The notion of a socio-technical system provides a further way of understanding and explaining history. In it one may visualize history as resulting from complex interactions of Persons, Ideas, Society (Societal Situations) and Technology. This may be roughly diagramed as in Figure 5.

Figure XX: An Engine of History

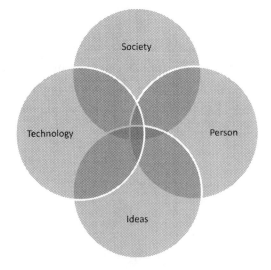

Thus, in order to explain history or, even more audaciously, to broadly predict future trends, one would take into account all of these factors.

For example, as suggested above, the civil rights movement of the 1960's in the USA results from the confluence of the **social situation** of segregation, the **idea** of civil rights, the **person** of Reverend Doctor Martin Luther King Junior and his colleagues and the enabling **technology** of television. Certainly, such protests as were witnessed in the Southern States of the USA had occurred before, Horne (2016) documents slave rebellions dating back to the very beginning of slavery in the United States. However, by the early 1960's household ownership of televisions had increased throughout much of the soon-to-be post-industrial world—a world predicated as MacLuhan suggests on a "cool", "participatory" media like television that was well on the way to creating a "global village". The scenes of violent suppression were not only witnessed by many through the medium of television, they were witnessed in a very immediate, "MacLuhanesque" fashion, as if the events were occurring close by and we were actually there. In this example the new technology enables or facilitates, through an individual or subgroup, the actualization of an idea, an idea that, although experienced as new, is many millennia old. We are close here to Heidegger's notion of technology (Heidegger, 2013) where technology is seen not only as an enabler or extender of human functions, but also as a revealer of what lies hidden in the human being. What lies hidden, as Freud and others warn us, is not always a pretty sight. A journey into the unconscious, Jung tells us, "is not a walk down a primrose path." Alluding to the concept of "imaginary groups (Hazell, 2005) we might thus argue that technology assists in the surfacing and submergence of these, propelling thus, certain ideas, individuals and movements into the public sphere.

A technology that occurs without the presence of enabling or facilitating factors in the other three domains (Person, Ideas and Situation) will not have the same powerful effects as we saw in the example above with the advent of television. Golding (1972) depicts wonderfully the way in which the steam engine is introduced in ancient Roman society only to be greeted with scorn, fear and derision. As the hapless inventor explains the possible uses of a stream engine in work and in war he is confronted with the harms this would bring about in Roman society. Why would we need slaves if we had engines to do all the work? How would we demonstrate our superiority over those we vanquished? What would we do with them? Similarly, the inventor is asked as to what would be the fate of personal valor and skill in fighting warfare was to be so mechanized by steam power that fighting could be carried on at a distance? The fictional inventor is exiled for his scurrilous and subversive ideas. The steam engine apparently was invented approximately two thousand years ago by Hero of Alexandria (McGinn, 1990) but was never scaled up and used only as a toy. Similar tales could be told of the invention of gunpowder in China which is used only for fireworks. When it arrives in Europe, where the political environment is much more turbulent and competitive, it is quickly put to use in warfare.

`Deploying this model to further examples we may posit that the breakup of the USSR and its satellites was due not only to the persons involved (Reagan, Yeltsin, Gorbachev) nor to the competing ideas of democracy, capitalism and communism and their relative effectiveness, nor even to the geographic advantages enjoyed by the USA, but also to the impact of technologies—sometimes seemingly innocuous ones—the photocopier enabling widespread inexpensive dissemination of information, the satellite television network, enabling the broadcasting of a variety of lifestyles, values and opinions and as such creating a more "novelistic", "dialogical" discourse (to employ the useful terms of Bahktin, 1982). Thus, the deployment of these technologies disrupted the more "epic" narratives of either side in the "cold war" of ideas.

The break-up of the USSR can be understood as resulting from the democratizing effect of these third wave, post-industrial technologies. The USSR in the 1980's was an industrial and agricultural economy that existed, to an ever increasing extent, in a post-industrial world. To sustain economic power it had to adopt post- industrial technologies, computers, the internet, satellite telecommunications, even the humble photocopier. However, if these technologies were adopted and deployed freely enough to aid productivity the grip of central planning would have to be loosened. The choice was clear: either adopt third wave technologies, and maintain economic power, but lose the political regime of post Stalinism or maintain the centrally planned political system and not keep up with the post-industrial world. Gorbachev's and Yeltsin's *perestroika* and *glasnost* can now be seen not as just a change in values, not just as a backing down to Reagan's "star wars" and hard-line-jawboning, but as a rational response to the demands of the post-industrial world order. Similar changes can be seen underway as China shifts from communism to a more centrally planned capitalistic market-based industrial and post-industrial economy.

More recently, we see Russia seeming to back off from the free flow of information one would hope to find in a representative democracy and opt for an oligarchic arrangement that seeks to enjoy the benefits of post-industrialism while incorporating authoritarian elements of Stalinism by having power focused in a ruling network of entrepreneurs and co-operative politicians.

We argue that almost any major "event" (to employ the term in the sense implied by Badiou, 2013) is propelled by the confluence, in a very complex manner, of forces emanating from all of the above-mentioned domains. More recently we might argue that the so-called "Arab Spring" was impelled no only by persons, situations and ideas but was catalyzed with the essential ingredients of cell telephones and related technologies that enabled the assembly and deployment of crowds and the high-speed dissemination of information on all levels—local, regional, international and global.

Erikson (1993b) shows how the corruption of the papacy combined with Martin Luther's anger at his father helps explain the origin of Protestantism. Luther, in attacking the papacy is argued to be symbolically attacking his father. The time is ripe for the change and Luther has the internal resources. He is up to the task of leadership. We thus have, in this formulation three of the elements in this model of history—the person (Luther), the ideas (ethical consistency and self-determination) and the situation (the corruption of the Pope and his colleagues). When we add to this mixture the new technology of the moveable type printing press widespread societal change ensues, redistributing power, activating ideas, changing culture, marginalizing some, while centralizing others.

The Gutenberg printing press in the late fifteenth century which facilitated the production of the Bible and the dissemination of translations of the Bible into languages other than Latin meant that the priesthood no longer held such a position of privilege with regard to the meaning of the Bible. An ever-growing group of people were capable of reading and interpreting the meaning of the Bible for themselves. This laid the groundwork for the burgeoning of diverse readings and renditions of the scripture. Although cloaked in ideology, these phenomena can be best understood as reactions to a redistribution of power resulting from the technology of the Gutenberg moveable type printing press. From a group relations perspective, all the elements of the FABART system (Hazell and Kiel, 2017) were impacted— fantasies, authority, affect, boundaries, roles and tasks were radically altered as the technology was deployed on a wider and wider basis. These changes were wrought at all levels—individual through to regional and national.

In many ways, even over 500 years later, the world is still attempting to cope with the revolutionary technology of moveable type presses (a technology which has, by the way, the disarming simplicity of a child's toy). We see for example wars being fought in cultures where the literacy rate is very low but growing (Afghanistan, for example with a literacy rate of about 40%). In a more recent parallel, we see tensions between those who have access to the 21st century's digital technology and those that do not—the so-called "digital divide".

If people read and are free to read from multiple sources, they develop ideas—ideas of dialogue, ideas of individuality, ideas of multiple narratives. The individual becomes a concept for more and more people. The stage is set for the great revolutions of human rights over the centuries that followed the development of the moveable type printing press, battles that are still rumbling around the world, like echoes of thunder.

Further ideas and concepts develop with a "knock-on" effect. If reading becomes important, so does literacy. Literacy takes time. It requires teaching, probably schools devoted to the education of younger persons. Thus the concept of childhood emerges as an increasing number of children spend years learning how to read. This concept itself goes to inform thinking in other realms, ethics, economics, labor, psychology and so on.

As the number of books increases so does a society's "social memory" and its capacity to reflect on itself and generate yet more transformative ideas and technology. The idea of history changes from one of myth to one of an evolving narrative with enormous implications. The snowball of the impacts of the technology starts to roll down the hill, gathering mass and speed.

The moveable type printing press is, like the internet, a technology with a tremendous potential for democratization in that, if fully deployed, it distributes information and power across a wide span of society. The wave of democratization posited by Fukuyama (2006) in the past few centuries was potentiated in many ways by the printing press and is being accelerated by the "third wave" technologies of the mini computer, satellites, cell phone television and the internet. Socio-political systems based on agrarian an industrial modes of production are resisting the changes wrought by these technologies, even today.

However, this constellation of technologies can also have an anti-democratic effect, some of which will be examined later. If the technologies of information distribution are taken over by a "big brother"-like enterprise, then the capacity of mass indoctrination is increased. In addition, and this especially poignant in the technologies of the 21st century which are so immediate and personal-seeming, there is, as one uses technological deployments such as, say, Facebook, the experience tantamount to that of entering a large group. This brings about regression, as is quite well documented (Kreeger, 1975; LeBon, 2002; Freud, 1921) and the result of this regression is splitting and projective identification of the kind described at the beginning of this book. This regression and splitting, common in large groups, occurs at all levels and society is placed in a vulnerable position where "siloes" of opinion are at odds with one another and discourse in the productive sense has all but ceased. The stage is then set for tragedy.

The showing of the Vietnam war on television made it more difficult to "sell" the war at home. People would see violence close up. They would see a young man, for example, wounded and in pain being dragged into a helicopter and would see a young man who looked like a relative, or a neighbor. The interpersonal distance was reduced so dramatically that the war was in one's living room. Grossman (2009) points out that when killing is done at a distance, the traumatic effect is reduced. Television reduced this distance, traumatizing the viewers. The human cost of the war was right in everyone's living room. Since then wars have not been televised in such a freewheeling, unfettered, close-up fashion. They are consequently not met with such resistance and the industries and interests vested in the continuance of war may proceed relatively unfettered.

These examples serve to demonstrate that while history is driven by great ideas, great people, great movements, a vital potentiating driver of change is technology. Much, perhaps, can be gained from adopting (at least temporarily, as a heuristic device) the perspective of a technology-driven history. It is important to recall, however, that the dynamic is reciprocal. On a very concrete level, it is easy to find examples of technologies being invoked but not deployed in fully transformative ways. Technologies may be resisted by a variegated set of forces—religious, social, psychological, economic, to name but a few.

Thus, sometimes societies actively seek a technology, sometimes unconsciously suppress the deployment of a technology or unconsciously repress even thinking about a technology.

3: Toffler's Model

Alvin Toffler in "The Third Wave" (1980) presents a model of history that has three phases; the first wave (agricultural), the second wave (industrial) and the third wave (service-based). While history is certainly more complex than this and while there were obviously several waves prior to the "first" agricultural wave (Paleolithic, Neolithic, pre-fire, bronze age, iron age etc.), Toffler's system has a certain compelling convenience and utility.

Below, in Figure 6, we see a simplified rendition of Toffler's model that looks solely at the proportion of people working in various sectors of an economy—agriculture, manufacturing and services. To these three posited by Toffler, we have added a post industrial sector which involves work in "Leisure and Entertainment" and a "post-post industrial sector" where we hypothesize the emergence of a "self-actualization" sector. We hypothesize that these are already emerging as the service sector and the entertainment sectors become more automated.

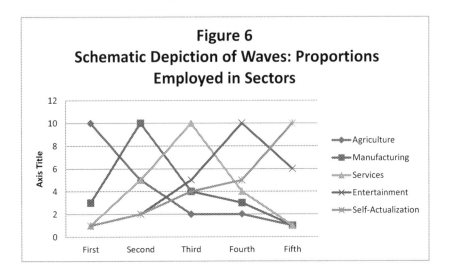

Figure 6
Schematic Depiction of Waves: Proportions
Employed in Sectors

With these shifts in employment patterns, which are potentiated by the innovation of defining technologies come radical changes i9n the socio-technical system—changes that Toffler elucidates in detail in his text, "The Third Wave".

Toffler's system, although it is a simplification and tends to lump together many socio-technical sub-phases, for example, small scale horticultural systems and larger scale agricultural systems or the multiple "industrial revolutions" besides the traditional "British" one, and does overlook other vital socio-technical systems such as that of the hunter-gatherer, still is an extremely useful approach insofar as it alerts us to the connection between the socio-technical system, with its defining technology, and the vast array of other social and psychological variables. One is also alerted to the fact that different social systems will operate in different "waves" and that intergroup and inter-regional tensions will result from these differences.

Toffler does not deploy what we here term group-as-a-whole theory in his disquisition, since his focus is more sociological. However we may see that each of his waves is associated with a different set of impacts on the conscious and unconscious elements of FABART (Fantasies, Affect, Boundaries, Authority, Role and

Task) system of a social system on all levels from the individual through to the civilizational.

As an example, we may take the example of the post-industrial classroom as a social system and how it is altered in the third wave, the wave of small computers, cell phones, the internet and ancillary technologies. The impacts are wide ranging but only a simple example will be given to demonstrate the overall idea.

Fantasies are affected insofar as access to knowledge is greatly increased. Fantasies of the teacher "knowing everything" and being the fount of knowledge will be eroded and the student will have fantasies connected with knowing, discovery and exploration beyond the confines of the classroom.

Affect will be affected insofar as exposure to emotionally stimulating material will be increased. Even if there is censorship of the internet, there will still be a far wider array of emotionally stimulating inputs.

Boundaries are radically impacted by these technologies. Students have access to world-class libraries and all sorts of information through their telephone in the room while the teacher is talking. Many types of monitoring can take place and the sense of privacy is altered dramatically.

Authority and power relations have been transformed. The teacher is not the only one in the room who knows stuff. The words of the teacher can be checked within seconds. Countervailing information can be found and shared by the students and shared immediately.

Roles will change. The teacher is not the only source of knowledge or even the sole evaluator of the students' work, since this might be done by a remote computer. The change in authority and boundaries will necessitate a change in the role of the student and the teacher.

The **task** will also change. In earlier waves the task might have been the straightforward transmission of knowledge which was to be remembered and repeated. This can now be done mechanically leaving room for another task—perhaps the critical evaluation of ideas, the operation at a higher cognitive level.

What Toffler and group relations theories alert us to is that these changes are not at all easy, especially since they are connected with unconscious anxieties—anxieties connected with the paranoid schizoid position.

For example, an aspect of the internal object relations matrix is the *institutional object*. This is an emotionally charged representation of an institution or a group with which one has a relationship. Examples of these are: a family, a company, a region, a nation, a church, a role (such as that of royalty) and so on. As technology impacts the socio-technical system, or, as a new wave, a new paradigm alters the framework of a society down to its roots, so these institutions are altered, usually in a dramatic way. Their boundaries will shift as the tasks change and the ideas that formed them become redundant and are replaced. These shifts not only occur in the "outside" world of social spaces, they also redound into the inner world of objects, creating a dramatic need for re-organization. This re-organization ricochets throughout the internal world of objects, pulling apart old connections and creating the demand for new ones. These changes decrease the integration, cohesiveness and stability of the internal world. Internal pieces of self and other are more likely to be projectively identified as the fear of falling apart increases. In addition there is the tremendous amount of mourning that has to be done as the old ways pass away. In reaction to these internal challenges, unfortunately, the response is often not accomplished via working through, but by acting out. Instead of working one's way, laboriously diagonally across Bion's matrix towards inquiry and theory, we see a straight horizontal movement from sense impressions to cell A6, which is mindless acting out, which has usually untoward, if not catastrophic, consequences.

A Fourth Wave?

When I present Toffler's system to students, however, the question invariably arises, "Is there a fourth wave?" This is an interesting and important question. It is important because if there is a fourth wave, economies that are based on previous waves may find it necessary to transition employment percentages into fourth-wave type jobs since as time passes smaller numbers of people are required to maintain higher levels of productions in any given wave. For example, in the early 21st century, less than 5% of the US population worked on farms, but farm productivity is currently much higher than a century before. The same applies to the industrial sector, thanks to control mechanisms and automation technologies. Figure 6 gives a schematic representation of shifts in employment with the passage of waves through an economy of shifts in employment with the passage of waves through an economy.

e see as industrialization takes hold, fewer people work on farms, as the third wave takes hold so fewer people work in the rapidly automating industrial sector and more into an ever-increasing number of jobs in the service sector.

However, there are many signs that even the service sector can be and is being automated, much like the industrial sector before it. Automatic teller machines, telephone registration systems, online retail purchasing, computer-based learning are just four examples of what could well be the next wave of structural unemployment. White collar jobs will decline in number the same way as farm work and blue collar jobs disappeared before it. What economic opportunities await these new landless, jobless?

We believe they will involve the work of the fourth wave, namely work in the leisure, entertainment and cultural industry. Infotainment, hospitality, tourism, edutainment, personal growth, arts, movies, cultural tourism, theme parks, these will be the work of the fourth wave. Some regional economies, such as Southern California and parts of Florida, for example, already have their economic bases in these industries. Chicago has managed somewhat to transition from an industrially based economy to one that relies on third and fourth wave types of economic activity. India, at the start of the 21st century, finds itself with significant parts of its economy in each of the four waves, agriculture, industry, services (much software code is written in Bangalore) and entertainment, with many movies being created in "Bollywood". The fourth wave is the wave where the "culture industry," gains hegemony and becomes a major employer. In the second wave, the idea of selling ring tones for telephones, seems ludicrous. In the fourth wave it is a multi-million dollar business. We also hypothesize a fifth wave, namely one where employment is centered around self-actualization. Again we see this in all of its forms already emerging in the form of the taking up of the self as a project and perfecting it in manifold ways. The question remains as to whether or not this too can be automated...

As waves pass, new ones arrive so job opportunities expand and contract. Blue collar jobs decline and service sector jobs increase as an economy passes from the second wave to the third wave. Similarly tertiary sector jobs decline in frequency and are replaced by quaternary sector (fourth wave) opportunities as an economy transitions from the third to the fourth wave.

The question arises, "What to do?" One could keep one's economy in a certain wave by not allowing or encouraging technologies of subsequent waves. This would keep jobs for people in the current wave, but would be costly and place one's economy in a weaker position *vis a vis* other economies. The lesser evil, would probably be to have one's economy move forward into the next phase while providing social, cultural, educational and economic supports for the structural unemployment brought on by this transition, this to ease the transition to the later, more productive phase. Examples of such supports would be: educational grants favoring the newer wave, shifts in cultural values towards values of lifelong learning and of constant change, unemployment benefits (perhaps re-labeled "redeployment benefits") as people move from the declining wave to the growing wave. A name that has been given to this type of security is "flexicurity", where it is culturally assumed that jobs will be rendered redundant by advances in technology and that one will inevitably have to train for new jobs and roles several times during one's lifetime. Adaptation of the individual to such a system would hypothetically require, however, a cohesive and coherent internal world and relative abeyance of a dependency culture.

History shows us that all too often, as a results of, say, racism, sexism, or class barriers, this transition is denied to certain groups, or at best, made very difficult. When one examines the history of African Americans in the United States, of America, for example, the recurrent pattern is the obverse of the ideal. African Americans gained entry into share cropping just as the nation is industrializing. They gain access to blue collar factory work, just as the industrial sector is about to be down-sized ("rationalized") as the economy shifts into the third wave.

Thus such programs as are designed and implemented, one must take care not to leave groups "behind the wave", on the wrong side of the "digital divide." This is important not only because of principles of fair play, socio-political stability and equality of opportunity, but also because a technologically productive society must utilize ideas from far and wide, from as many people as possible participating in the "technology game."

And, following the model of the socio-technical system outlined previously, we posit that the changes in the fourth wave will be as wide ranging (and as unanticipated and difficult to cope with) as the transitions of the previous three waves. The entire "PIBSCREAM" will be affected as the new defining technologies reverberate throughout the system—values, behavior, boundaries, ideas, classes, politics, the arts, culture, religion and material bases—all will change at the fairly readily observable level. At the unconscious level equally far ranging and potentially traumatic changes will occur as old ties are attenuated and broken, as new connections need to be made, as new images of self, other, society and world have to wrought and re-wrought, often in the face of a largely unacknowledged and misidentified crisis.

As an example of one thread that may be followed through these shifts brought about by the introduction of defining technologies we may outline the different types of authority associated with each of Toffler's waves with an addendum of some of the ways authority might emerge in the emerging fourth wave.

4: Forms of Oppression

The oppression of one human by another or of one group of humans by another is commonplace. The concept of oppression can be understood as one form of "authority" in the FABART scheme. This oppression may be regarded, in shorthand form, as a usage of one person or a group by another, in what might be regarded as a violation of Kant's second categorical imperative (Kant,2008). (Why this edict is so frequently overlooked and violated is in itself an interesting question.) Superficially the oppression and usage of others is understood as a form of laziness, or as the maintenance of status. At a deeper level it may be traced to what Laing (1965) terms "ontological insecurity" which itself stems from a fragile integration of the internal world of object relations, a locking into the paranoid-schizoid position.

What will be argued here is that the form of this oppression and thus, the exercise of a form of authority changes each of the waves described by Toffler (1980) and the fourth and fifth waves being posited here.

Oppression in the First Wave

The first wave, the agricultural era, was characterized by inherited power-- aristocracies, the fusion of the church and state, an era of monarchial theocracy. Power was wielded (and is wielded) in these socio-technical systems by brute physical force, overt threats of dire physical punishment, either in the here and now, or in the afterlife. One is born into one's social class with little chance of change. Social class is given, is accepted as part of a cosmic divine order. To challenge it is to challenge this divine order, and place oneself at risk. There are minimal opportunities for reflection upon or critical analysis of the social order, largely resulting from the aforementioned belief system and also because in this system, the bourgeoisie and correspondingly, the intelligentsia is very small.

Oppression in this context has a fateful, given quality. God or the gods appoint the aristocracy and they dominate and exploit the peasantry with some complicity from a yeoman landowning class, or a network of guilds, trades or merchants.

One does see rebellions on occasion. Wat Tyler leads a revolt of the peasants in England in 1381 and is soon killed. John Wycliffe publishes a Bible translated into Middle English and is deemed a heretic. Successful rebellion as in the Magna Carta emerges from an ever-growing upper middle class of landowners but by and large, the lowest classes toil and suffer and are kept in ignorance by virtue of exhaustion, coercive threat, mass illiteracy and consequent narrow horizons.

Oppression in the Second Wave

In this, the industrial wave, the class system has changed, and along with it, the form of oppression. The aristocracy may still exist, but has been joined by an emerging wealthy class of technocrats and capitalists who have grown wealthy and powerful off the fruits of industrialization. The aristocracy either joins in with this wave of technology or attempts to maintain its wealth and power alongside the newly-emerged upper class.

At the other end of the social ladder, the peasants and farm laborers have receded in numbers and we now find an ever growing number of factory workers, the proletariat.

Another new feature on the social scene in this the industrial age, is the middle class, the bourgeoisie. As the second wave progresses this class grows in size. It can be seen as the group that has been "recruited" by the upper classes to manage, to invent, to rationalize, to run the factories and emerging massive bureaucracies, to train, educate and socialize the vast socio-technical system of the industrial age.

The task of this middle class is to manage the proletariat, the working classes. The working classes, at the outset of the second wave, typically are unorganized and in desperate circumstances, fresh off the farm, as it were. With the passage of time, the working classes organize themselves, gain power and improve their situation. The history of the rise of the labor unions is the story of this dramatic empowerment.

Oppression in this era is secular in nature. Nietzsche's pronouncement that "God is dead" is the hallmark of the second wave. The monarchial theocracy has been replaced with the rational state. Government has been technicized. Oppression is now carried out now in the name of rationality. The logic may be flawed but the reverence for rationality is the prime mover. Taylorism (2016), time and motion studies, bureaucratization all render the person as a machine and legitimize the domination of others.

This rationality underlies both the industrialized capitalism of liberal and totalitarian states. In one system it was the rationality of the "invisible hand of the market" that was trusted. In another, it was communist or pseudo-communist ideology and the rationality of the "central committee" that was seen as the seat of truth. The industrial system and its associated socio-political structures require literacy and education, thus one can no longer dominate through the near-complete ignorance of the masses.

Domination still has a brutal physical quality, insofar as workers are exhausted, and operate under what Marx calls "wage slavery" and debt slavery while the middle classes are rendered anxious lest they slip down the social ladder. Volsinov (2013), in his telling critique of Freudianism, argues that psychoanalysis is mainly aimed at these very anxieties.

Persuasion, what Althusser (2014) terms, "the reproduction of ideology" becomes extremely important in the second wave. Persuasion, indoctrination, propaganda to capture the hearts and minds of the masses. Newspapers, radio and later film are used to create a mass psychology that facilitates this domination. Such "reproduction" of beliefs and ideology is dealt with not only by Althusser (2014) at length, but also by Adorno (2001).

In the second wave, however, there is an ever growing middle class and owing to the demands of an ever more technologizing society, an ever growing intelligentsia. This intelligentsia, during the second wave, is fairly capable of reflecting on social conditions. William Cobbett, Karl Marx, Weber, the Hamburg School of Critical Theory among many others—thinkers and artists alike--who are all examples of this capacity for critical reflection are to be found in the second wave. Some of these thinkers will be handmaidens of the powers-that-be and some will be critical of the system, those that Marx called, "the progressive elements of the bourgeoisie".

Thus, while there is enduring inequality and oppression, there is also a growing quantum of criticism. It is possible for the individual (usually a member of the "progressive elements of the bourgeoisie", as Marx would have it) to be alienated, to feel like something is wrong and the system needs to be adjusted. This critical capacity will change in the next, the third wave.

To dominate in the second wave, one must gain access to capital, technology and means of indoctrination, while to dominate in the first wave, one must gain access to God, the land, physical power and the aristocracy. We recall that these patterns at the macro level will manifest throughout the social system— affecting nations, regions, communities, families, institutions and individuals.

Oppression in the Third Wave

In the third wave, the factory-based blue collar worker has all but disappeared as workers have been displaced from automated factories into the service sector. Much of the time, these second wave jobs have migrated to other economies which are transitioning from an earlier wave. The middle class has grown, not only in numbers but also in dimensions. Many service sectors jobs "look" middle class (telemarketing, retail) but are lower in pay than many blue collar jobs.

The aristocracy has receded in visibility and prominence and the super wealthy of the second wave have usually adapted to the new conditions in the post-industrial era. One of these new features is a very high level of dynamic change in the socio-technical system. Change, wrought by the army of technologists in the middle classes, comes thick and fast - -the new rich emerge and join the ranks of the super wealthy at a rapid clip while the middle class has the range and depth of a Dickensian novel where one finds middle class landed gentlemen rubbing shoulders with Mr. Micawber and even, perhaps, Bill Sykes.

A new form of oppression emerges in this phase – third wave oppression. Instead of aristocracy and religion, instead of capital, wage slavery and overt coercion to conformity we find the creation (to use Marcuse's term) of "one dimensional man" (Marcuse, 1991). In part through the creation of what Adorno (2001) calls the "culture industry," the capacity to escape the indoctrination of the masses is reduced so dramatically that fewer and fewer people manage to feel, to observe and reflect upon their alienation from society and its structures. In this incapacity to see through the contradictions in the socio-technical system, people become brainwashed and subjugated, but do not know it. While this was true of the masses in the second wave, it is even more widespread and thoroughgoing in the third wave. It is furthermore achieved by "soft", seemingly innocuous means. The second wave jackbooted rantings of Hitler or Mussolini or the vast military parades of a Stalin would not work in a "cool" "Macluhanesque" third wave society. We find this anticipated in the Orwellian assertion (2009) "all art is propaganda". In third wave societies, the techniques would be that of a soft machine: a television ad campaign, movies with product placement ads, changes in style, television situation comedies, public relations campaigns, reputation management, preying upon the narcissism of small differences, "doublespeak" (Orwell, 1950)--all these and more would warp and bend thought so as to flow along conventional lines. Every so often an alternative form, a spontaneous gesture, a dissident voice might emerge, but these are very quickly assimilated into the conventional forms of the culture industry. The radical, critical gesture of today shows up in the fashionable commercial of tomorrow. It is somewhat analogous to a mall, a controlled environment, devoted to consumption, giving the illusion of diversity where there is the appearance of alterity (Hazell, 2009) but no true appreciation of difference.

The movie "The Matrix" (1999) metaphorically captures this condition insofar as the bulk of the population is utterly unaware of their condition of subjugation and only achieves realization of this at great cost and risk. The likelihood of the consciousness of alienation, as Marcuse asserts, is extremely low, if not nil. We have thus become, in the third wave, one-dimensional.

Oppression in the Fourth Wave

In the fourth wave, of which we already see signs, the contradictions that were to some extent available in the previous waves have all but disappeared. Baudrillard (1994) writes of this situation and its consequences. His approach is to examine the relationship between signifier and signified. In the early waves there is a strong relationship between the two insofar as it is believed that the name one gives something will affect the thing in itself. Conversely the very name of the thing is said to have a connection, amounting to an identity with the thing it symbolizes. Thus, the flag of a country is equivalent to the country, the name of a god is that god. Both the symbol and the thing in itself are treated as if they shared qualities. We find this attitude in early childhood development. This attitude is superseded by the growing awareness and belief in the arbitrary nature of signs and the relative independence of signifier and signified. Through the second wave and into the third wave the technologies enable an ever greater realization of the object such that films, for example, come to approximate, more and more, the "real". As Baudrillard points out, by the time we enter the fourth wave the representation of the real has increased to the point of being a simulacrum. We reach the era of the "deep fake". This has the effect of "abolishing" the real as a separate category and we then live in a world that is itself a simulacrum, a matrix of simulacra. Thus, if one gains power over these simulacra, one has power. Such an eventuality is anticipated comedically in the advent of "mockumentaries" such as "This is Spinal Tap" (1984) and "The Office" (2001-2003) and in acts such as Andy Kaufmann as (perhaps) the apocryphal Tony Clifton (MaTeOWaN, 2018) and the "Ted Talk" of Sam Hyde (2013). Debord (2002) anticipates this scenario very early in his depiction of the society of the "spectacle", as do Deleuze and Guattari (1986,1987,2009) with the concept of the "plane of immanence". Those still remembering the sense of reality that obtained in the earlier waves will ask, when confronted with this simulacrum, in wonderment, "Is this real?" thus expressing in their bafflement the "deterritorialization" (Deleuze and Guattari, 2009) consequent to the cultural displacement wrought by the new socio-technical era.

How each wave manifests in groups and organizations

The first wave will manifest in a tendency towards a hierarchical system of authority. Authority or power is inherited or appointed and may manifest in something of a caste, dynasty or feudal system. Knowledge is viewed as centralized in those in the know and the sense of deindividualization that is located in the bulk of the members results in speedy, summary decisions carried out by one or a few select members of the elite.

The second wave will resemble the functional organizational chart of the business world of mid-stage capitalism. There is a hierarchical system, but it is more complex and less centralized and more dendritic. There is an emergent bureaucracy or its equivalent. The dialectic of oppressor and oppressed is more visible and lasts longer than in the previous stage as there is a greater reliance, in this scheme, on the expertise of the emerging middle class for the management and development of the socio-technical system.

In the third wave, we find markers in the language used and there is an apparent change in the organizational chart, be it explicit or implicit. This is the age of "soft management", the age where employees are called "team-members" or "associates" and they labor in "teams", or in a "matrix management" system and they are encouraged to develop their "empowerment" and to work in "flex-time" formats and "cross-train". In this system, the rhetoric is that of collaboration and equality, but this is usually a mask for more subtle forms of domination and power. In important ways, this is powered by the traditional means of "wage slavery" and "debt slavery" but it is enabled to a great extent by the expansion of technologies that permit the almost full-time indoctrination of values that keep the system going. This is the age of the "one dimensional man" of Marcuse (1991). Systems of management and leadership theory emerge to accommodate the complexity of this situation, such as the "situational leadership" scheme of Hersey and Blanchard (2012).

In the fourth wave we may turn to Deleuze and Guattari (1987,

2009) for guidance. A helpful image is that of the "rhizome." A rhizome has properties that are different from the seed (which capture the previous eras). A rhizome may sprout in almost any direction. It is a whole, but it is also fractal in that half a rhizome may still sprout. A rhizome lacks the dendritic, hierarchical structure we find in the other socio-technical forms. What this means, on a practical level is that things may turn up anywhere. The world is more Kafkaesque (Deleuze and Guattari, 1986). In the deterritorialization wrought by the fourth-wave technologies we feel a sense of bizarreness, unless we are fully acculturated to it, as are, perhaps, elements of the younger generations. A metaphor that captures this is found, to a great extent, in the fiction of Kafka and in much modern entertainment where a protagonist enters a different room and is confronted with a bizarre set of circumstances where they do not feel "at home" insofar as it feels uncanny (Freud, 1919). A telling example of this is found at the end of Kafka's "Amerika" (2019) where Karl finds employment at "The Nature Theater of Oklahoma."

In addition we note that, in this fourth-wave socio-technical system in a rhizome-like fashion that small events like nodules on a rhizome may very quickly emerge and blossom. These emergences take the mentality that is accustomed to the frameworks of analysis found in the previous waves by surprise and are seen as random. However, we may apply the theory of imaginary groups (Hazell, 2005) and see that they do show up, only in very small ways, sometimes microscopic. (One is put in mind of the attention paid by interpersonal psychodynamic psychotherapy to the microscopic.) These small signs can be seen as potential emergences of an unconscious imaginary group. The observation of such signs can be carried out by any of the techniques (note, technique is related to a technology and technology reveals) mentioned in this book, such as listening posts, social dreaming, open space, group relations conferences, reflexive ethnography and so on.

As examples of this we may cite the "Arab Spring" phenomenon which may be seen as emanating from one disgruntled stallholder

(Mohammed Bouazizi) who dramatically protests the kickbacks and corruption he has to deal with on a daily basis. This individual protest seems to set off a conflagration throughout the middle east and the consequences are still being played out at the time of writing, years later. More recently we see in 2018 the eruption of the *"gilets jaunes"* in France which started off as a small demonstration, but then suddenly grew until it became internationally acknowledged. These precipitants, "small" though they are, could be anticipated by attention being paid to even smaller signs and symptoms, if the models and approach described here and elsewhere were to be used. Just as an individual might improve their functioning and adaptation to reality by keeping note of their dreams and using this data stream as a guide to consciously unacknowledged issues that need attention, so a group, society or planet might benefit from attention to its group unconscious in its various, often microscopic manifestations. Deleuze and Guattari would enjoin us to pay attention not only to the molar, but also to the molecular.

The previous examples show how the fourth wave socio-technical system might be seen as operating on a large scale but the system can be scaled down. For example, Semmelhack *et al* (2013) describe a case where, in a nursing home one woman expressed an intense desire for a women's support group. This request was hypothesized to come from an unconscious "imaginary group" of women (or "female part objects") that wished to agglomerate. Correspondingly, a group was scheduled and gained good attendance. Through this mechanism, arguably, powerful issues could be spoken about and metabolized in a group before symptoms emerged at any level from individual through to community and beyond.

Thus, we may, as we interact with a family, group, organization or region, encounter a socio-technical system that operates according to one or more, or all of these templates. Acknowledging this as a possibility might enhance our understanding of what is going on. In addition, as has been argued and as will be argued next, all of this is expressed historically and, thus, spatially.

These forms have an historical and a geographical dimension. Unfortunately, these dimensions are not frequently emphasized or even acknowledged in the field of mental health and group dynamics. One might do well to recall Bachmann-Medick (2016) who amplifies Jameseson's (1981) edict, "always historicize" with her own, "always spatialize!"

5: Participation in Technology: Who Plays This Game?

Who plays this game, the game of technology? Who gets to invent? Who decides which inventions will be sponsored and how they will be deployed? Given that technology will shape society, this is an important question. We posit that technology is such a potent shaper of society and of history that it functions like a block of votes, votes for a certain way of life, certain values, politics, social and economic systems. If this is the case and if we wish to have a democratic society, these "technological votes" would be shared equally, or at least have a democratic mandate. We see, however, when we look at the history of technology, that participation in the development, deployment and use of technology is profoundly affected by "isms" of various kinds. Thus, sexism, racism, class prejudice, nationalism, ethnocentrism can all dramatically exclude certain groups from the technology process. Women, children, certain races, the aged, the poor and persons from certain regions of the planet are significantly under-represented in the pantheon of inventors and technocrats. Most inventors are white, middle class males and of those a significant proportion are driven, competitive, isolative and often suspicious. Thus, society is being shaped in important ways by this relatively small group. History has examples of individuals who managed, often against all odds, to become players in the technological process. Garret Morgan, an African American, invented the traffic light, and the gas mask, but had great difficulty, owing to racism, gaining any recognition for his work, especially for his gas mask. He only gained some recognition when finally newspapers finally printed photographs of him helping a rescue team don these masks before going into a mine to save some trapped miners.

One is led to a set of questions. What would the world look like if women had invented more of our technology? What would the world look like if children, the working classes, the aged or the poor were more involved in the technology process? The theory proposed here predicts that the world would be different, since these groups are driven by different values, priorities and aims and these would result in different technologies. Using the "Heideggerian" model outlined below, it is quite likely that different enframings of standing reserves would have occurred. Applying the Marxist notion that technology is a weapon used by the bourgeoisie against the proletariat, especially the craftspersons, to render their skills redundant and thus devalued, we again reach the position that the history of technology might well have been different and the world a different place.

For example, women are typically socialized to value human relationships, intimacy and continuity in social groups (Gilligan 2016, Chodorow, 1991). Perhaps the technology that women, thus socialized, would develop would both reflect and facilitate these values. Men, on the other hand are often socialized to value rationality, autonomy and competitiveness. One could argue that those values indeed are reflected in much of the technology developed and deployed by men.

A similar case could be made for children and the technology children use. Many schools constructed during the industrial era mimic factories and are singularly "child unfriendly." Doors are heavy, banisters too fat for tiny hands, colors are drab, surfaces often hard, smells and sounds unpleasant. What would this technology look like if children, its primary users, were involved in the design process? What would facilities used by the old look like if they were involved in the technology design and deployment process. To be engaged in this process of developing and deploying technology is to gain, in an important sense, a franchise in what one's world will look like. To exclude individuals and groups from this process is to disenfranchise them.

6: The Personality of the Inventor

A similar argument could be forwarded with regard to the types of people who come to dominate the technology scene. When we examine the personality types of inventors we find a high proportion of individuals who are highly driven, competitive, logically-minded, often prone to isolation and not infrequently, suspicious. They often have many of the qualities of the obsessive personality.

If the world is shaped by technology and much technology is shaped by obsessive personalities, then the world is, in significant ways, being designed by obsessives. Even if this sequence of assertions is only partially true, it is worthy of careful consideration. Is this the kind of world we wish to inhabit? What technology, what world would be shaped if technology was in the hands of say "histrionic" personalities, or "dependent" personalities or "self-actualized" personalities? Might these worlds be preferable in some ways? If it were, what could be done, for example, in schools, colleges, companies, foundations and governments to affect the balance to alter the representativeness of those who get to play the technology game? Competitions, prizes, grants, projects, courses, departments for example could be devoted to, say, "self actualizing technology," "technologies of human contact and collaboration," "non-isolative technologies," "archetypal technology" or "intuitive technology." Perhaps this would induct personalities into the realm of technology that they otherwise would not have considered.

For example, typically when one administers the Myers-Briggs Type Inventory (Briggs-Myers, 1995) to a group of engineers or technologists, one finds a high incidence of "STJ's," meaning sensing, thinking & judging types – practical, logical and organized. Every so often one will encounter an "NFP," an intuitive, feeling, perceptive type, imaginative, emotional and spontaneous. Usually these individuals feel like the "odd one out," but usually with encouragement, they can be helped to see they have a valid and important contribution to make to the technological realm, one that emphasizes spontaneous life, human values, feeling and possibilities for different ways of being.

It is sad indeed when people such as these opt out of the technology game, taking with them their valuable balancing contributions. Career guidance counselors would be wise, I believe, to bear these possibilities in mind when working with individuals who express an interest in technology but who identify as an "NFP" on the Myers Briggs Type Inventory. Gifts differing (Briggs-Myers, 1995) provides an overview of this instrument and its implications.

The Inventor: Container and Contained

When asking the question, "Who invents?" we may also deploy Bion's theory of container and contained. The inventor can be seen as the individual who contains a "wild thought" about a new technology or technique. The society which the inventor inhabits contains both the inventor and his or her wild idea. Bion posits that individuals will vary in their capacity to "tame wild thoughts" (Bion, 1997). Similarly, groups and societies will vary in their capacity to contain and tame wild thoughts and will accordingly vary widely in their reaction to such ideas. At one extreme we find societies where such wild ideas might be encouraged, much in the way a company might foment change by installing and maintaining a research and development department. Again, this department might vary widely in its "wildness" depending on the containing capacities of its surrounding context. At the other extreme, we find groups and societies where there is what might be termed a phobia of letting the wild thoughts take root, of ensuring that no "bats settle in the belfry." In such a society the inventor will contain their wild idea on their own, with varying degrees of success depending on a range of variables. Perhaps they become the proverbial "mad scientist." Perhaps they become a prophet of the technological type in another land. One is put in mind here of Nikola Tesla who moves from Serbia to the USA and how even in America many of his ideas are met with terrific resistance and are, arguably, even under-utilized today. For example, the wireless transmission of electric power or derivatives of the Wardenclyffe experiment would have, if successful and widely enough deployed, a radically transformative impact on society. One could argue that even the relative lack of acknowledgment of the huge contributions of Tesla's inventions (the induction motor, hydro-electric power, radio, radio control, mag-lev transportation, alternating current, the Tesla coil—to name a few of the hundreds of his inventions) to modern and post-modern society is in part due to a social repression of that which these inventions unleashed or, if mobilized, would have unleashed.

From a Marxist perspective, the function of technology is to act as a weapon in class warfare insofar as it aims at systematically reducing the value of the labor of the craftsman or craftswoman. Technology takes the craft of, say, the blacksmith and replaces it with the moving production line on which the blacksmith then works as a semi-skilled or unskilled, lower-paid laborer who is easily replaced. In this framework, the inventor, the container of the wild thought is typically recruited from the ranks of the bourgeoisie to place these ideas at the service of the ruling classes. For these individuals adequate containment will be provided so long as the technology serves the purposes of the ruling elites.

For those containing ideas that do not serve those purposes, such containment will be in short shrift. They will have to fend for themselves with scant social resources aimed at containment of their wild ideas.

We may posit then that the inventor may be viewed as a potential tamer of wild thoughts and, like the individual who has untamed ideas of any sort (aesthetic, spiritual, socio-psychological, economic and so on) is placed in a potentially vulnerable position in a society or group. In both cases the new idea may be seen as disruptive and may be repressed. The individual may then come to serve as a repository, as a scapegoat. This will be especially true where the idea, be it abstract or concrete, cultural or technological, disrupts the status quo. If, however, the idea is seen to bolster the position of the ruling classes the container of the new idea, of the "wild thought" is placed, to some extent, in a more favourable position. Several works of fiction and science fiction capture these dynamics, for example, Mamet's "The Water Engine" (1977).

7: Integration: The Psychodynamics of the Socio-Technical System

Each element in the model of the socio-technical system is affected by unconscious forces. Some, such as the connection between unconscious psychodynamics and culture have been explored in great depth elsewhere (Roheim, 1971,1974,2010; Devereux, 1951,1961,1980; Kardiner, 1939; Erikson, 1993a). Others, such as the connection between, say, invention and unconscious dynamics, not so much.

Once some tendrils of connection between the socio-technical system and psychodynamics have been drawn, we will then be able to place this in a spatial context, to begin to provide additional explanations, beyond the standard geographical ones, for the persistence of differences and tensions between regions at every scale—from the city block, to the campus, to the village, to the county, state, nation and on to the level of the civilization (to use this latter term, to some extent, as employed by Huntington, 1996).

When we employ the checklist advanced by Hazell and Kiel (2016)— FABART/Rules--Fantasy, Affect, Boundaries, Authority, Roles, Tasks and the Rules that govern them--and juxtapose it to technological developments we may bring about a certain set of notions regarding the inter-relations of technology and the psychodynamics of social systems. Technology evokes changes in all of these domains on the individual and the group level. Here we will focus on the group-as-a-whole impacts of technology in these domains.

Fantasy: Fantasies, both conscious and unconscious, are stimulated by the advent of technology. For example, the technology of robotics has stimulated a wide array of fantasies, as witnessed by the burgeoning of science fiction novels and films depicting future scenarios, for including, Bicentennial Man (1999), AI (2001), Terminator (1984) etc. Some myths speak to the unconscious meanings of technologies, witness Prometheus and his eternal punishment for stealing fire from the gods. Here we see that the fantasies might involve dreams of immense power and the dangers of usurping and taking hold of its "magic," We see such anxieties expressed in the Promethean myth captured in Mary Shelley's "Frankenstein" presciently written at the beginning of the industrial revolution.

Affect: Technology is clearly related to affect and such emotional reactions are often depicted aesthetically. In the movie, "2001-A Space Odyssey" (1968), we witness the re-enactment of the invention of the club and the attendant joy released in the proto-human as its power and utility are recognized. We also see the fear of the new as the obelisk makes its appearance and in the culminating scenes where space, time, place and person become warped in a baffling moebius-like continuum. In Orwell's "1984" (1950) we witness the depression brought on by the depersonalization of post-industrial technology, while in Huxley's, "Island" (2002) we witness a harmonious, transcendent culture where emotional trauma is worked through with the use of the drug "soma."

All of the domains of FABART interact. Thus the fantasies stimulated by technology, which might have to do with mastery, offending the father, castration, immortality, loss of identity and so on, will all have emotional correlates—fear, anticipation, dread, hope, joy, anger and so on. Groups will have, to a greater or lesser extent, avenues for the expression and management of these emotions and will flourish or founder depending on their effectiveness. As hinted at above, aesthetic activity is one extremely important avenue for documenting, sharing and processing emotional responses to technologies, both technologies already present and those about to come. As McLuhan, with typical acerbity, informs us, "Artists look into the future using a rear-view mirror" (McLuhan, 2011).

Boundaries: Technologies change boundaries. And when a boundary is changed around an individual, group or institution there will be effects throughout every aspect of that system— throughout every element of FABART and the rules that govern it.

The previously-mentioned post-industrial classroom provides an example. Students with cell phones can communicate easily with the outside world. They can chat with friends, check Facebook or look up what is being covered in the class by the teacher. Thus the hermetic seal of the "sacred chamber" of the classroom has been broken. Notably, the authority position of the teacher has been altered—no longer is she the sole fount of knowledge in the room. And there will be emotional responses to this as the teacher feels something of a let-down in their central position. Perhaps rules need to be changed. Perhaps no cell phones should be allowed in the classroom, but isn't this simply a clinging to the old model of education? Perhaps the whole structure of the educational enterprise should be examined. This will probably require re-examining the task of the group which may need to be reformulated in the light of the new socio-technical system and new demands being placed upon it and the individuals who inhabit it.

Boundary management: We can see in the foregoing example of the classroom how intimately bound together are issues of boundary and authority. As technology enables the transgression of the traditional boundaries around the classroom, so the position of the professor and her authority is altered. We see a similar engagement in, say, families where, for example, a child might have access through their cell phone to all sorts of information, people and experiences through the internet and multiple applications. In the days of dominance of print media, the inflow and outflow of information across the family's boundaries was far more easily controlled and monitored. With the advent of cellphones hooked into the world wide web the boundary situation has changed, not only for families but for all scales of social groups. Once the boundary of a group undergoes a qualitative change every other aspect of that group is affected. We see this in the enactment of everyday scenarios in families where parental concerns over the children's use of information technologies occur with as high a frequency as, say, governmental concerns over citizen's usage of informational technologies, and vice versa.

The beating of citizens by the police or their apprehension and murder can now be captured on cell-phones such that the "whole world is watching", to quote the shouts of those protesting in the streets of Chicago in recent technological times. Thus the boundaries around the everyday are altered, as are the boundaries around the role of those in power. The advent of inexpensive drones equipped with cameras and all sorts of easily hidden surveillance devices radically alter one's assumptions regarding privacy and boundaries. Again, the concept of boundaries is very closely linked with ideas about all the other elements in the FABART matrix—to change boundaries is to change affect, authority, roles, rules and tasks.

A vital boundary in group life is the boundary between the individual and the group. It is a classic issue confronted in the decades-long psychodynamic study of groups. The individual, upon entering a group, feels conflicting urges—the wish to belong and the fear of being engulfed. Much of group dynamics, especially in a group's early stages, can be understood as emanating from the attempts of its members to reconcile these twin drives. With the addition of technology that can effectively accomplish both of these aims (i.e. a technology that enables one to join and one that makes one feel that one cannot leave or feel unique or have a private self), this conflictual human predicament is amplified such that one would predict oscillations back and forth from the extremes of "being a part of" to "being apart from" until the individual and the group culture achieves some sort of dynamic equilibrium. Unfortunately, not all groups, individuals and organizations are equally well-equipped to cope and along the way one could predict one will find casualties of the changes wrought by the social impacts of technological innovation. These casualties lie beyond the usually employed category included in the notion of "structural unemployment" (that is, unemployment and redundancy brought about by technological innovation) and therefore are usually overlooked and explained in some other way; often these reactions are pathologized.

Authority: Power derives from several sources (French and Raven, 1959)—Legitimate, Reward, Expert, Referent and Coercive. Each of these are influenced by access to information. The greater one's access to information, the more power and influence one might wield. A plethora of technologies alter access to information and to the reliability with which one may regard that information. The internet enables one to have access to global sources of information—information that once might only be held by those seeking or holding power. We saw this in in the previous example in the small scale of the classroom. We see it also operating at the larger scale of nations where highly centralized authoritarian governments see their power as being potentially undermined through the widespread utilization of information-sharing technologies, such as the internet and its applications-- Facebook, YouTube, Twitter and Instagram. The power of these information-sharing technologies is magnified when combined with small video cameras that send images of news with extreme ease. Those wishing to stay in power will use these technologies to further their ends. Thus we see the president of the United States of America routinely "tweeting" in an attempt to alter the perceptions of events occurring in the world—sometimes to recast the meaning of an event, sometimes to challenge the veracity of information shared, sometimes to attack the reliability of the disseminator of the information. This technology is used in many political ploys. One is put in mind of the expertise with which Hitler utilized the then nascent technologies of film and radio to promulgate his political ends. On an international basis we see authority relations being affected by the use of technologies through trolling.

Technology can radically alter power relations and it places groups on something of a knife edge, for while it promises much in the way of additional information, improved adaptation, improved communication, it can also provide opportunities for increased disinformation, reduced adaptation and increased exploitation. In this, too, we see echoes of Heidegger's notion of the revelatory function of technology, namely, that a technology, much like psychoanalysis, can serve an uncovering function, exposing what lies beneath the surface of society.

Roles: At the most concrete level, new technologies create new roles and eradicate old ones. Flint-knapping moves from being a profession to becoming a hobby and blacksmithing becomes a profession with the advent of metals. Typesetting and web design, whaling and oil-drilling bear similar relationships. Beyond this, all the changes in other aspects of the socio-technical system (fantasies, affect, boundaries, authority, tasks and the rules that govern them) bring about shifts in roles—shifts at the formal and informal level. This in turn, creates all sorts of role tensions—the tensions experienced by individuals and groups as they shift roles and the tensions that are now created between the person and their role they must now play (are they really "cut out" for this type of work?). The same demand is placed upon the organization, group or subgroup and its role (Can this organization shift in its role adequately in order to keep up with the new role demands?).

Again the 21st century classroom provides examples. As information becomes more freely available to students through online media, the professor is called upon to change her role from "fount of knowledge" and "dispenser of information" to "facilitator of the gathering, evaluation and synthesis of information." This can be an exciting shift. It can also be an arduous one.

In addition, as the classroom becomes increasingly an online experience, the professor may find that their job comes to resemble more that of a call center operative as they field emails and telephone queries from students around the world and quizzes are graded by a computer. They also may find their job is monitored by someone in a distant city who is counting the number of their posts in online discussions and their response speed to student inquiries, much in the way such things are monitored in call centers. Again for some, this "clerical shift" may be quite rewarding as it aligns with what be measured as "Conventional Interest" on the Strong Interest Inventory (Donnay, 1997) and, since it is efficient, they are comfortable and they take up the roles easily. For others, it may be experienced as boring and deprofessionalizing as it takes them away from the interpersonally intense matrix of the classroom and the elements of performance art found in the lecture hall and they thus find the new role very difficult to adjust to.

Tasks: Technological innovation changes tasks. New tasks are created. We see this reflected in the commonly cited statistic that most of the jobs of, say, ten years in the future, do not exist today. Similarly, many jobs and their associated tasks will disappear as technology is innovated. Everything in the FABART/Rules system is inter-related. This is especially true when it comes to tasks. When we ask about the functionality of fantasies, boundaries and affect, or question the legitimacy of authority, one benchmark to which we may refer, in a pragmatic fashion, is the way in which such relate to the performance of the task. Once again, we notice powerful "knock-on" effects in the socio-technical system. Technological innovation alters the tasks of a group and this change rolls through the system, altering everything else, both at a conscious and unconscious level.

Rules: The changes wrought by technology call for changes in the rules that govern the socio-technical system. Examples of the relatively "anarchic" early phases in the development and deployment of technologies are quite plentiful. In the early days of the automobile, there were few, if any rules of the road or even driving licenses. In organizations that introduced the internet and email one frequently observed six months or so of "free usage" with free visitation of websites and emails of all sorts zipping about. Soon however, companies realized that their code of conduct had to extend to the usage of this technology. Certain sites were off-limits, employees activities online were monitored and guidelines given as to how email should be used. This pattern repeats itself as technologies move through the early "anarchistic" phase to a more rule bound phase and, sometimes, on to an "appropriate technology" phase where the impact of the technology on things such as the environment, civil rights, physical and mental health or the political climate are examined and the rules become ever more refined and a subject for often, quite complex debate. At the time of writing this, "sex robots" of some sophistication are being developed. No doubt this new technology will call for shifts in rules and will have effects that reverberate throughout the socio-technical system, both the "PIBSCREAM" and "FABART/Rules."

8: Lacan and Technology

Technology may be fruitfully regarded through the lens of the ideas of Lacan. First, one may look upon technology as a *sinthome* (Lacan, 2018). From this perspective technology is seen as a symptom, first in the classic Freudian sense and secondly in the re-interpretation offered by Lacan. This idea is explored in Romayshyn's "Technology as Symptom and Dream" (1989).We see, for example, the use of technology in the *fort-da* game (Freud, 1920) where the child expresses and at the same time achieves some mastery and understanding of the thoughts, feelings and fantasies associated with the separation-individuation process. The technology, in this case, is the spool attached to a string that is tossed away and retrieved. The technology (which involves, we recall, not only the tool but also the procedures associated with the tool and its deployment) thus can be "read" in much the same way a symptom (or a dream) can be read—as containing a code to the underlying desire, defenses against the desire and a solution to the conflict between the two. We are close here to the concept of the transitional object of Winnicott (1965), the soft object that fills in the gap between the mother and the child. This object as Winnicott points out elaborates through time into all cultural, aesthetic and spiritual activities. In short it develops into what makes life feel worthwhile.

The deployment of the technology in both of these cases (and here we introduce a Lacanian concept) leads to the experience of *jouissance*, which is a complex experience involving the joy and satisfaction of the moments of orgasm. In these moments, so brief and yet so vital, there is a fading away of the object; there is the experience of "only me." In French, only me translates into *"seulement mo "* and then forms a pun with *"sur le mont, moi"* which translates back into English as, "On the mountain, me," which captures the exaltation of jouissance. We thus arrive at the position where technology, as a sinthome, enables the experience

115

of jouissance, the temporary imaginary mastery and satiation of desire, the eradication of the gap (the *"beance,"* in Lacan's terminology) between desire and its realization.

The sinthome can be diagrammed, utilizing Lacan's Borromean Knot in several ways, one of which is seen below:

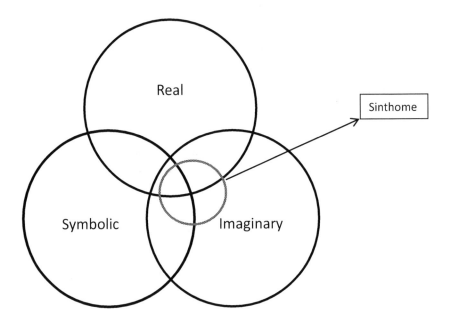

Figure 7: Representation of the sinthome in the spaces of the Borromean Knot

The sinthome, pictured thus, lies entirely within the realm of the imaginary so that parts of it are entirely imaginary. It does, however include elements of the Real, the Symbolic and part of the region where Real and Symbolic overlap. None of the sinthome lies in the region of the purely Symbolic or the Purely Real. In this, the sinthome can be understood as a retreat from the Symbolic (in everyday terms, it does not "want" to be understood symbolically) and as a retreat, in addition, from the Real (it "resists" encounters with the truth of the Real). It can be understood as a construction, predominantly imaginary, that, in the manner of a *bricolage*, patches together whatever is available in the Symbolic and Real as a means of mastering anxiety, dread, desire, conflict and the other panoply of anguishes that beset the human being.

We argue that technology, viewed as a sinthome can be profitably regarded in this same (Lacanian/neo-Freudian) manner. The Real is traumatic (Lacan, 1997). The Symbolic involves following the rules of a language of some sort and adapting to reality, in short, psychological work and frustration. The sinthome takes elements of the Real and Symbolic and weaves them into an imaginary narrative or, in this case, a device and a set of procedures to recoil from both of these pains and achieve, in addition, a sense of perfect mastery over the exigencies they present. This narrative then becomes woven into the story of an individual's and society's identity and can then be identified as an element of the *"falsifying function of the ego"* or group identity.

This is not to argue that societies where technologies are avoided are more capable of confronting the Real and the Symbolic for we will often find that they rely on a subset of acceptable technologies or spend a good deal of time thinking about technologies that might be acceptable. The sinthome remains, even in its virulent rejection, in what might be considered an obsessional form.

A homely, everyday narrative might show how these dynamics play out close at hand.

X and D with no wifi:

We recently went on a week-long vacation to the Upper Peninsula of Michigan. We stayed in a beautiful remote lakefront cabin, situated right on the beach. As soon as we arrived, our grandson and his friend hived off to their rooms, only to return in a few minutes exclaiming, "There is no wifi! We cannot play our games!" To the older couple in the group, this was no big problem. It was welcome, in fact since it enforced peace and quiet upon us, an opportunity to go within, perhaps a chance to engage in intimate conversation or simply "space out" in nature. Not so for the two youngsters for whom it was a catastrophe. One could almost sense the yawning chasm of emptiness, of understimulation they foresaw. It was so bad that when asked if they would like to return to this bucolic paradise, with nature and a perfect beach for swimming, running, sand-castling, they replied, "Only if it has wifi!"

What do we get when we apply Lacanian (and Heideggerian) ideas to this vignette, which is almost commonplace?

First, what is wifi as a sinthome? What anxieties and depressions does it symptomatically "solve"? Perhaps the fear of emptiness, of under-stimulation. Perhaps the dread of disconnection with others and, at the same time, since it envelops one in an isolated cocoon of "the game", an anxiety of intimacy and all of the truths that can emerge when one shares interpersonally. The game involves competition and mastery and its content is often of a paranoid nature, where subjects are pursued and attempt to escape through labyrinths. Perhaps it is this that one is left with in its raw, undigested state without the technology of wifi. In a different register, when one plays the game one is drawn into a community of other gamers with whom one might converse at a later time— when one goes back home, through social media, in conversation. Thus participation in the game helps one develop social currency and join a group. Perhaps it was this that was felt to be at risk in the absence of Wi-Fi. For the late middle-age adults, social isolation was something to be enjoyed. For middle-school boys it is something to be feared, much as Sullivan (1953) posits ostracism as the key to much anxiety in this (and other) age-groups.

9: Heidegger on Technology

Heidegger (1977) points out that his definition of technology is different from that which is usually held; that is to say, he does not see technology solely as a means to an end or as a tool. In several ways his ideas help form a connection between technology and the psychodynamic theory of social systems. Heidegger's quest, in his essay, is to grasp the "essence" of technology, or, in other words, to capture what is it about technology that "endures" (since this quality of "going on" is an essential component of being—of essence). What is it that is always present in technology? What lies at the core of technologies? When we follow his argument, we find some ideas that have tremendous impact on our understanding of groups and of the manner in which technology impacts the individual and the group. We may then proceed to inquire as to how this impact will have a spatial dimension.

Heidegger arrives at the conclusion that, "technology is a way of revealing" —"It is a way of revealing i.e. of truth"(1977, p12). Technology takes up this role since it causes things to come into being. It thus takes its place alongside the arts, poetry and science. In addition, we would argue that technology, in its revelatory function, stands alongside psychoanalysis, poetry and speculative philosophical systems as a potential revealer of truth or truths. Framed this way, technology may be seen as a revealer much in the way that psychoanalysis or some forms of psychotherapy can be "revealers." That which is hidden as potential, in the individual, group, institution, community and society is revealed by technology.

This uncovering reveals and releases what Heidegger calls a "standing reserve" (1977, p19) which is uncovered via a technology through a process called "enframing" (1977, p19). This process might be compared to a dam on a river, which holds the standing reserve, the potential energy of the mass of water behind it, or a bomb, which contains within it the standing reserve of energy in its contained materials. It is this release and revelation of contained energy that constitutes an essential aspect of the impact of technology on humans. "The essence of modern technology shows itself in what we call enframing" (1977, p23).

But this enframing is not purely technological, not just about tools, devices, procedures and machines, for "man stands within the essential realm of enframing" (1977, p24). Thus, once again, we arrive at the revelatory function of technology where the tool reveals humanity to itself. Much as the lifting of repressions reveals previously unknown areas of the self, so technology uncovers hidden aspects of the mind which were held in abeyance as "standing reserves" in a manner similar to the repressed drives, wishes, fantasies of the psychodynamic unconscious. These "standing reserves" may also, we would argue, be seen as pools of information in the information processing sense, information that has yet to be coded by the more rational functions operating at all levels from individual through to social. Much as when an individual can become flooded with unconscious material by a sudden insight and become temporarily overwhelmed, so might technology release a welter of new information that can temporarily engulf an individual, group, community, society or civilization. In the same way that therapy or psychoanalysis might reveal a long-standing individual or family secret that has brought about an array of adjustments in the individual or family, so technology will reveal societal, institutional and humanitarian secrets that have been driving many social and institutional phenomena. These revelations can be very disruptive, re-traumatizing even, especially if unanticipated and experienced without supports. In both cases supportive metabolizing structures would be of great help. If these are not present, the potential for acting out, paroxysms of pained and confused activity, might be expected.

However, these standing reserves are usually released without humans understanding what they are, where they are or what the consequences of their release will be. It is as if, metaphorically, humanity throws a boomerang out into the sky and then turns its back, busying itself with other things and is then stunned and shocked when hit on the back of the head by an object they do not recognize, a transformed boomerang. In yet another way, this process can be compared to a "wild analysis," where unconscious material is revealed, willy-nilly, at all levels of society from individual through to civilizational and global. As Heidegger

(1977, p24) states, "Thus the question as to how we are to arrive at relationship to the essence of technology, asked in this way, always comes too late." In everyday language, technology, without any prior warning, reveals something to us something about ourselves as individuals and groups. We then are called upon to cope with this new information, trying to play catch-up, coming to terms with what are usually uncomfortable, if not painful, truths.

Another metaphor helps illustrate further aspects of Heidegger's idea. It is as if technology operates like the stressor that can suddenly reveal that a person has a latent illness, say, tuberculosis. In many poor countries many people, especially women, are infected with tuberculosis, but do not have any of its symptoms and do not know they have it. When, however, they are visited with a stress of some sort, say, a pregnancy which weakens their immune system, the underlying illness manifests itself and symptoms, sometimes fatal, emerge. Technology operates like the stress in the above narrative. An individual, or a group or a society may hold within itself, unrecognized, a deep trauma, conflict or drive. A technology is introduced into this system, often enthusiastically, and this technology erodes the previously-shored-up defenses and symptoms emerge. These symptoms, however, unlike those of tuberculosis, are not recognized as resulting from the stress and are not even recognized as symptoms emanating from a previous infection. They are thus treated ineffectually, much as tuberculosis was before the discovery of its causes and antibiotics.

The U.S.A may perhaps serve as an example. Horne (2016) argues quite convincingly that the founding of the country was based upon a counter-revolution by the founding fathers and their cohorts in order to prevent abolition of slavery, recognition of the legal rights of Africans in America and to stem the tide of growing enfranchisement which seemed to be coming across the Atlantic from Britain. The country was, according to this narrative, founded upon white supremacist assumptions, much in the same way as the unilateral declaration of independence of Southern Rhodesia on November 11th, 1963 was an attempt to maintain the power and privilege of the ruling white minority in that country. If Horne is to be credited then the founding myth of the country, which posits that it was a fight for freedom from a colonial oppressor, is false or, at best, a half-truth, and based upon repression, distortion and denial. Thus, the repressed narrative takes the place of the standing reserve of Heidegger. It is a hidden truth and, just as a hidden family secret can create a multiplicity of poorly understood symptoms in a family, so a social secret will create a litany of mysterious ailments in a group, region or nation.

When a technological ensemble is introduced into a society or group, the consequences are structurally similar to the events that take place upon the revelation of a family secret and these too, with the advent of geneology software and the internet can be revealed at a much quicker pace than before, causing serious disruptions and adjustments in many inter-weaving social networks. When we add the advent of technological deployments and applications such as Facebook, Twitter, Instagram, Youtube, allied with the capacity to document with a cellphone, to the mix this massive denial and repression, this standing reserve, is revealed. The white supremacist mentality that previously was lying under cover is uncovered. Unfortunately, because of inadequate understandings of the dynamics of the socio-technical system, this was unanticipated. It never can be fully anticipated because one is always surprised and shocked by the unconscious when it shows its face. However, the fact that some form of traumatic emergency would have taken place could have been anticipated and mechanisms for coping with the pathological exudations could have been provided. For example, each year in the USA we are encouraged to get flu shots. Exactly which flu virus will strike is a calculated guess, necessarily so because the virus mutates so quickly. But at least some effort is made to anticipate the disease. Similarly, various agencies practice for the emergencies they might face in the future, such as floods, fires, storms and attacks of various sorts. Similarly a society or any group for that matter could work explicitly on the assumption that the introduction of a significant technology into its operations will reveal the "standing reserve". This "reserve" is not known, although perhaps it is anticipated by artists and the like, but is something distressing and inconvenient will be revealed can be reckoned upon and generic mechanisms established to cope with these revelations—mechanisms such as those discussed later in this text.

Heidegger then continues and examines what consequences this line of thought might have upon the notion of freedom which itself is founded upon the uncovering of truths. The enframing of which Heidegger speaks throws the individual and group into a reactive position as technology reveals qualities heretofore undreamt of, except, perhaps in science fiction.

In addition, Heidegger points out the dangers inherent in the revelatory function of technology. One can know too much too soon. This can be traumatic and can cause immense and tragic disruptions on all levels. One is reminded of Oedipus who suffers so much from his curiosity and his uncovering of truths. In this sense, technology can be seen as contributor to what Badiou (2013) terms an "event"—that which can increase the intensity of being, sometimes to unbearable heights.

Heidegger (1977, pS33) further argues that this revelatory function is double-edged. On the one hand, it presents a great danger, but on the other, it presents an opportunity to grow, to increase one's power. Here we are witnessing not the familiar trope of "technology can be used for good or evil" but a warning in a different register. Technology disrupts the psychodynamic equilibrium of the individual, group and society by revealing that which lies hidden, by bringing that which is hidden or only a potential, into being. It thus presents a crisis—a dangerous opportunity. This crisis can result in positive or negative disintegration, to employ Dabrowski's (1970, 1977) useful distinction. In this it parallels the potentials for growth that can arise in individuals and groups as they cope with stress and trauma. Some systems become more complex, that is, more differentiated and integrated, while others fragment, close or tend towards entropy—negative disintegration.

In all these cases, the likelihood of the trauma, strain or stress resolving with the system being in a higher state of complexity is increased if that system is aware of those dynamics. That is, if the individual or the group has some way of monitoring, anticipating and processing that which is revealed by technology in addition to dealing with the practical problems introduced by its advent.

For example, mobile phones introduced a plethora of social, practical technical adjustments. The list is long—tracking devices, illicit usage, redundancy of phone booths, privacy, impact on interpersonal relations and driving, and so on. What Heidegger is alerting us to is that mobile phones revealed what was previously only a standing reserve. This included a strong urge towards community, as witnessed by the popularity of social media. It also included a good deal of hatred and paranoia, as witnessed by cyber bullying, and online hate speech. Here, we seem close to a revelation of the drives of the Freudian id—love and hate—the Empedoclean twinning of forces of integration and disintegration. In addition we also see in the usage of cellphones a revelation of the wish to numb oneself, as witnessed by online games and by droves of people on the streets glued to their tiny screens as if to shut out a world, which is perhaps too much to bear. Here we see perhaps, the revelation, through technology, of a massive defense against trauma of all types, where the mobile phone and its apps are used as an anodyne or analgesic, much in the way the technology of opioids is used. The mobile phone, even with this scant perusal, seems to reveal a humanity that is traumatized, wishes for numbness and isolation but yearns for community and approval while terrified of its own hatred and that of others. This technology has revealed deep neurotic and psychotic anxieties and conflicts. Psychodynamic psychology informs us that if these conflicts are not thought through, put into some code, they will be acted out, usually blindly and usually at great cost.

Unfortunately such analysis rarely takes place at either the conscious or unconscious level. Recently there are more college courses and several publications on "society and technology" (McGinn, 1990) but as to the more psychological, especially the psychodynamic, impacts, there is very little. Metaphorically, this leaves humanity and the individual in the unfortunate situation of being recurrently traumatized, re-traumatized and deterritorialized, without any acknowledgment, support, treatment or even explanation.

To examine how these ideas might throw light from a different angle on historical events we might look at the rise of fascism in Europe prior to World War Two. What "enframing" took place during that era? What technologies liberated the standing reserves? What was the content of the standing reserves? Does such an analysis offer an additional explanation of those catastrophic decades?

Nancy (1991) provides us with a clue as to the content of standing reserve when he suggests that the Nazi movement was a paroxysmal response to a deep, powerful and frustrated drive towards community. Hazell and Kiel (2017) suggest that this "drive toward community" might be added to the classic list of deep human drives. If thwarted, it results in neurosis or psychosis much in the same way as if the other drives, as the symptoms that can emerge in too-brutal thwarting of Eros and Thanatos. This frustrated drive towards community, perhaps engendered by the rampant depersonalization of mid-to-late-stage industrial capitalism, erupted in the deep, cultish cohesion of the Nazi movement.

In addition, the standing reserve of this era seems to contain profound yearnings for identity, ambition, recognition and honor. These might be conveniently translated into the terms of Kohut's theory of narcissism (Kohut; 1971, 1977) in this case, applied to a community-as-a-whole. Hitler stood out as a symptom of wounded narcissism and an avenger of wounded pride that he would reclaim.

The pre-war standing reserve also can be seen to contain anxieties about engulfment, or of being swallowed up, of losing one's identity. This is reflected in part in the quest for "*lebensraum.*" That the standing reserve was indeed complex and deep can be seen in the way in which evidence is found for pent up rage, destructiveness, fear of the stranger, ontological insecurity, splitting and persecutory anxiety.

An additional component of the "standing reserve" that was revealed in the decades leading up to the mid-twentieth century— revealed by the constellation of technologies and techniques of late capitalist-industrialism, for example the moving production line of Henry Ford—was the experience of emptiness. As Hazell (1984, 2003) argues, this experience is repressed for the most part, emerging as emotional development takes place. It can also be seen as socially repressed, emerging as a standing reserve when the certain groupings of technologies are deployed.

Thus, the technologies of mid-to-late capitalism, especially those involving mass production, both created and revealed a standing reserve of thwarted needs for community, self-esteem, self-differentiation and boundary management. The deployment of the technologies of moving pictures and radio and "mechanical reproduction" (Benjamin, 2008) not only accentuated the revelation of these drives but also enabled the formation of movements, groups and institutions that paroxysmally attempted to meet them and satisfy them. The results were disastrous.

In the second decade of the twenty-first century, the defining technologies would seem to be those revolving around "social media". The conscious expectations of such technologies as Facebook, Snapchat, Twitter, Tik-Tok and related technologies were that social interaction would be increased and with it, social cohesion. Applying the Heideggerian theorem, however, we would expect an "enframing," namely, a revealing of that which lies in reserve, in the social unconscious. What we see is not only a drive for community, but also a drive for recognition, a wish to be reflected, to be noticed and admired, as if the standing reserve contained enormous wells of unrequited narcissistic desire. This pool narcissistic hunger seems related to a profound "ontological insecurity," to use Laing's felicitous term, (1965) which in turn is related to Winnicott's notion of "going on being." It is as if a tremendous anxiety regarding continuity and cohesion of the self (Kohut, 1971, 1977; Stern, 2000) has been tapped into and revealed by these technologies. Related, and in addition, we may observe that there is much space given over in these technologies to pets, especially cute and cuddly ones. In this we may surmise a somewhat frantic and sad quest for transitional objects that will stem the tide of narcissistic deprivation, abandonment and ontological insecurity.

The social media technologies also reveal a vast store, a standing reserve, of hatred and paranoia and to understand this we may deploy the theory of Klein. For we see splitting into "good" and "bad", tremendous surges of persecutory anxiety, deep threats to personal boundaries consistent with rampant projective identification and a pronounced tendency towards an incapacity to think which is the result of envious attacks on linking as described by Bion (1978).

In parallel fashion we may see the standing reserve as linked to a regression to preoperational thought as described by Piaget (1969), characterized by animism, egocentrism, syncretism, transduction, irreversibility of operations and an incapacity to decenter from one's own perceptions or hold in the mind more than one dimension at a time when making judgments (lack of conservation). In straightforward classroom operations and with young children, this is all quite charming and to be expected. However, when occurring in adults and combined with the paranoid schizoid process delineated above, it is potentially catastrophic. These issues have probably always been present in the mind, be it individual or social. Technology reveals these undercurrents at a more rapid pace while at the same time dismantling the culture, religion, social structure that once helped contain them, leaving both the individual and the group to face up to a torrent of unconscious urgings without preparation, support or guidance.

A metaphor that captures some of the dynamic of these

technologies is that of the public bathroom wall and the graffiti writings upon it. Prior to these technologies, these were kept in the bathroom, as secrets. Now, they are broadcast, for all to see. The secret is out, with all its capacity to retraumatize; with all its demands upon the ego and the "ego-like" functions of society (to refer to Edelson's typology,1970). Thus a crisis is created. Will there be growth or re-integration? Will there be extra forceful repression, in a nostalgic attempt to get the writings back into the bathroom stall? Will there be pain and multi-facetted attempts at reducing it? Will there be negative disintegration or positive disintegration? (Dabrowski, 1970, 1977)

Technology thus, much like a trauma or a PTSD trigger, weakens the defense mechanisms, both individual and social. The repressed material—psychotic-like, paranoid, preoperational, split, fragmented and unbearably intense—flows out into the social discourse in a flood of unprocessed information. Information, however, that contains not only that which is dreadfully unthinkable but also that which is best in humans, that which is vital to its survival. Much like a kidney, or a dialysis machine, the individual, group and society is charged with the task of sorting through the discharge and making sense of it, structuring around it as best it can.

We may thus view the technology as revelatory of the group unconscious much as a symptom or projective test is revelatory. What is left is to provide social structures and dynamisms to aid in the resolution, abatement or containment of the contents. Now we play catch-up. Will the processing devices—art, therapy, education, debate, discourse, conversation, institutional dynamics—be powerful enough to metabolize this outpouring.

This explanation does not replace the more traditional ones that are used to explain social unrest and individual disquiet. It does not replace the explanation of the anguish current in the USA in the early twenty-first century as having much to do with reduced social mobility, high rates of income inequality, increased risks of redundancy of one's skill set owing to robotization or computerization of tasks. It simply stands alongside with those explanations. In doing so it makes one perhaps more aware of the immense magnitude of the challenges borne by the socio-technical system and its inhabitants at multiple levels and in myriad domains. These strains are typically underestimated, at great cost and risk.

At the time of writing, two further crises are existent in the USA: Opioid addiction and mass shootings. The Heideggerian model may be applied to both, perhaps offering some further useful insight and ideas for solutions.

Opioids were used during the United States during the civil war. However, when we apply the socio-technical model we may observe that the sponsorship and deployment of opioids has increased dramatically over the past two decades. Conventional approaches to the problem involve legislation, treatment and regulation and these meet with varying degrees of success. However, if we ask the Heideggerian question, "What has been enframed and what is the standing reserve unleashed by this technology?" we take a different approach. We arrive at a different set of ideas and different solutions. Opioids are painkillers. In addition they can give a deep sense of tranquility. They act as a powerful anxiolytic. People might start off taking them for a bad pain but become addicted to the overall reduction of pain and the deep euphoric feeling they afford. As the addiction deepens the sense of euphoria declines and the person simply takes the opioid in order to avoid the terrible withdrawal symptoms. Now they are addicted, and, unfortunately, are not enjoying any of the original pleasure. They are simply avoiding the withdrawal symptoms. One could argue that the standing reserve revealed by the widespread sponsorship and deployment of this technology is that of a deep pain and anxiety from which many people suffer. This, however is rarely asked in the discussions of how to deal with the problem. Why, for example do some people, who have access to opioids, not take them? The usual answer is that they have a higher set of standards or make better decisions than those who do. This leads to efforts at moral and other forms of education and attitudinal shifts which might well be successful but do not address the underlying issue of widespread pain and anxiety. The pain is not only physical pain; it is a deep emotional pain and a profound anxiety, so powerful that it overwhelms the rational decision making of many individuals. Given this idea that opioids have simply revealed a deep pain that was always there, we are led to different ideas regarding solutions—ideas that would address the underlying cause of the pain. Why are so many people in pain and suffering? What causes this? An accumulation of everyday worries? Trauma? Conditions of labour? Widespread insecurity? Transgenerational trauma? Childrearing practices that feed into anxious attachments?

Personally, my favorite candidate is that of widespread trauma, especially the last item on the list, the trauma of anxious or avoidant attachment patterns in infancy and early childhood. Perhaps the "War on drugs" is being fought on the wrong fronts when we fight suppliers and attempt to alter the attitudes of children, adolescents and adults towards drug usage. Research shows that when an infant is cradled in the arms of a loving mother and is exchanging gazes, endorphins, oxytocin and dopamine levels rise (Strathearn, 2011, Machin and Dunbar, 2011).Further, these hormones are strongly implicated in the addiction process. A secure attachment helps us secrete and modulate our own pleasure-givers and pain killers. When we have a nation where so many suffer from insecure attachment, emotional neglect, and ensuing profound loneliness we will have a nation of many individuals whose bodies are less able to manufacture their own painkillers (or a plethora of other pleasurable endogenous hormones). They will then walk the surface of the earth feeling ontological insecurity, unsure of themselves and in pain. They will also be less resilient to pain and, in pain, less able to pause and think things through. They become more liable to "act out," to move rapidly to cell A6 on Bion's grid. They will then turn to external supplies of painkiller. A securely attached individual will be highly unlikely to see much use for painkillers except as a recourse to pain reduction in an acute, short lived situation. The opioid crisis is revealing to us at a group level, the deep anxieties residing in a large proportion of our society. This argument has a certain rationality to it and it is not a particularly new one. The importance of infantile attachment has been recognized for a long while. There are, however, terrific resistances to acknowledging its importance (witness the resistance Bowlby, the seminal researcher on attachment faced in getting these ideas accepted). For to acknowledge this would require social changes that would disrupt the status quo in multiple ways. It would also involve a remorseful recognition of pains, deep pains. Such recognition can be personally and socially troubling.

We may also fruitfully apply the Heideggerian concepts of enframing and standing reserve to the "mass shootings." What of the community mind is revealed in these events? What are typical solution-sets? What might the more dynamic approach suggest? Again, we may use the quaternity of "Idea/Technology/Person/ Situation." (ITPS) These events can be explained as resulting from the horrifying confluence of the idea of mass slaughter of humans, an enabling technology, a situation and a person or group of persons who enact the scene. The idea of mass slaughter is as old as the hills. Such things are described in ancient texts. The enabling technology is assault weapons and their ilk. These have been around since the middle of the 19th century, were widely deployed in warfare during World War One and have become readily available in chain stores in the USA since the latter part of the twentieth century. There is ample discussion of the persons who commit these atrocities and of their victims, but little discussion of the situation that served as the context for these shootings. Thus, remedial measures are aimed at regulation of the technology, identification of potential perpetrators and some attempts at comprehending the idea of mass slaughter. The latter is usually quite superficial, perhaps because it interacts so powerfully with the understanding of the fourth, scantily examined element, the situation. True, the situational variables, such as bullying, social ostracism and certain familial variables have been called in to help account for these events but very little of the systems-structural-psychodynamic-spatial analysis that is being forwarded here.

What is being revealed by this confluence of Idea/Technology/Person/Situation (ITPS)? What standing reserve is being enframed? In what way is this acting out derived from the level of the community? What beta elements are being transposed rapidly and without thought to cell A6 of Bion's grid? The immediate answer would seem to be that these scenes are acting out of massive destructive, indiscriminate rage—the expression of a profound hatred. But hatred of what? Superficially, it seems to be hatred of those who ridiculed or ostracized, but it also might be the murder of innocence and of hope, for often the targets are innocent and stand for youth, childhood and naïve hopefulness for the future. We then arrive at the hypothesis that the shooting is an action resulting from deep despair and rageful envious attacks on those that contain hope and innocence. The group-as-a-whole is suffering from a nihilism, a negativism resulting from broken dreams of the deepest sort, that there is something good in the world. Again we arrive at stages of early childhood development since in Erikson's system (1993a) the first year of life yields the virtue of hope and the distortion of idolism. The result of this despair is, following Klein (1975), a paranoid state where good and bad are pathologically split and the bad is extruded into others where it menaces the remaining good. The frantic holder of these last remnants of good then feels a frantic persecutory anxiety such that they are compelled to destroy that which is seen to contain the bad or that which might be selfishly holding on to the good he or she so desperately lacks. In either case, the result is destructive rage. This line of analysis works not only at the level of the despairing individual, but also for the group as a whole which will find a repository for these unbearable emotional pains and then will act in shock and horror as the individual, overwhelmed by the power of the projectively identified paranoid contents, acts them out. The predisposition toward becoming a repository of this underlying social despair and consequent nihilistic rage is determined in large part by social experiences, especially those in the first year of life when, as Erikson (1993a) hypothesizes basic trust is developed and solidified or as Piaget informs us (1969) object permanence is established, or as Mahler (1975) tells us, we enjoy a positive sustaining symbiosis, or, to follow Klein, we are able to achieve the depressive position and take the rough with the smooth. Given this psychodynamically informed social systems approach, we would direct our remedial activities not only at regulation of guns, not only at bullying, not only at identifying and bringing back to health individuals who are prone to become school shooters, but also at the deeper unconscious causes of these events. They are manifestations of deep underlying social conflicts. In this case the remedial efforts would be aimed at asking what are the factors leading to this despair? How might they be ameliorated? The list might be quite similar to the list generated for the opioid epidemic. As is so frequently the case there would have to be an initial expenditure of time, effort and money, this being committed to in the hope that significant payoffs would occur in the future, not only in the reduction of the incidence of the problems identified but also on a much wider social and socio-technical front.

We might be well advised, therefore to follow not only Jameson's (1981) dictum, namely "always historicize," but also, "always spatialize" and, in addition, honoring the following imperative: "always technologize!" in the sense of taking into account technological influences on the individual, group and social psyche.

We now examine some additional ideas on the essence of technology, its meaning and implications for the individual, culture and society.

10: Technology and Surplus Anxiety

In this section we will examine the following argument: advances in technology frequently create a surplus. Humans frequently become anxious in the presence of a surplus, often so anxious that they feel compelled to destroy it.

Humans often find themselves confronted with a surplus. Certain physical environments are exceptionally abundant and people can find they have more than they need. For example, the Kwakiatl of North-West America find themselves frequently in a situation of super abundance of salmon, wood, furs, skins, tools and wealth owing to the extreme productivity of their physical environment. Georges Bataille, in "The Accursed Share" (1991) argues that this surplus creates an anxiety such that rituals involving ceremonial destruction of this wealth are instituted so as to allay the anxiety of having such an excess. It is almost as if humans operate according to some unconscious inverse talionic principle, namely that such wealth will have to be paid for, so it is best to destroy it before bad luck, or ill fortune overtakes you. Bataille argues that this surplus anxiety is a universal phenomenon and that in modern and post-modern societies the preferred means of destruction of the surplus is through war and the large-scale construction of prisons, both non-productive means of disposing of surpluses. This list of Bataille's can probably be extended. Perhaps much of what could be considered "conspicuous waste" (Veblen 2009) falls into this category, for example.

We may perhaps extend Bataille's theory so that it can be applied to surpluses created not only by "mother nature" but also to those created by advances in technology. When we look at technological revolutions we notice one of their main features is the creation of a surplus. The agricultural revolution, the industrial revolution, the post industrial revolution, all increased productivity dramatically.

On the other hand a recurring question: "If there is such a surplus, why isn't life so much better? Why isn't there more leisure?" Perhaps Bataille's argument provides a partial answer. Perhaps our attitude toward the technologically created surplus is just as anxious and ambivalent as it is towards the abundance of nature. Perhaps in this anxiety we do in fact create rituals and social mechanisms all aimed at destroying or eating up the surplus – wars, prisons, and manufacture of pseudo problems, as if to atone for the gift or to preemptively pay back the super abundance, the over-payment.

Mauss (2000) compellingly argues that gifts must be exchanged, that a gift, not reciprocated places the receiver in an exceptionally vulnerable position. They could be seen as low status, stingy and lacking in every way, perhaps lacking in humanity. This vulnerability can only be fully eradicated by giving another gift, perhaps back to the original giver, or perhaps to someone else who is part of a gift giving circle, such that ultimately the gift is "returned." Perhaps the abundant gifts of technology create a similar anxiety. An anxiety that is in part left unprocessed and in part is allayed by the symbolic destruction of excess or conspicuous waste.

If these hypotheses hold true, it behooves us to create more productive, or at least less painful, ways of evening the score of eradicating the indebtedness we feel as the result of the abundance born of technology. For example, programs where we symbolically "give back", to the environment, or pay forward this indebtedness to future generations. Existing "gift giving" programs could be expanded and reframed to allay the anxiety of the "accursed share," of excess, or surplus.

III

Theory of Positive Disintegration and the Socio-Technical System

Introduction

The aim of this section is to bring together several domains of theory: Dabrowski's theory of emotional development, group relations theory, socio-technical systems theory, Heidegger's theory of technology and geographic notions of spatiality. This may be diagrammed as below:

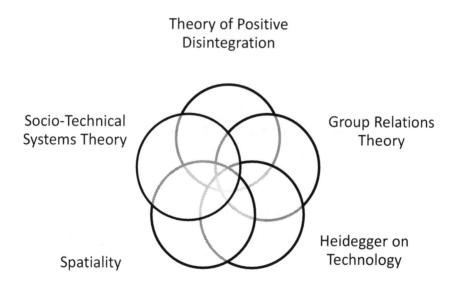

Theory of Positive
Disintegration

Socio-Technical
Systems Theory

Group Relations
Theory

Heidegger on
Technology

Spatiality

Diagram 8: Interaction of Five Domains in Group Relations Work

Many of the phenomena we encounter in social systems at all scales can be usefully explained when we apply the concepts, ideas and hypotheses of Kazimierz Dabrowski's theory of emotional development, the theory of positive disintegration (Dabrowski, 1971970; Dabrowski and Piechowski, 1977).

This theory has been used elsewhere (Hazell, 2003, 2008, 2009) to explain other phenomena, for example, group processes and the experience of emptiness. In this section, we will give a brief description of the theory of positive disintegration (the same one used in Hazell, 2003). Then we will examine several of the ideas in the theory as they can be applied to explain fairly common occurrences in socio-technical systems. This will involve linking Dabrowski's theory with group-as-a-whole theory and Heidegger's conceptions of the revelatory function served by technology. In a further integrative step we will attempt to integrate these ideas with concepts of spatiality.

Theory of Emotional Development or The Theory of Positive Disintegration

The theory of positive disintegration, or aspects of it, is delineated in a number of volumes including Dabrowski, Kawczak and Piechowski (1970) and Dabrowski and Piechowski (1977).

The theory of positive disintegration (TPD) states that there are five hierarchically organized levels of development. The theory is aimed at explaining behavior in the individual but it is our belief that it can also be used to explain group-as-a-whole phenomena. The process of development involves a transcending of an earlier structure through its disintegration and ultimate reconfiguration into a new and more complex system of organization. Thus, disintegration is seen as potentially positive, as being a necessary process for development to occur. One of Dabrowski's books is entitled *Psychoneurosis is Not a Disease*. In it, he argues that many things that are understood as "neurotic" are, in fact, breakdown phenomena resulting from emotional development; they are signs that psychological growth is occurring.

The Levels of Development

<u>Level I - Primary Integration</u>:

At this level the person is organized around the meeting of basic survival needs. The person at this stage feels relatively well integrated, and has as his primary purpose the meeting of "instinctual needs," e.g. hunger, sex, safety, shelter, comfort. It seems as though the person is dealing primarily with what Maslow (1968) termed "basic needs" and not "meta-needs," or higher level needs. The individual at this level of development is unaware of meta-needs, or if he is aware of them, assimilates them to his primary orientation of meeting basic needs. This would occur in much the same fashion that Kohlberg (1976) has demonstrated that people of lower levels of moral development interpret and assimilate the acts of higher moral development entirely in the terms of lower moral development, that is, for example, they may interpret altruistic acts as being acts of meeting basic needs. Level I is the level of the confident, unconflicted, self-serving individual. They are untroubled by a conscience or concern for others.

<u>Level II - Unilevel Disintegration</u>:

At this level the relatively smooth functioning of Level I breaks up, disintegrates and leaves the person with a predominantly wavering attitude. The previously well-bound and integrated structure now becomes loose, resulting in the individual feeling attacks of directionlessness and chaos. There is a difficulty in making decisions; forces within the person push against one another so that the person vacillates. In the absence of an internal hierarchical organization (the disintegration is unilevel) the forces do not resolve into smooth and deliberate action. The person at this state is very subject to polarities of emotion. Sometimes the disintegration can be extreme and result in psychosis. In other instances, the person can "pull themselves together" and manage to function in a seemingly integrated way. Under pressure, however, the disintegration returns. Frequently people at this stage long for a return to the "good old days" of Primary Integration, when things seemed, by comparison, simple. The words of Yeats' poem (1989) seem to capture Unilevel Disintegration quite aptly:

"Things fall apart, the center cannot hold,
Mere anarchy is loosed upon the world."

The hallmarks of this level are ambivalence, mixed feelings, ambitendency, confused and conflictual activity, and the sense of having multiple selves. The individual is unsure as to what is really important, as to what should take precedence. Most individuals are at this level of development. (Hazell 1984) This last assertion is buttressed by findings associated with Kohlberg's theory of moral development, namely, that most people occupy level two of his developmental continuum. That is most people are "conventional" in their moral judgment. This level corresponds roughly to Level Two of Dabrowski's scheme.

Level III - Spontaneous Multilevel Disintegration:

At this level of development, things are still fallen apart, but there is a growing hierarchization within the person. Instead of equipotent forces acting upon each other, resulting in a wavering, vacillating directionlessness, there is a developing sense of a hierarchy of values, with certain values and forces emerging as prepotent. The person begins to feel "inferiority towards himself," that is, he starts to experience the difference between what he is and what he ought to be. This develops out of the newly-emerging hierarch of aims and values. Among some of the other "dynamisms" (or experiences that can facilitate and encourage further development) are: positive maladjustment, feelings of guilt, feelings of shame, astonishment with oneself, hierarchization, subject-object in oneself, inner psychic transformation and self-awareness, self-control, autopsychotherapy and education-of-oneself. Dabrowski and Piechowski, 1977)

Level IV - Organized Multilevel Disintegration:

In this stage the person has developed an organized and consistent hierarchy within him or herself. In the words of Ogburn (1976):

He has transcended the problem of becoming
And tackles the problems of being. (Ogburn, 1976)

The basic needs are generally well taken care of at this stage or have receded into the background; the individual is concerned largely with the meta-needs of which Maslow speaks (Maslow, 1968, p. 210). In fact, Piechowski (1982) argues that there is a strong correspondence between the Self Actualizing person of Maslow's thinking and the person who has achieved Level IV. Thus, some of the active dynamisms are: self-awareness, knowledge of one's uniqueness, developmental needs, existential responsibility, self-control, regulating one's own development, education-of-oneself, self-induced programs of systematic development. The primary task of the individual at this stage of development is to solidify the structure that emerges from the previous disintegrated stage.

The locus of control for the individual at Level IV is very firmly an internal one—she can act independently of the external environment if she so chooses.

Level V – Secondary Integration:

Only a few rare individuals reach this level of development. At this stage, the "ought" has become unified with "what is." The personality ideal has been achieved. The planful self-development of Level IV has been successfully completed. Individuals at this level seem to experience self, other, time, being and the world in radically different ways. Thus, persons at the other levels often have difficulty understanding them.

Overexcitabilities

Development through the stages is related, in large part, to the level and profile of excitabilities in the person. Dabrowski posits five types of overexcitabilities: Emotional, Psychomotor, Sensual, Intellectual and Imaginational. An overexcitability is a predisposition in the individual, largely inherited, to respond to certain types of stimuli in an above average manner. For example, a person with sensual overexcitability will be more responsive than average to cutaneous stimulation. He or she will also tend, if this tends to be his or her dominant type of overexcitability, to transform other types of experience, e.g., emotional, intellectual, imaginational into sensual types of experience. For example, the emotion of affection will be readily transformed into stroking for a person with sensual overexcitability. Similarly, the emotion of rage may be transformed into self-harm.

Perhaps another term for overexcitability would be sensitivity, perhaps analogous to photographic paper which can be varied in its sensitivity to various types of light input. The pronounced overexcitability would correspond to a finely grained, highly sensitized paper—the impression of reality gained when there is an overexcitability that is correspondingly sharp, intense and vivid.

Following is a brief overview of the manifestations of the various forms of overexcitabilities (OEs):

Sensual:
This manifests through a heightened sensitivity to sensual experience—skin stimulation, sexual excitability, the desire for stroking, physical comfort, tastes, sights, colors, etc.

Psychomotor:

This manifests itself in a tendency for vigorous movement, violent games and sports, rapid talk and a pressure to be moving. Emotional excitement is converted into movement that is highly charged with energy. Dancers and athletes might have a high degree of this OE.

Imaginational:

This is shown in a sensitivity to the imagined possibilities of things. There is a rich association of images and metaphors flow freely. People with high levels of this OE might easily confuse reality and imagination.

Intellectual:

In this the individual displays a voracious curiosity and a strong desire to learn and understand. There is a persistence in asking probing questions and a reverence for logic. There is a love of theory and an enjoyment of thinking.

Emotional:

This is the most important overexcitability in that if this is absent or weak, it is unlikely that development will proceed. Emotional overexcitability is manifested in the person's ability to form strong emotional attachments to others, and living things and places. Also present with emotional overexcitability are: concern about death, strong affective memory, concern for others, empathy, exclusive relationships and feelings of loneliness. People with high levels of this OE often say they are "too emotional."

The level of development the individual reaches is dependent upon three factors. The first factor is the person's hereditary endowment, namely, the configuration of his overexcitabilities and other genetic inheritances. The second factor is the environment in which the individual lives and the extent to which it supports or impedes that individual's development, for example, family, school, community. The third factor consists of the individual's response to his or her situation—the decisions he or she makes in response to the life situation they find themselves in and the genetic heritage that they possess.

The third factor is only found at Level III or above, that is, persons at levels I and II are molded entirely by genetic and environmental factors. Only at Level III does the individual start to take hold of their situation (in an almost "existential" way) and make a conscious, self-determined choice as to how they will act.

Progression through the levels of development depends on three factors—first, second and third. The first factor is one's genetic inheritance. This determines the profile of Overexcitabilities—one's sensitivity to different forms of stimulations; imagination, sensual, psychomotor, intellectual and emotional. Of these the level of emotional overexcitability is the one that has the greatest effect on the developmental potential of the individual—the higher it is the greater the potential for development.

The second factor has to do with the environment one inhabits—one's familial influences, schooling, society, culture, location and so on. Finally, there is the third factor, namely, that of individual choice—free will, one's decisions. This factor only emerges in force at level three of development and continues to strengthen in levels four and five. Those individual and social systems located at levels one and two are dominated by the first two factors—genetic inheritance interacting with external social forces.

Attributes of the levels

Following is a listing, with brief definitions of the attributes of each of the levels of development.

Level One
- Lack of inner conflict
- Low level of introspection
- Domination by physical motivations

Level Two
- Other-directedness, motivation for conformity
- Multiple "selves," identity confusion
- Ambitendency, vacillating behavior and moods
- Ambivalence, confused and mixed feelings and valuations
- Unclear values hierarchy

Level Three
- Emergence of the Third Factor—decisions begin to be driven more by free will than basic needs and convention
- Subject-object in oneself—self-observation, self-criticism, the observing ego
- Positive maladjustment—being a misfit an outsider, but in a morally elevating way
- Astonishment at oneself—being surprised by one's own attributes and experiences
- Feelings of inferiority—feeling that one is not living up to one's own expectations
- Emotional intensity
- Concern for others, empathy
- Autonomy—self directedness
- Existential anxiety and depression
- Confusion since the values hierarchy has not yet solidified and integrated

Level Four
- On the way to a coherent, consistent hierarchy of values
- Consistent autonomous behavior
- Autopsychotherapy—bringing about one's own growth
- Spontaneous authenticity
- Self actualization*
- Full functioning*

Level Five

- Personality Ideal—the project of level four is close to completion

*The terms self actualization and full functioning refer to the concepts of Maslow (2013) and Rogers (2003). Many Dabrowskian theorists argue that these terms are not coterminous in meaning. We, however, see much utility in arguing for their equivalence.

In addition, the switiching on and off of these psychological functions is not digital. They taper in and out as the individual, group or social system moves back and forth through the stages. Thus, an individual at the higher end of Level One will start to display some of the ambitendency and ambivalence of Level Two. This, by the way, is a frequent trope of "gangster" narratives. We see Tony Soprano (*The Sopranos*, 1997-2007) for example, as a Level One personality, manifest conflicts, anxieties and confusions typical of a Level Two. He goes to see a therapist with the wish to return to the relative comfort of an "integrated" Level One. For several reasons, the effort fails. In addition, one may see that the different levels exist simultaneously in any individual or social system, frequently vying for dominance—this is what is meant by Multilevelness. The degree of Multilevelness increases with the overall level of emotional development.

Object Relations and TPD

In this, the next step in our integration, we will bring together TPD and object relations theory, especially in the generic form in which it was laid out in chapter one.

The Differentiation of Selves:

The theory of positive disintegration posits an increasing awareness of the multiplicity of selves or sub-personalities as development proceeds throughout the levels. In levels 4 and 5 these selves are increasingly integrated such that they come to resemble a well co-ordinated committee.

Whence, however, the multiplicity of selves? How are they created? Fairbairn (1952) provides an answer. In the earliest stages of the mind, we have, according to Fairbairn, a "pristine unified ego"—a unified mind free from splits. The early mind retains this integrity by forming memories of experiences. If the experiences are not, for the baby (or any person), too painful, then they do not have to be split off as if into another part of the self. They are simply encoded, in a more or less accessible form as memories, in the still unified, but no longer pristine, ego.

If, however, the infant is exposed to traumatically painful experiences, these will not be internalized by memory, as memories, but by wholesale introjection, followed by splitting. These introjections, of both the object and the part of the ego that was connected to that object, operate in the unconscious as autonomous or semi-autonomous sub-personalities. Although Fairbairn provides broad categories of these objects, we find it more helpful to think of a cornucopia of variegated internalizations— often much more resembling a chaotic median or large group than a small committee.

We now reach an important theoretical juncture. At least two points emerge.

i)   The multiple selves observed and experienced at levels 2 and 3 of TPD are created, in part, through the mechanisms described by Fairbairn. They are manifestations of the second factor in Dabrowski's theory in that they originate from the environment via the introjection of bad objects or the "thingification" of bad experiences..

Further, the fewer the introjected bad objects, the less their power and the greater the power of memory with its tendency towards accessibility, internal dialogue and cohesion. This growth in the potency of "memory objects" as opposed to "introjection objects" increases the likelihood of a) becoming aware of different selves and b) feeling more confident in the ultimate cohesion of the entire self. The first of these leads to a richer interior milieu and the second results in a deeper "ontological security" (Laing, 1965). In addition the Love (L) links (Bion, 1978) will tend to be more potent and these hold the worlds, both inner and outer together.

This, *ceteris paribus*, increases the likelihood of the individual becoming aware of their many selves and of being able to integrate them, that is, of proceeding to a higher level in the Dabrowskian scheme. Thus, emotional development in TPD relies upon good enough object relations (secure attachments, holding, handling and sensitivity) and freedom from other traumata especially in early life, (Winnicott, 1965a). Emotional development rests upon these factors as well as the first factor variables such as emotional overexcitability. We may anticipate the next steps in our reasoning by pointing out that the individual who has a relatively well integrated set of internalized objects is less likely to projectively identify these into the group mentality, scapegoats, imaginary groups and other people, places and things than the individual who, by virtue of a traumatic early life, must resort to these defense mechanisms to preserve their psychodynamic equilibrium.

ii) The second point involves the concept of primary integration and here we part company with traditional Dabrowskian theory. The concept of "pristine unified ego" is certainly "primary" and certainly "integrated" or at least "unified" but it is not what Dabrowski means by Primary Integration. In fact, the concept of "pristine unified ego" bears some relation to the concept of Secondary Integration. Juxtaposing Fairbairn and Dabrowski leads to the following formulation:

The Pristine Unified Ego is more "primary," that is, developmentally earlier, than primary integration. Primary integration in TPD is a defensive posture of integration to protect from what is felt to be certain disintegration in the face of an overwhelming amount of negative introjects. In primary integration, the person is desperately holding himself or herself together out of fear that if they let up, they will go to pieces. Thus the integration is only superficial—only a hard shell containing a frightening, loosely held-together bag of bad objects. This explains the brittleness of certain types of Level 1 individuals and groups, the fear of introspection, the proneness to paranoia, the use of hate as in Bion's (1978) H links, sometimes coupled with forceful intellectualism (hypercathexis of K Links) and overall closedness—all this being aimed at keeping awareness of self-object multiplicity and friability at or near zero.

If the individual is to develop to Level 2, memories will link subselves and the painful awareness thus evoked may be worked with or the individual will seek to blot out the memory—through now-familiar techniques—the litany of defense mechanisms, acting out, alcohol, consumption, drugs, violence, frenzied activity.

Thus the primary integration as posited and described by Dabrowski, operates like a brittle defensive shell held together by H and, to a lesser extent, K links that contain, split off and out of awareness, a Pandora's Box of bad objects threatening to overwhelm from within, or, if projectively identified, from without. Also, these individuals or groups are far more likely to split off and projectively identify these frightening and deeply distressing subpersonalities into people, places, things and into the group mentality.

Remembering, Repeating and Working Through:

At level 1, as conceived here, namely, as a defensive arrangement, awareness of emotionally charged memories is reduced. This lack of memory-objects means that the individual is more likely to repeat—to have a compulsion to repeat as a substitute for memory—action being used as a replacement for memory, as a way of enacting the memory in a concretized manner (Freud, 1914). The memory is "lived out" rather than remembered. In this, repetition compulsion bears resemblance to Piaget's sensori-motor stage (Piaget, 1969).

Beginning at level 2, and strengthening in level 3, memories start to link subselves, link past to present and the individual becomes aware of their repetitions. It is at this point—feeling empty, despairing and helpless—that individuals may turn to therapy, open themselves to mourning, work through, fully remember, metabolize the bad objects, and start to live a life not so dominated by repetition. These processes may also be mapped out on Bion's grid insofar as there is a reduction of the individual swiftly moving from beta bits to cell A6 and an increase in thought, implying a movement across and down the grid. This process continues throughout level 3 and, if we are lucky, gives us a glimpse of level 4. Often, however the pain is so great and the task of integration so daunting that individuals veer off the path of re-integration and turn to painkillers or consciousness-blunters of all kinds, often developing symptoms instead.

Thus the sequence of repeating, remembering and working through, along with all their appurtenances, parallels the shift from level 1 to 2 to 3 of TPD. It is also during the levels 2 and 3 that parts of the self that have been split off into the group mentality will be reclaimed by the individual and, perhaps, worked on by the group as a whole. This reclamation will replay, again and again, the depressive dynamics aptly described by Klein (1975).

Redefinition of the Concept of Self:

Corresponding to the developmental shifts through the levels, there is a redefinition of the concept of self. These redefinitions and the accompanying shifts in the sense of otherness, or alterity are described in Hazell (2009).

At level 1, when defined in the defensive and not the "pristine" fashion, the notion of a unitary, physically defined, "essential" self is maintained, often desperately, as a defense against the chaos of the inner world.

As the individual enters level 2, the illusion of a unitary sense of self breaks up and the individual experiences himself as having multiple, disparate and disintegrated selves. There is also an emerging awareness that the sense of subjectivity, of "who I am," shifts from one of the sub-personalities to another with a disquieting rapidity.

As the individual progresses through level 2 and closes in on level 3, there is an emerging awareness that much of the sense of subjectivity has been based upon introjects, upon foreign objects taken into the self in an attempt (following Fairbairn) to master them. There is also a growing awareness that that which is taken to be "other" is based upon projective identifications of unwanted parts of the self into other people, places and things.

These two realizations, at first faltering and evanescent, have the effect of making the individual aware that much of what he had taken for self and other was imaginary—based on introjection and projective identification. They also become aware that the psychic boundaries are not as certain and clear as the physicalistic approach endorsed by level one would have us believe.

These realizations throw the individual further off balance. The age-old "deep" questions emerge; "Who am I?" "What is really me?" "Who are you?" "What is the nature of our relationship?" "Who is doing this?" "Who is really speaking or listening?"

These issues are the hallmark of level 3 concerns. As level 4 approaches, so the individual will get glimpses of a "new self"—perhaps akin to the "transcendent" self of Levinas (1999)—perhaps adumbrations of the "thou art that" (Gurdjieff, 1975 and Ouspensky, 1998). This is very much akin to the notion of "true self" of Winnicott (1965) which is itself based upon spontaneity. Thus, the concepts of self and other evolve as one progresses through the Dabrowskian levels.

Similarly, the concepts of self and other change as a group evolves and examines itself in a group-as-a-whole modality. As concepts of self and other, of subjectivity, authenticity and alterity shift, so must many other concepts, concerns, processes and dynamics undergo radical change.

Having now discussed several threads of development (the differentiation of selves, repeating, remembering and working through, redefinition of the concepts of self, other and authenticity) in terms of both TPD and object relations theory, we may now describe how this may manifest itself in groups operating under the aegis of the five levels of TPD.

The Group: From One to Many to One and Many:

Just as the self, throughout the course of development, shifts from the "one" of primary integration or the zen-like emptiness of the pristine unified ego to the "many" of unilevel and multilevel disintegration and proceeds towards organized and then secondary integration, so a developmental group can be seen to shift from "one" to "many" and then on to the "one and many" of reintegration.

By no means is this a lock-step, formulaic procedure. It is multilevel, involving regressions, saccades, conflicts and all of the complexity of any dynamic flow process. This procession is not equifinal. Progress occurs through a critical evaluation of current dynamics. That which emerges is unknown at the outset. This enables the emergence of the true self, which is spontaneous.

In addition, the group relations consultant to the group, in her role as interpreter and observer of covert processes, functions as an agent that disrupts primary integration by making the part objects, part selves and imaginary groups that are formed unconsciously, visible. Thus, this challenges the level one mythology of pseudo-integration that seems to be the aim of so many groups, especially when under stress and strain or when traumatized.

For this reason, in addition to the many reasons cited elsewhere in group dynamics literature (Colman and Bexton, 1975; Colman and Geller, 1985), the role of consultant is routinely attacked as the group attempts to neutralize their disruptive, destabilizing function, in an attempt to maintain the Level 1 group mythology of primary integration, which is so often held on to tenaciously as a defense against re-experiencing group-as-a-whole trauma. In some ways, as I have argued elsewhere (Hazell, 2003) this is an attempt to blot out the painful experience of emptiness that is connected with Level 2 functioning, both at the individual and the group level.

Examples of Groups at Different TPD Levels

Once again, we emphasize that the levels are perhaps best viewed as synchronic and phasic rather than diachronic and sequential, that is, as occupying parts of the group mentality to be activated or deactivated as the group goes through other processes. These levels can be regarded as imaginary groups, residing in the group mentality, vying and interacting with one another, comprised of split-off parts of members, yoked to a greater or lesser extent to conscious processes in the group and to its tasks. Consultants are enjoined not to let these conceptualizations take on the "numbing sense of reality" (Bion, 1961).

We may now examine brief capsule descriptions of the groups that typify the different levels of TPD. We first focus on how groups may operate at the different Dabrowskian levels, then we will give illustrations of families functioning at each of the levels.

The Level 1 Group:

The Level 1 group aims at the condition of primary integration in the defensive sense defined previously. It seeks to blot out internal differences and manifests angry anxiety when such differences of opinion or vertices of interpretation arise.

Bion's basic assumption dependency seeks primary integration through achieving a longed-for coalescence with the all-powerful leader. Basic assumption fight flight seeks primary integration via a paranoid exclusion of "bad parts" and a fearful, suspicious and brittle cohesion. Such cohesion is maintained through the mobilization of all the techniques described by Adorno *et al* (1983) as applied to the authoritarian personality. The only differences arise in that these defensive maneuvers are deployed as social defenses. Common examples of such groups would be cults, gangs, mobs, enmeshed families and social systems operating as closed systems where denial, fear of differences and novel information often results in the group operating with unaddressed contradictions, double standards, double binds and everyday hypocrisy. Such groups, because they have strong tendencies towards closedness do not operate well as "complex adaptive systems" (Gell-Mann, 1995). They thus tend towards entropy, maladaptation to the external environment and internal chaos. History shows us, unfortunately, that while this is the inevitable result of such closed systems, the pathway to self-destruction is long in terms of human lifetimes and saturated with agonizing tragedy. Just as individuals rely upon the "back-up position" of primary integration as a means of protecting the self from disintegration and further harm, so we see in groups that the emergence of the Level 1 group is a response to trauma—either trauma to the group as a whole or as a result of a coming together of traumatized individuals attracted by the Level 1 form of social defense mechanisms.

The Level 2 Group:

This form of group is very common. The predominant characteristics are ambivalence, ambitendency, confusion, conflict and floundering—one step forward three back. There are many parts in the group and the group cannot come to a decision as to what is most important or of most value.

There may be an uneasy, stertorous emerging awareness of hypocrisy or double standards or the group may at times reverses its position on "important" issues—seeming to undo work done, working against its own best interests; but these awarenesses are fleeting and cause anxiety, depression, emptiness and, frequently, demoralization.

As is the case for individuals at Level 2 there is a social, public longing for cohesion, as if a "strong leader" would return the group to Level 1 and its relative lack of awareness of disquieting conflict. At times the Level 2 group will make excursions into Level 1 functioning, but these are often only excursions—the unilevel disintegration returns with its distressing, unstable polyvocity and unintegrated, disorganized multiplicity.

In group relations work, the Level 2 group will be frustrated with the consultant for not providing an integrating framework or language. The Level 1 group will be similarly frustrated and in addition will disparage or attack the consultant role as in, for example, "negative K culture" (Hazell, 2005).

Examples of Level 2 groups are legion: corporations with stated missions that are self-sabotaged by other activities, study groups in the Tavistock tradition that have not become "working" or "sophisticated" groups and families where there is a low degree of cohesion and where a fairly routine undermining of each other's activities and goals. Leaderless groups or groups with an unintegrated guiding ideology or inchoate hierarchy of values are prone to operate along Level 2 lines. Individuals in these groups often feel like the metaphorical "crabs in a bucket." They may struggle for escape, for differentiation, often clawing at one another, but as soon as one is almost free, the others will pull him back in again.

The Level 3 Group:

The Level 3 group is still disintegrated, but there is an emerging sense of hierarchy, a sense of values accompanied by an acceptance of internal differentiation. The group becomes concerned with "moral" issues that are related to an emergent ethical ideology and, as a result, there is a depressive atmosphere (in the Kleinian sense). There is a sense of guilt over harm done to others, a sense of concern and a wish to repair and integrate—a wish for some sort of atonement.

Dynamically, there is a reclamation of split-off selves, and a mourning process is activated as a result of this. Psychological safety is much higher but still not guaranteed. As a result of this, and powering this, there is a higher degree of emotional overexcitability, or sensitivity, in the group. Those parts of the group that have this emotional overexcitability start to emerge in leadership roles.

The group starts to activate the Third Factor; it starts to encounter and countenance explicit conscious choice as to how it will operate. This involves the taking of responsibility and the remorse that this entails. Frequently, there is a guilty acknowledgment of the intensity of unconscious psychological violence in the group.

The Level 3 group corresponds with one form of Bion's sophisticated group. The Level 4 group provides another example of this. Examples of Level 3 groups can be found in emergent psychotherapy groups and almost-functioning self-study groups, families that have worked through many underlying issues and well-functioning technological teams. These groups are often positively maladjusted to the prevailing culture of Level 1 and 2 groups in which they are found. That is to say, they will often be seen as "misfits". However, from this perspective, they are to be positively valued "misfits." They often suffer from conflicts as to how they might preserve their identity, boundaries, organization, authority structures and survive without compromising their core values and "regressing" to Level 1 and 2 functioning.

The Level 4 Group:

This group will have initiated and be working on the process of re-integration of the multiple selves in the group. As mentioned before, radical reorganization of basic concepts of self and other (Hazell, 2009) will have occurred, leading to a dramatically different group process. Groups and individuals at this level are extremely rare, perhaps only existing in fictional accounts such as Hesse's *Magister Ludi* (1949) or Aldous Huxley's *Island*, (1962), or in philosophical accounts such as Buber (1958) and Levinas (1969, 2005). Humanity has yet to explore this domain in any thoroughgoing fashion. It is strongly desired, however and often individuals at Level 1 will capitalize on this deep longing and form pseudo Level 4 groups which turn out to be, in reality, Level 1 groups, often cults or crypto-fascist and cult-like.

The Level 5 Group:

The group at Level 5 is even more of an unknown entity. The basic concepts of group, self and other, to name but a few, have been so radically reformulated that the languages of Levels 1 through 3 fail to capture it. Even the language and concepts of the Level 4 group or individual can only hint at it—only provide adumbrations. We are perhaps her in the realm of "sanghas" in Buddhism or the "anjos sobre Berlim" depicted in the movie, "Wings of Desire" (1987)—spiritual groups that exist outside of conventional materialistic notions of time, place and person.

It is to be recalled that these five levels of groups are not to be understood in a simplistic diachronic, developmental scheme alone. That is, we should not form cubby holes of these five categories where developmental programs are established to promote shifts throughout the levels. To do so exclusively would miss the point or useful hypothesis that all the levels exist synchronously in all groups and persons at all times.

Following the postulates of imaginary groups, we see all levels existing at all times in all groups. Parts of members are projectively identified into imaginary groups existing in the group mentality and these groups will correspond to varying degrees to the five levels of groups just described. These groups will interact with one another in the group mentality and will find members who will act as their spokespersons. The prominence or recession of the imaginary group will depend on multiple factors—group stresses, group history, location and composition, group culture and technology to name a few. The imaginary groups will thus rise and fall in the consciousness of the group, in its shared reality— sometimes speaking up loudly and coherently, sometimes brokenly, perhaps stifled and silenced, with its spokespersons deemed outcasts, unworthy or perhaps, mad. (One is reminded here, for example of Nietzsche, who might be seen as a spokesperson for the higher level group mentality.) Each of these five imaginary groups will have their "leaders" and spokespersons who will rise and fall depending on the multiple vicissitudes of group life.

Framed this way, the consultant's, therapist's or leader's task shifts to one of listening to the many multiple groups within the group and reflecting these awarenesses back to the group. Here, we argue that these groups are organized hierarchically along lines described by Dabrowski (1971) and Dabrowski and Piechowski (1977), each level manifesting its own constellation of anxieties and potentialities.

Equipped with this brief overview of TPD (the theory of positive disintegration) and how it may be applied to groups, let us now examine how some of these ideas might apply to examples from family life.

Multilevelness and Families

In *Imaginary Groups*, Hazell (2005) describes and explains how the levels of TPD can be seen as existing contemporaneously in all people and as dynamics in all groups. Further, individuals and groups are in constant tensional states as to whichLlevel (1 through 5) will dominate their ideation and behavior. These processes are manifested in families, organizations and societies. Just as one may have a Level I individual (who has latent, or unconscious capacities for Levels 2-5), so one may have a Level 1 family (with analogously latent capacities for levels 2-5). Much of the drama of group life (if not all human life and history) can be understood as emanating from the dynamic tensions existing between the levels. Let us quickly examine some simple examples utilizing the family group for illustrative purposes.

<u>**Level 1 Families**</u>

These families are very common in the popular media. Often the "gangster" family is a predominantly Level1 phenomenon. "The Godfather (1972)," "The Sopranos" (1997-2007), "Scarface" (1983), all depict families organized mostly around Level I ideals of brute force, lack of introspection and the ambivalence it might bring on, all accompanied by primitive physicalistic motivations.

Interesting and poignant dynamisms are depicted in these narratives insofar as each of them involves elements of <u>positive maladjustment</u> where an individual does not fit in, but their not fitting in is because of the emergence of higher level, more developed structures in their personality. Thus, in each narrative we do not find a completely smooth surface, nor the absolute opacity of Level 1. There is an element of a key personality or an individual that is at odds with the reigning psychopathic paradigm. That is, someone is maladjusted, but in a positive way, in a way that betokens a higher level dynamic.

Michael Corleone (in "The Godfather Part III" (1990)) tries to get out of the family business, but they "keep pulling him back." His wife has serious moral compunctions over the gangster way of life.

Tony Soprano has bad dreams, has anxiety attacks, and is seeing a psychotherapist. These dreams indicate conflicts which are not Level 1 phenomena and their presence adds powerfully to the pathos of his personality. In addition, his wife, a classic Level 2, whilst in denial much of the time, does have an occasional (Level 3) pang of conscience.

Tony Montana of "Scarface", who so robustly exemplifies Level1 behaviour ("Say hello to my little friend."), shows distinct signs of multilevelness in his conflict over his ultimate refusal to kill children. (Interestingly, it is this refusal that leads to his death. Tony Montana died because of his conscience.) Tony's beautiful "say hello to the bad guy" speech, delivered to a bemused and anxious (yet perhaps admiring) restaurant crowd, is an eloquent indictment of the duplicity of Level 2. Sadly for Tony he has nothing readily available to put in the place of the empty hole burned out by his skepticism. Tony Montana's wife loses herself in a negative disintegration, in an unfortunately common Level 2 fashion to drugs and alcohol. Unable to maintain a full-blown psychopathic lifestyle, she is, as yet, unable to move on to Levels 3 and 4 and suffers unilevel negative disintegration—she goes to pieces in front of our eyes, as does Tony in the final scenes.

Not all Level 1 families are gangsters in the usual sense of the word. Many are simply unambivalent conformists that manage frequently to pass under the social radar. For example, World War II death camps were often run by people who went home after work was done and lived a harmonious "ordinary" life. Several of Hitler's henchmen came from quite ordinary, conventional, bourgeois backgrounds. The families in the early chapters of "Gone With the Wind" (Mitchell, 1936), prior to the arrival of William Tecumseh Sherman in Atlanta, are similarly free from disquietude and angst regarding their moral position.

These examples should serve to remind us that Level 1 is not something always "out there." It is a potentiality available to all individuals and groups. It even, in its very simplicity, has a certain allure to it. When it is socially derogated, it is similarly tempting to see it, not as a potential in oneself, one's family or one's reference group, but as being "other," as existing only "over there," in the other individual, family, group or nation. Freud's comment, which gains so much more meaning in German or French, is apt: *"La ou ça etait, le je doit être."* ("There, where "that" was, the "I" must be."

Level 2 Families

The Level 2 family dynamic can be described as much "storm and fury, signifying nothing." Families dominated by this dynamic will be confused, conflicted, ambivalent and ambitendent.

Examples from popular culture are again readily available. Most "soap operas" depict the Level 2 dynamic. Characters shift and change values, even identities, "on a dime"; the conflict is never-ending and, at the end of the day, little or nothing has been accomplished or learned, it's back onto the same old treadmill. Love triangles, competition, fear of ostracism, anxiety over conformity and the panoply of Level 2 motivations hold sway.

Many classic examples of Level 2 families can be found in television situation comedies. Notable amongst them is "The Simpsons" (1989-present). Homer changes value systems sometimes several times in a sentence. Marge plays the role of conventional, caretaking woman while demonstrating at times an alarming capability of being very different, and Bart and Lisa both like to laugh at the violence of the "Itchy and Scratchy Show" while at other times they show the capacity for empathy, shame and guilt.

However, in the Simpsons we find significant multilevel tensions within individuals, within the family and between their family and others. Lisa frequently speaks for Level 3 concerns and is positively maladjusted. She is concerned about justice, cruelty to animals, aesthetics, consciousness, meaning; all the Level 3 dynamics are in evidence.

Bart sells his soul but has a moral crisis and each member (except Maggie?) has evidence of hierarchization, that is, of feeling that there are parts of themselves, dynamics that are of greater worth than others. I would argue that it is the presence of these multilevel dynamics that engages so many people and creates the sense of life we find in "The Simpsons." Mr. Burns, however, seems to reside obdurately in the realm of level 1.

Dabrowski pointed out that Level 2 was the most commonly occurring level; that it was a very vulnerable level, insofar as many people (and here, families, groups and institutions) could not retain their integration throughout this stage; and that it required a tremendous amount of psychological energy to transform oneself (or by extension, one's family or group) into an individual, family or group functioning at Level 3.

Thus, the Level 2 family dynamic will be very common, frequently riddled with problems of disintegration (addictions, neuroses, crises, psychoses, personality disorders), and requiring great and often uncomfortable effort to change.

Level 3 Families

Applying TPD to family systems, we arrive at the following formulations for the Level 3 family. The Level3I family will have tensions and breakdown phenomena, but these will be different from the Level 2 family insofar as they will be more <u>multilevel</u>. There will be a tension between what *is* in the family and what *ought to be*. This *ought to be* will not originate from social norms, or mores, such as "keeping up with the Joneses," or from a desire to conform. It will stem from an internal moral imperative, a "calling," as it were. Something stirs, either in the family as a whole, or perhaps in one or several members of the family. For example, a mother may feel a strong urge to help in the community; a daughter wishes to study religions to resolve a crisis of meaning; a family as a whole looks at its lifestyle and sees that much of it, although materially comfortable, is empty; an adolescent son challenges his parents' way of life and its many masks and feels profoundly alienated. In each of these tensional conflicts there is a clear opportunity for the family to grow, and the Level 3 family, since it has other elements of Level 3 functioning such as self-observation and autonomy, is sometimes able to capitalize on these tensions and mobilize their energy to potentiate growth. Such conflicts are, as we see in the case of the Simpson family, common enough in Level 2 systems. However, in the Level 3 system, the conflict, the tension and resulting motivation is persistent, sometimes painfully so.

This growth may not always be along tried and well-worn pathways, for Level 3 functioning necessarily involves *positive maladjustment*, where the individual (or social system or subsystem) does not fit into the *status quo* because it represents something of greater complexity than the *status quo*. The Level 3 family is either itself a "misfit" or has members that are "misfits." These "square pegs in round holes," however, are not rebels without causes, nor are they seeking attention or working towards other secondary gains emanating from gainsaying conventional wisdom.

Upon inquiry, we find their maladjustment is, stands for, or is striving for something of a higher order of complexity. (For a further elaboration of the concept of complexity, Gell-Mann (1995) and Harvey, Hunt and Schroder (1961) provide a useful approach. In addition, increased complexity may be mathematized through graph theory (Trudeau, 1993).

Another aspect of Level 3 functioning is that of self-observation. A social system operating at Level 3 will examine its own process critically much in the way a level 3 individual observes themselves (or in the language of TPD, experiences "subject-object" in themselves). This self-observation may show up in self-reflection, self-examination, retreats, journaling or an openness to examination by others.

As we can see, Level 3 is very rich in dynamisms and these will be reflected in the energy and complexity of the Level 3 family. A key difference between the Level2I and the Level 3 family is that the Level 3 family, for all its confusion, is, deep down, headed somewhere in a fairly sustained fashion, while the Level 2 family is torn by ambivalence and ambitendency. This is a key difference, and especially important for anyone seeking to understand families.

Level 4 Families

These families will be very rare. The Level 4 family will be more organized, less chaotic and more directed in its activities in a sustained way toward it goals. This may sound like this family is a single-minded automaton and that it achieves its aims like a robot. This is not the case. In fact, the robot family is more like the Level 1 family. The Level 4 family is variegated and diverse on all levels. Individuals in it are internally complex and multifaceted and the group is comprised of different personalities. These differences are, however, accepted. The tensions created between the different parts and the different levels of complexity they embody potentiate dialog, discourse and, ultimately, growth. In fact, this "growth ethic" may be (explicitly or implicitly) part of the "family philosophy." This level corresponds roughly to what Bion (1961) describes as the sophisticated group or what is described in the Tavistock tradition (Colman and Geller, 1985) as a working group. This family is self-directed, autonomous and self-correcting. It is an open system, ever growing in complexity and facilitating the growth of all the parts of all its members.

Level 5 Families

Families operating at this level will be extremely rare; so rare, in fact, that they are more usually objects of imagination or visionary experience. The Level 5 family is perhaps rendered even rarer since so many sacred stories involve the transcendence or forsaking of family ties. Nonetheless, one can find examples of "holy families" or families of gods and demi-gods in various religions.

TPD and Groups

We may now proceed and attempt to integrate the theory of imaginary groups and Dabrowski's theory of positive disintegration. One pathway is through the notion that each individual is an assemblage of "multiple selves," some likely to be split off into the group mentality and thenceforward, others less likely to be so ejected. As previously noted, some of these "unwanted selves" or part-objects might have to do with sex, aggression, dependency, pairing or responses to trauma. In addition, we may posit that these internal object relation units will belong to the different Dabrowskian levels—some will be akin to level one, with its hostility towards introspection and its clamouring for dogmatic cohesion; some will be confused, other-directed and subject to conflicting influences; some will be suffering moral conflicts, aware of a tension between what is and what ought to be, feeling positive maladjustment; yet others will sense some organization and relatively calm hierarchization of the many selves inhabiting the internal world while yet others will be able to glimpse, perhaps if only fleetingly, the possibility of mystical calm.

Various tensions in the group and the socio-technical system will lead to the encouragement of certain of these part object assemblages to be brought out into the open so that they may become part of the public discourse, while others are repressed and then, further, projectively identified into the group mentality whence they take up residence in a selected individual, subgroup, thing, region or "atmosphere."

Thus an imaginary group is formed in the group mentality that corresponds to these split off parts—a Level 1 group, a Level 2 group and so on. Further, this imaginary group becomes embodied in a person, group, place, region or thing. Once this dynamic is established, it takes on the numbing sense of reality and then conflicts typical of the strains between the levels take place. These tensions take place at all levels—individual, dyadic, group as a whole, institutional, regional, societal, civilizational.

The most common tension between the levels is that between the "Four's" and the "One's" for the minds of the "Two's". The labeling of this conflict varies from time to time and place to place: authoritarianism/totalitarianism versus self-determination, indoctrination versus discourse and so on and the maneuvers used in this battle are various—deceit, persuasion, reasoning, terror, discrediting, propaganda, fake news, leaks, sentimentalism, nostalgia--to name but a few. History swings back and forth as now the One's hold sway, now the Four's and the Twos veer this way and that depending on the course of the battle. In many ways the struggle is driven by technology which (following Heidegger) serves a revelatory, traumatizing function in that it uncovers what is a "standing reserve" in the group mentality. Thus, through an individual or group, or in a specific region and a certain time in a certain situation certain ideas in the group mentality are uncovered and given realization through the advent of a technology. In recent times the bifurcation of Two's into those who nostaligically wish for the seeming calm integration of primary integration (Level 1) and those who ardently pine for the seeming calm of Level 4 has been accentuated by the advent of online technologies and their deployment of social media in conjunction with robotization. In addition, the massive increases in productivity brought about by the cybernetic age has not been evenly shared throughout society because of an unwillingness to share which in turn is driven by the underlying sense of greed, envy and ontological insecurity. In this way the computer age has revealed the vast, powerful imaginary group that is terrifyingly anxious about its continued existence (it's capacity for "going on being" (Winnicott, 1965)) and the accompany psychotic paranoid dreads of envy, greed and spoiling (Klein, 1975).

As mentioned earlier, history is replete with such schisms surfacing as a result of the deployment of technology—television, civil rights and the Vietnam War, the moveable type printing press and the religious schisms in Europe. This notion is not terribly novel. What is novel is that these schisms can be understood through a Dabrowskian lens. When we integrate these ideas with the model of history previously posited (history as a result of the interfacing of Ideas, Individuals, Technology and Situation) we may append to this that the ideas can be arranged hierarchically according to the Dabrowskian model, that the individuals and leaders can be understood as representatives of imaginary groups comprised, to varying degrees, of split of parts of all members of the group and that technology, especially if it is a defining technology, will uncover these imaginary groups usually in a traumatizing or, more correctly, re-traumatizing way.

Dabrowski's theory and the Tavistock Study Group

We may call the Tavistock study group a technology, given the broad definition being used here which includes procedures. Such procedures might include, for example, crop rotation, irrigation and logistics. The Tavistock self-study group is a technique that aims to uncover the unconscious dynamics operating in groups. Typically, such uncovering is related to psychodynamic theories such as Freud and Klein. More recently one might see references to object relations theories such as Fairbairn, Kohut and Winnicott or even the models of infant development posited by Stern. Thus what is revealed in the unconscious corresponds to those theories—repressed sexual and destructive urges, splitting, projective identification, envy, dread, psychotic and neurotic anxieties. Hazell and Kiel (2017) posit further paradigms that might be fruitfully used to expand our notions of unconscious group dynamics. This same process of extended theoretical application can be used with Dabrowski's theory.

Under many circumstances in organizations, groups are held together and some sense of cohesion and comprehension are maintained by the formal organization and the informal culture of the institution. These operating rules help maintain the notion of coherence while repressing, suppressing or otherwise defending against what might be impulses and wishes and realities that might present problems for the short-term operational functioning of the organization. At the same time, the organization's rules and culture will sometimes use its structures to channel such unconscious dynamics into activities that might further the ends of the organization. Thus, for example, there will be rules, explicit and covert, in the organization that suppress or deny the existence of hatred of management while also channeling these negative impulses, via, say displacement, towards that which is seen as hostile to the organization—competitors, untoward ideas or ignorance. If the culture and regulatory system in place in the organization is up to the task, this will give the appearance of unanimity—an appearance of what might approximate, on the surface, Level 1 or, if so portrayed, Level 4 of Dabrowski's scheme. One might take, for example, countries that seem united and peaceful because they are being effectively "unified" by an autocratic force. As soon as that autocratic force is removed, so the internal differentiation of that country emerges and conflict can easily arise. One often witnesses this phenomenon in those regions that lie at the boundaries of the "great empires." As these empires wax and wane, so these regions will experience a decline in the hegemonic influence of one imperial system and lapse into a conflictual state as the underlying schisms, which were previously repressed, emerge. Sooner or later, four things can occur. One, the region is taken over by another imperial force which suppresses the differentiation once again; two, chronic warfare as the various factions fight for hegemonic influence in that region, or fight for their very existence; three, the internal differentiation is worked through dialogically and the internal map of the region is redrawn so as to reasonably well delineate the cultural, economic, geographical and political divisions that make sense to the inhabitants or four; the previous empire returns and re-establishes or attempts to re-establish its hegemony.

The Tavistock group, although far from an "imperial" force,

has an analogous uncovering effect in groups. People seem to enter a group with the hope and expectation that it will provide an integrative experience. The analytic comments of the consultant, combined with the technological constraints of the Tavistock model, serve to disrupt this desire and reveal the underlying multiplicity. The revelation of this differentiation is typically resisted as it is uncomfortable. It is uncomfortable in much the way that Level 2 of Dabrowski's scheme is uncomfortable. It is a unilevel disintegration. It tends to expose the individual and the group to its ambitendency, its ambivalence, its wavering uncertainty, its confusion as to what is truly worthwhile, its polycentrism, polyvocity and a pervasive vacuous sense of pointlessness. Oftentimes the group will feel like a prolonged scene in "Waiting for Godot" (1982), a famous example of the theatre of the absurd. The latent absurdity of the group is revealed.

However, this disintegration is potentially positive for it provides a pathway to hierarchization and to organization at a higher level. Sometimes, in a Tavistock group, a Level 3 or 4 leadership might emerge. It might emerge as the group works through its primitive frightening impulses stemming from deep ontological insecurities. This working through is beautifully captured in the work of de Mare (2011) who offers hope that, even in median and perhaps in large groups the "hatred" we find just under the surface can be worked through and a sense of community achieved. This model of de Mare's is indeed interesting because it is homologous in form to the model of Reich (1980a,b) who argues that the "emotional plague" of spitefulness and despair can indeed be worked through (in his case through bodily-based therapy) and an underlying sense of good will be arrived at. The pathway, however, is long for a tremendous amount of work has to be done to traverse the "dark night of the soul" of Level 3 to get to the relative calm of Level 4.

When viewed this way, the Tavistock group relations conference may be viewed as part of the struggle between Level 1 imaginary groups and Level 4 imaginary groups for the minds of the Level 2 imaginary groups. Most people are at Level 2 (Hazell, 1984). Furthermore, most people at Level 2 do not see themselves as fragmented, that is, at Level 2. This is in part due to the relative absence of the dynamism of "subject-object within oneself" posited by Dabrowski. Perhaps, following Lacan's concept of the "falsifying function of the ego," (Lacan, 1997) they carry a far more cohesive and coherent self-image than is, in fact, warranted. Given that most people appear to be functioning at Level 2, we might expect that many people entering a group relations conference will be at Level 2. The experience of the conference will expose at the level of the group as a whole the underlying level of incoherence and fragmentation. This will be re-traumatizing. However, the conference offers opportunities to work through, or at least examine, this trauma—a trauma that involves an uncovering of the falsifying function of the ego both at the individual and group level—and also offers opportunities for the individual in their own way to integrate these new insights at a higher level of complexity.

Just as one can read Marx and learn how to better exploit and use others, so one might be able to similarly use the insight gained from a Tavistock group to better manipulate others. Here, perhaps, one has to work the odds. The number of individuals with such antisocial tendencies will be far outnumbered by those who gain such insights into the vulnerabilities of humans and use this knowledge in the interests of an "open society" (Popper, 2013), or at least, so one might hope.

Thus, to summarize, the technology of the Tavistock group operates in a manner similar to all other technologies as posited by Heidegger (2013), namely that it uncovers. What is revealed is the underlying Level-2-ness of groups. However, the group relations conference offers opportunities to examine this revelation and work them through. This working through may be fruitfully mapped by the scheme forwarded by Kazimierz Dabrowski and Piechowski (1977) among others.

Developmental Potential

As mentioned earlier, a very important concept in TPD is "developmental potential." Developmental potential refers to the amount of available energy in the person or system that is particularly suited to the task of increased development through the Levels 1,2,3,4 and 5. While energy for humans and social systems can be categorized into the five "overexcitabilites" (OEs): psychomotor, sensual, imaginational, intellectual and emotional, it is only the emotional OE that provides the kind of energy that results in the increased complexity we see at the higher levels.

It is therefore extremely important to know what happens to the emotional energy in not only individuals but also in groups, for not only will this give a reading of what level the group is operating on, but also of the developmental potential of the group, how far it can go and what measures might have to be taken in order to mobilize and deploy its energetic resources. The level of emotional OE in an individual is determined in part by genetics and epigenetics, in part by social and interpersonal experiences, such as trauma, or challenges that can encourage or stunt emotional life, and finally, and this is especially true for progression to the higher levels of development, by decisions made by individuals and groups.

Especially important second factor determinants of emotional OE would be the amount of *unworked trauma* in an individual, family or social system. Unworked trauma, insofar as it results in defenses, both individual and social, creates a sort of psychic "scar tissue" that can dampen emotional responsiveness even in the most resilient person or social system. In addition, secure attachments in childhood are especially important in sustaining emotional OE. It is thus very important, from this perspective, to support empathic attachments, if one wishes to promote development in the group, this being done in addition to working through societal level trauma.

Groups are tensional fields. Tensions operate between generations, genders, roles, in the field of authority and between the conscious and unconscious, to mention just a few domains. This section opens up the possibility that there is another tensional field in the group—a tensional field between the different levels of Dabrowski's Theory of Positive Disintegration.

These tensions exist within and between individuals. Each individual contains within them elements of each of Dabrowski's five levels. Some of these levels predominate and may exert hegemony and others may be virtually silenced, but there is always the potential for multilevel dialogue—this is Dabrowski's notion of *developmental potential*.

Similarly, multilevel tensions exist to a greater or lesser extent, and with greater or lesser degrees of consciousness, between individuals in the group, no matter what the size. Thus, an individual may, if they are sufficiently "multilevel," hear an array of voices inside themselves, voices emanating from different parts of the self, at different levels of emotional development. And a group or community, too, may manifest a panoply of "voices" coming from different levels—the confident psychopathic voice of Level 1, the wavering, drifting voice of Level 2, the moral anguish of Level 3, the visionary inspiration, perhaps, of Level 4, and the ineffable mystery of Level 5. One is reminded here of the many voices of the novel, of which Bahktin (1982) reminds us and which are captured so intensely by Dostoyevsky(2002) in "The Brothers Karamazov"—the spiritual Alyosha, the conflicted Mitya, the confident unreflective innkeeper and his cohorts, Father Zosima and so on.

The theory of positive disintegration thus offers another template, another useful map, to chart the complexities of the socio-technical system. In addition, these variations in level and the nature of the tensions operating between levels are expressed spatially. Different levels and relationships between the levels will be found in different regions of the earth. Some regions will tend to operate on a more authoritarian basis. This would correspond to Level 1 in Dabrowski's scheme. Within this region, one would perhaps find areas where there was greater diversity, such as in a multi-ethnic city. This might promote a more level 2 or 3 type of social system. In turn, within this matrix one might find evidence of smaller social networks and regions organized around Levels 3 and 4. These inter-regional differences would express themselves throughout the socio-technical system— politically, culturally aesthetically, economically, socially and so on. These variations occur in response to a multiplicity of factors, geographical, historical, sociological and technological. We now move to integrate Dabrowski's ideas with some hypothesized impacts of technology.

The relationship between technology and TPD

Perhaps the simplest and quickest way to enter this complex domain is to view the first twenty minutes or so of Chaplin's movie, "Modern Times" (1936) for this movie, with stunning accuracy and prescience, outlines the impact of the early twentieth century's technologies on the human psyche and community.

After seeing a flock of sheep being herded into work under a large clock, we see the "little tramp" working at a production line that moves faster and faster. He is under constant surveillance, fed "fast food", pitted against his fellow workers, depersonalized and under excruciating pressure. He ultimately "goes to pieces" (has a "nervous breakdown," in the words of the film). He behaves erratically, develops something that might be called a transient sexual "perversion" and is hospitalized. Supposedly "cured," he is put out on the streets where he is unwittingly involved in a demonstration and is imprisoned as the leader of a subversive group. In prison, he unwittingly takes cocaine and helps thwart an escape attempt. As a side-plot, we see the "waif of the docksides" stealing to help her bereaved and despondent father and her hungry siblings. The first twenty minutes of this movie are hilarious and at the same time tragically prophetic in that they seem to anticipate in an eerie fashion—(a fashion often encountered in great art as McLuhan (2011) points out)--the upcoming decades— an epidemic of mental illness, drug addiction, social conflict, mass incarceration, invasion of the private sphere, sexual dysfunction, destruction of the sense of community, intrapsychic fragmentation, emptiness, polarization of viewpoints, love relations under siege, dissolution of stressed-out families and randomness.

The film is made in 1936 and is remarkable in many ways. It is the first film to use soundtrack, this being enabled through the application of amplification devices developed as a result of the invention of the triode tube by de Forest. This invention enables a multiplicity of other technologies involving amplification— communication, control devices, computational machines and so on. The previous fifty years had ushered in a host of technological developments that, together, would slam into the socio-technical system in much the way an asteroid slammed into planet earth some 65 million years ago—creating a mass extinction—in the one case of flora and fauna—in the other case, of social forms. Such inventions as, to name but a few; powered flight, radio, bicycle, internal combustion engine, moving assembly line, alternating current electricity, the induction motor (along with the some 700 other patents by the all-too unheralded Nikola Tesla), the perfection of the machine gun, the tank, high tensile steel and so on, and so on.

Referring back to the socio technical model of chapter 2 we can see how such innovations impacted all of its elements— politics, ideas, religion, behavior, social structures, culture, ethics, aesthetics and material—such changes, arguably, to reverberate for centuries to come, much as the impact of the moveable type printing press is still reverberating through some planetary socio-technical systems some five hundred years later in the 21st century.

If we treat "Modern Times" as a thought experiment and juxtapose it to TPD and Heidegger's theory of technology we generate the following hypothesis:

Technology, while often having the superficial impact of social integration, has the covert, uncovering effect, through "enframing," of creating social disintegration at all scales. This is paralleled by a disintegration in the individual such that there is an increase in the manifestation of Level 2 unilevel disintegration. The disquiet created by this creates both a longing for unilevel integration and for organized multilevel disintegration. This increases the likelihood of a bifurcation in society where there is a headlong rush into defensive primary integration and an enthusiasm for quick fixes to Level 3 multilevel disintegration as people strive for Level 4 organized multilevel disintegration. We thus witness, with each technological revolution, an increase in the intensity and scale of the age-old conflict between agents of Level 4 and agents of Level 1 for the hearts, minds and souls of the majority--those at Level 2 of Dabrowski's hierarchy.

In a practical sense, technology, through the disruptions in relational matrices at all levels from intrapsychic through to civilizational, creates an increased likelihood for the emergence of Level 1 "true believers"—authoritarianism, cultism, closed mindedness in all its variegated forms as a nostalgic wish of protecting oneself as an individual and as a group from the onslaught of new information. This is akin to the response of the traumatized individual when they rigidify. Technology is alteric and acts with the impact of trauma, which is also alteric. Trauma studies show us that some individuals respond to trauma by rigidifying while others respond by "spacing out." Thus we will also see groups devoted to "floppiness," looseness, fuzzy boundaries and pretenses of lifelessness, much as individuals sometimes respond to trauma by going into a fog or "playing possum". This will be some individuals' and groups' response to the crisis of meaning brought about by the traumatic revelatory impact of technology—by the "shock of the new." Thus, the introduction of a defining technology can be seen as akin to "wild analysis" where the therapist delivers an ill-timed interpretation, too soon, before the client's ego is able to cope. The response of the client is to become angrily defensive, to dig in or to space out—to lose track of time, place, person and not to recall what was said. Another parallel might be that of an individual who takes an hallucinogen, unsupervised and unprepared, and has, as a consequence a "bad trip."

Chaplin captures this adaptation to the trauma of technology in his depiction of the company boss (a classic Level 1, similar to Mr. Burns of the Simpsons), overseeing the entire plant, enjoying his luxury without any concern for the workers and their plight. We also see it in the bosses, fellow inmates, prison guards, policemen and other workers, who, obediently, have internalized the rigid authoritarianism of their supervisors, possibly through the defense mechanism of identification with the aggressor.

Chaplin also demonstrates Level 2 fragmentation as we watch the little tramp go to pieces on the production line. He cannot keep up. His body starts to twitch. He hallucinates and rushes around the factory, randomly turning valves and nozzles. Going this way and that, he ends up chasing a woman down the street in a sort of addled sex-frenzy. A hint of Level 3 or 4 is provided in the calm intermezzo with the waif of the waterfront helping her bereaved penniless father and starving siblings.

If we create an intersection here between Heidegger's notion of technology as "enframing" (or revealing that which was previously hidden in human potentialities, that is, of bringing into being that which was previously only a potential) and TPD, we arrive at the notion that technologies will have a tendency to reveal the underlying unilevel disintegration that is found in most individuals and groups. This unilevel disintegration is usually held in check, or obscured, or channeled by the rites, rituals and culture of the pre-existing social system. The reaction to the revelation brought on by technology is one of a defensive retreat into primary integration (of the traumatic kind) or a somewhat fervid quest for some organization and hierarchization, perhaps in the form of a race to imagined states of secondary integration. This rush to a quick-fix secondary integration is often heralded by "false prophets," money-making gurus eager and able to capitalize on the surge of vulnerabilities and confusion.

Facebook: An Example

The technological ensemble of Facebook demonstrates these dynamics. At first blush, this technology holds out the promise of further social integration, of more extended and integrated social networks—perhaps of some harmonized "global village." The result has been far more complex, for Facebook did help people find long lost friends and family, make new acquaintances and form online communities. At the same time there was the shock of alterity as people saw things, and encountered things, people, behavior and attitudes that were very different from their own. To some this provided an opportunity for increased learning, for increased complexity and growth. To others, it was traumatizing and led to the formation of "informational siloes"—the creation of networks that reinforced one's own beliefs and ideas and the attacking of anything that was different, that was experienced as alien. In turn this polarization was encouraged by some who sought to gain power and influence from the ensuing disarray. The technology had a similar uncovering effect to the procedural technology of the "Large Group" experience in a Tavistock-based Group Relations Conference. Unfortunately, this occurred without the task of learning from the experience and without the assistance of consultation.

The technology also revealed an underlying hunger for approval from others, manifested in individuals seeking the "hit," the dopamine rush—akin to winning on a slot machine— of receiving a comforting bundle of "likes" on one's postings. The technology revealed an underlying narcissistic craving—a vulnerable self- structure longing for mirroring, twinning and idealization (Kohut, 1971,1977). Viewed this way, the technology can be seen as ostensibly providing a solution for social problems only to reveal that the underlying issues were far deeper than almost anyone had anticipated. The metaphor might be that of someone going to the doctor with a skin rash only to discover they have a serious metastasized cancer, or an autoimmune disease. The discovery is traumatic in and of itself. Technology is alteric in and of itself; it reveals the alteric and the alteric is traumatic. The traumatic effect is multiplied insofar as it is unexpected and then denied.

Returning to the example of Facebook we can further integrate these ideas with group relations work. Decades of experience in this field have demonstrated that the regressive tug of the large group, as opposed to the small group is enormous (Kreeger, 1975 ; de Mare, 2011). This regressive tug involves a regression to more infantile forms of thinking and psychological operation. One notes manifestations of what Piaget (1969) calls pre-operational thinking, of what Matte-Blanco calls the thinking of "infinite sets" and of what Klein calls the paranoid schizoid position. In addition, the profile of the defense mechanisms utilized becomes more costly both energetically and in terms of contact with reality. We note an emergence of primitive defense mechanisms, utilizing Vaillant's scheme (1998), such as denial and delusion and a reduction of and even a hostility towards the more sophisticated defense mechanisms, such as altruism, anticipation and humour. Facebook, while it offered the promise of Level 4 of Dabrowski's scheme, also created a regressive tug towards Level 2, as individuals found their identities being questioned on all fronts. Some individuals and groups, reacting in fear to this disintegration—at root a fear of going to pieces—of becoming psychotically dispersed—took refuge in the "castle keeps" of Level 1.

Facebook had the effect of suddenly creating a large group—a group full of the promise of togetherness and community but also saturated in the regressive tugs mentioned above. The response is that while there are tremendous benefits in terms of human connectedness, there is also a seeming flood of primitive thinking, splitting, paranoia and overall regression. This is remarkably parallel to de Mare's findings with regard to the median group (de

Mare, 2011). What he found was (in line with previous discoveries) a frightening emergence of hatred. More optimistically, he also found that this hatred could be worked through if there was sufficient support for dialogue. A median group is comprised of a membership of about 25 people. With Facebook we are dealing with much larger numbers. The task of coping with the emerging unconscious on this scale is daunting. The parallel between these musings and Reich's conception of the "emotional plague" is quite telling and, perhaps, apposite.

Spatiality, Technology, Group Relations and Disintegration; Positive or Negative

The speed at which transformations occur in the socio-technical system found in Figure 4 will vary by region. This speed of transformation can be affected by any of the variables in the system. For example, a social system with a rigid class system, political system, values system and religious mores that might be challenged by the introduction of a technology will put up resistance to that innovation. This is captured elegantly in the previously mentioned short story by William Golding (1972) where individuals present the emperor, at the height of the Roman empire, with the new invention of the steam engine (which was invented by Hero of Alexandria about 15 B.C.) The invention is roundly rejected and the inventor punished because it was seen to interfere with the slavery upon which the empire depended. The same sad plight occurred for several other inventions that were "ahead of their time."

When we take these regional, national and civilizational differences in the rate of adoption of technologies, and juxtapose it to the previous assertions regarding the impact of technology on the Dabrowskian levels, we arrive at the hypothesis that regions will vary in the extent to which the different levels are a) achieved and b) in conflict. Those regions where technological advances are embraced will endure a greater degree of conflict between the Dabrowskian levels of development. The fate of this conflict will depend on a host of other variables that contribute towards or subtract from the integrative capacities of that society. In addition, those regions where technological advance is more avidly embraced will present greater opportunities for both psychological development and regression, insofar as technology reveals the standing reserve in the human personality and societies and this standing reserve, in all its complexity and potential for chaos, will either be integrated into higher degrees of complexity of all levels of human organization or, defensively, will result in a flight into the rigid forms of Dabrowski's Level 1.

Examples of this formulation are numerous. The introduction of the photocopier, satellite television and the internet on the Soviet Union; the introduction of railways and all the ancillary technologies of the industrial revolution into the northern states of the U.S.A at a faster rate than the agrarian, plantation-based south are but two examples of this dynamic. Some regions remain "locked down" at all levels, from the individual through to the civilizational, as if there is the tacit knowledge that these organizations will be radically disrupted by the introduction of a new technology. This is especially the case of informational technologies. This locking down results in a relative stabilization of the Dabrowskian levels and even a routinization of the tensions that exist between them. With the advent of the new technological set, if it constitutes a "defining technology," that is, a technology with many knock-on effects, these routines are disrupted and the underlying tensions are uncovered as Heidegger suggests. The "standing reserve," with all its immense power, often built up over the ages, is unleashed, often with catastrophic, tragic consequences.

Perhaps some of these tragedies could be averted, or at least, ameliorated, if we were to recognize the vital dynamics being outlined here. When a new technology is introduced into a society, it uncovers the group mentality and the individual unconscious. If this is left unacknowledged and no mechanisms provided for the "working through" of that which is uncovered to such traumatic effect, the result is more human misery and waste.

"Gone With the Wind" (Mitchell, 1936) provides us with a literary example. This is a complex and even, one might say, troubled text. For the purposes of illustration here, however, we will simply draw out some of the lineaments that illustrate the connections between the paradigms of geography, technology, group relations and the theory of positive disintegration.

The imaginary landscape depicted by Mitchell in the early chapters is characteristic of a Level 1 social organization, if we apply Dabrowski's conceptualization of levels to a socio-technical system. Its structure is authoritarian. It lacks introspection. It is other-directed and blithely ignores the possibilities of conflict that lie behind the white supremacist institutions. It corresponds, roughly to the "magnolias and moonlight" depiction of the old south, referred to by Horne (2016). The technological system is agrarian, and of the plantation type. Industrialization is low, as Rhett Butler points out to those he deems overly confident of a quick victory of the southern states. Rhett Butler stands out like a sore thumb in this superficially tranquil slave state, for he has had contact with the rapidly industrializing north and its accompanying differences in mores, lifestyles and values; in short, its different "second wave," to use Tofflers nomenclature, socio-technical system. Butler's irony places him closer to a Level 2 type and he is excoriated by the Level 1's who deem his new ways unholy. Butler is aware of his two-sidedness and is capable of looking upon himself and others with some circumspection. This ability is shared by Ashley Wilkes, who also is less caught up in war fever. However, despite these adumbrations of "positive maladjustment," we cannot promote either to a level three, at least in the early stages of the novel, because they show little hierarchization and the conflicts between how things are and how they ought to be that we find in the troubled souls of the Level 3 individual, group, family, community or region. It might be there. If it is, it would be energized by his emotional sensitivity, his empathy, or as Dabrowski would have it, his Emotional Overexcitability.

By the time we are a few chapters into the book and General William Tecumseh Sherman's army has cut its destructive swathe across Georgia on its march to the sea, this superficially idyllic, crypto-fascistic slave state has been destroyed and all is in disarray. The heroine, Scarlett O'Hara is the chief exemplar of this disintegration which occurs at all levels of organization. She finds herself doing things, saying things, feeling things, sensing things that she has never experienced before. The incursion of Sherman's army, which is a truly traumatic incursion of a radically different socio-technical system, has activated a disintegration. For many, this will be a negative disintegration and they will remain deterritorialized, perhaps rigidifying, perhaps fragmenting. For some, it will provide an opportunity for growth and transformation into higher levels of development as they endure the trials and tribulations and take up the tasks of levels 2, 3 and beyond. For many, too, it will result in a nostalgic longing for the old days, the "glory days" of primary integration, of the fantasies of moonlight and magnolias. Thus we see, on a regional basis, a recapitulation of what Dabrowski posits for the individual and what has been here posited for the family and the group. We also see, and this appears to be novel, that these manifestations are potentiated, catalyzed, even caused by technological innovations and the different rates of technological adoption at the regional level.

Table 1: Intersections of Group Relations Theory, Theory of Emotional Development, Heidegger on Technology, Spatiality and the Socio-Technical System.

	Group Relations Theory	Theory of Emotional Development	Heidegger on Technology	Spatiality	Socio-Technical Systems Theory
Group Relations Theory		*Groups and subgroups operate at multiple levels of emotional development.*	*The group mentality, as "standing reserve," is revealed by technology.*	*Regional differences exist not only in observable "geography" but also in the group mentality.*	*Dynamics of Socio-Technical Systems affect the group mentality— FABART, Ps-D position, basic Assumptions etc.*
Theory of Emotional Development			*With the introduction of defining technologies, there is an increase in unilevel disintegration leading to polarization of levels 1 and 4.*	*Since technology is introduced at different rates spatially, there will be regional variations in distribution of levels and tensions between them.*	*There is a reciprocal relationship between all aspects of the Socio-Technical System and the levels of emotional development.*

Heidegger on Technology					*The revelation of the standing reserve and, thus, of the group mentality will vary from region to region.*	*The Socio Technical System works at different "speeds" with impacts that are both visible and "invisible".*
Spatiality						*The S-T-S varies by region.*

Table 1 gives a sketch outline of how the five different approaches mentioned at the outset of this section might intersect and offer useful insights into individual through to group, through to regional and societal dynamics. As to methods that might be of help in charting these complex waters, some are referred to in chapters 5, 6 and 7 of this text and in Hazell and Kiel (2017). These techniques basically involve the purposeful creation and maintenance, for a period of time, a "space of differance" wherein a dialogue might occur that allows for the emergence of elements brewing in the group mentality. These elements can then be worked through in such a manner that they become coherent thoughts around which the individual and the group might be able to generate practical plans. As mentioned elsewhere, these techniques include, but are not limited to, things like social dreaming (Lawrence, 2003), open space (Harrison, 2008), dialogical encounters in social networks (Siekkula, 2006), group relations conferences, listening posts, and the broad and vibrant field of cultural criticism.

Example: Socio-technical systems and where the baby sleeps

A study by Pye (1986) revealed some interesting differences in cultural constructions as to where it was appropriate for the baby to sleep. Amongst the Maya, much of this had to do with the parents' ideas on the relationship of the baby to its soul. This resulted in a more attentive relationship to the infant and its vicissitudes of mood. Such ideation and concern is not as frequently found in suburban dwellers in the USA who, when sampled, responded frequently that the baby might, for example, have its own room, separate from the parents. Often this was seen as a necessity and sums of money might be spent on decorating it with baby-friendly furniture. When Maya of Central America were asked the same question, they replied that the baby slept with its mother until the next baby arrived at which point it moved over and slept next to the father. When Maya were informed of the sleeping arrangements of their suburban counterparts, they reacted with surprise and concern, often asking if the babies liked it or not, since they felt that babies did not like to be separated from their caregivers. When told that, yes, the babies often protested and that the separation was often enabled by a walkie-talkie device so the parents could respond if the baby became distressed, they were further puzzled as to why such an unpleasant, inconvenient, costly arrangement should be pursued since it also put the baby's soul at risk of being lost. Why indeed? Perhaps the application of analytic procedures similar to those used by Erikson (1993) will yield some ideas. In the USA, the child is taught from the earliest period of its life that attachments are not so important. It is as if the infant is being prepared for a semi-schizoidal lifestyle that fits in nicely with industrial and post-industrial capitalism which relies on humans being used as replaceable parts that can be moved from one location to another and from one place in the production process to another without too much of a protest in the way of broken ties with others, families, persons or communities. Such depersonalized mobility is not required in a subsistence-based socio-technical system, such as we find amongst the Maya.

Every socio-technical system will have its advantages and disadvantages. The disadvantage of the system that systematically devalues attachments will generate its own set of social and interpersonal problems. Here one is reminded also of the young English who were sent to boarding schools, typically at about age seven, so that they might sever familial interpersonal ties and be all the more ready to serve in some far-flung realm of the empire. Similarly, a socio-technical system that encourages attachments will have its own set of issues.

In the "low attachment" socio-technical system one will see methods of compensating for the pains of premature separation, of what might be called premature ego development—the litany of pain-killers, chemical, interpersonal and social-- aimed at filling the gap left by the absent object. In the "high attachment" society we might see signs and symptoms akin to those found by Durkheim—low anomie but high degree of enmeshment and perhaps the sense of suffocation.

Winnicott's notion of transitional space (1965) is helpful here also. In low attachment systems there is an abundance of empty space, between people, between places and people and between people and institutions. Affects like loyalty and community spirit are at a low ebb and there is a corresponding expansion of the experience of emptiness. (This is touched upon by Hazell (2003)). Some individuals find this spaciousness exhilarating. Perhaps these might be counted among the "philobats" of Balint (1979). They respond to this vacuum with a creative response, much as a muralist can fill an empty wall with a vast painting. These individuals create cultural and technological "artifacts" that can fill this space much in the way a transitional object fills the empty gap between mother and infant. The socio-technical system then becomes one driven by these changes. On the other hand, for individuals in this society who are "ocnophiles", for whom the emptiness is a "horrid empty space" (Balint, 1955), this socio-technical system is a nightmare and they are at risk of becoming a casualty, especially if they are pathologized, if they are seen as having something wrong with them, rather than being seen as participating in a socio-technical system with which they have great difficulty articulating valued parts of themselves.

At the other extreme, in a "high attachment" society, the transitional space is constricted. The empty spaces are few and far between. Metaphorically, it is as if a muralist has been given a corner of a postage stamp upon which to create. Again, for some, this will be fine and they will thrive in such a system. For others this would be a suffocating nightmare.

Geography again can be brought to bear upon this. For some, America might be beautiful for its "spacious skies" because these symbolize a vast empty canvas onto which they may create. For others, it is too much. For some, the cozy English pub, with its snug nook, is heaven on earth. For others, it is a confining straitjacket. The situation, once we start to examine it, becomes ever more complex and interesting, for it is possible to live under spacious skies in a deserted landscape, but find oneself in a constricted social world, or to live in the narrow canyons of skyscrapers delimited by a few city blocks and yet feel as if one is the wide open spaces. It is these complexities that we may turn to the still nascent, yet fertile field of psychogeography (Self, 2017; Debord, 2002).

IV

Spatiality of Social Systems Psychodynamics

1: Introduction

In this section we attempt to introduce the spatial dimension to social systems. Social systems (which themselves involve technological features and developmental attributes) occupy space—from the dimensions of seating in a room, through the arrangements in a building, a campus, neighbourhood, region, nation, continent and the globe. This section thus integrates the discipline of geography into the areas covered thus far in this text. Since geography itself is one of the most interdisciplinary of all subject areas, this is no small task. However, the application of spatial or geographical knowledge to problems of counseling psychology, at any level of organization—individual through group and institutional--is quite rare. This is to be regretted because the geographical dimension can provide many powerful explanations for human behavior. In what follows, we will provide some notes towards such an integration. First we will provide a general systems model and then we will provide several examples of individual counseling with clients where the spatial, geographic dimension is prominent and helpful in both understanding and resolving the issues at hand. Figure 8 below is an adaptation of that offered by Blaikie (2003). The significant addition we have made to his model is that of the existence of a social unconscious and all that entails.

At the top of the chart we see the natural environment, with its variations across space and through time. This is the domain of the readily observable causal relationships we see in our attempts to explain regional differences and inter-relationships. The natural environment exposes different groups to different levels of resources and hazards. In turn, this exposure is affected by social and political processes. What lies at the base of this diagram, and this is crucial, is that these social dynamics are informed in addition, by unconscious factors such as those delineated thus far in this text. These forces, especially those of the paranoid-schizoid type involving splitting and projective identification have the effect of binding and deepening the regional differences driven by environmental and political forces. They thus intensify competition, suspicion, scapegoating and prejudice in addition to creating deeper rifts between perception and reality testing.

We note that it is not only opportunities that are differentially distributed across space and through time. The same is true of hazards. We thus see that when a disaster strikes it will affect some regions more than others. In addition, different zones within that region will be hit harder than others while, after the disaster, different areas will receive different levels of aid. While these differences are often driven by geographical factors, they are also driven by societal hidden agendas and, beneath and beyond that, powerful unconscious forces operating in the group mentality. We see such dynamics at work in many instances. Recent examples would be the differential impacts and rates of assistance with Hurricane Katrina in New Orleans and Hurricane Maria in Puerto Rico. In both regions it was the disadvantaged who were most devastated and those also who in turn received the least and slowest-in-arriving aid.

Such differences can be found in the language used to describe areas and regions. Often the underlying paranoid dynamics are covered in bureaucratic language but when social pressures create regression, the underlying psychotic-like phantasies are right on the surface and it does not take much in the way of psychodynamic interpretation to see where the underlying anxieties and fixations lie. Poorer countries might be referred to as "shit-hole nations," a "caravan" is depicted as an "invasion," foreign aid will be "cut off," and so on.

Given the power of the lowest element in the diagram, the "social unconscious" we argue that all attempts to solve social problems at any level of organization—small group through to global— that do not take these forces into account are bound to fail. Further, given the power of the social unconscious and its trans-generational properties, we argue that attempts to resolve such group, social and global problems that do attempt to take these formidable and painful forces into account face a gargantuan task; probably the most challenging humanity has to face. Currently, those who seem willing to take up this task are in a miniscule minority.

Figure 8: Spatiality of Psychodynamics of Social Systems

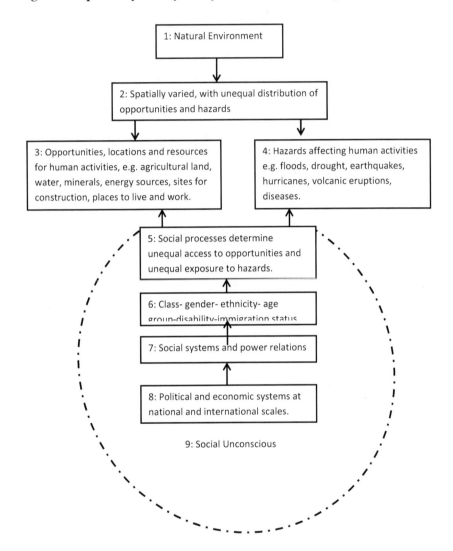

1: Natural Environment

2: Spatially varied, with unequal distribution of opportunities and hazards

3: Opportunities, locations and resources for human activities, e.g. agricultural land, water, minerals, energy sources, sites for construction, places to live and work.

4: Hazards affecting human activities e.g. floods, drought, earthquakes, hurricanes, volcanic eruptions, diseases.

5: Social processes determine unequal access to opportunities and unequal exposure to hazards.

6: Class- gender- ethnicity- age group-disability-immigration status

7: Social systems and power relations

8: Political and economic systems at national and international scales.

9: Social Unconscious

Spatial Implications of Heidegger's Theory of Technological Revelation

Technological innovation necessarily has a spatial as well as a temporal dimension. Innovations occur at certain times and in certain places. Thus the revelations of the "standing reserves" occur at different rates, in different regions and in regions that are more or less capable, by virtue of the organization of their socio-technical systems, to cope with the changes thus wrought, these changes being, as argued before, both of a material and ideational nature. Thus, for example, if a technological innovation occurs in region A but not in region B, certain socio economic and production changes will occur in region A and not in Region B. This, in itself will lead to inter-regional tensions that are well documented—tensions having to do with trade, power and migration, for example. However there will occur, in addition, a revelation of a standing reserve in region A, that will not occur in region B. This standing reserve will involve the revelation of hitherto repressed thoughts, feelings and fantasies at all levels of society. This revelation will not occur at the same rate in region B. Now the situation has become infinitely more complex. Can region A manage the "enframing" of the standing reserve? How will this be done? What changes will this in turn bring to the socio-technical system of Region A? How will this affect relations between the two regions. An analogy might be that of a married couple where one partner goes into psychotherapy, opens up and changes. How will they manage this change? How will it affect the relationship? Surely many things will change. The combinations and permutations of these systems are manifold and can be used to provide explanations for inter-regional as well as intergroup and inter-organizational tensions. Understanding these dynamics becomes yet more pressing as the pace of technological innovation and the resultant changes to the socio-technical systems increase.

The immense complexity of the situation existing between the individual and the socio-technical system is amplified when we consider that the individual is a system also—a system that can be depicted multiple ways—as a constellation of internalized object relations, for example, as shown in Figure 9, as comprised of layers, layers that are constantly attempting to adapt and adjust to each other and within themselves and also with other layers of the self. Multiple models of these layers have been forwarded. For the sake of illustration, those components depicted in Figure 9 are derived somewhat from Reich (1980 b).

Figure 9: The relation of the Individual to the socio-Technical System

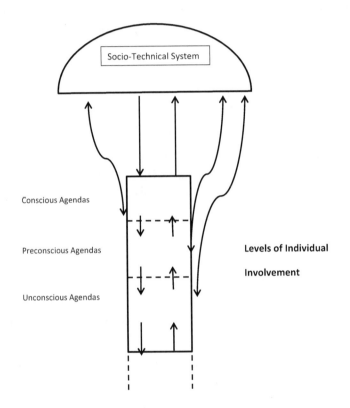

We have the mask, which corresponds to the conscious agenda--the superficial self which is very attuned to the performances expected of it in social situations. Below this layer we have the region which might be referred to as the zone of the "hidden agenda." This is the back of the mind where preconscious to unconscious motives are harbored—infantile wishes such as those depicted in psychoanalytic theories. Below this zone, we may posit a core where we find deeply repressed urges. Much has been written on these and we are left primarily with speculation since the layer above is so opaque and poorly examined. This would be the arena of primal desire. What do we find here? Social interest? Object seeking? Love and hate? Sex and Death? Or simply love? Perhaps time and further exploration will tell. At the time of writing it is difficult to get behind the mask into the hinterlands of the hidden agendas.

The flow diagram of the socio technical system (Figure 4) showed that the task of the individual in keeping up with the changes going on around him or her is indeed complex and increasing in complexity at an accelerating rate. When we add yet another dimension to the individual, namely the layers of the self and the co-ordination required among those and the socio-technical system, we start to appreciate the overwhelming complexity of the situation into which the human being is thrown. When we add to this the fact that the socio-technical system, driven by rampant technological change, is accelerating in its rate of change, we gain additional empathy and understanding of why things seem to be going wrong at such a pace. Indeed, as an upcoming section may illustrate, perhaps much of what passes for "mental illness" is the struggle at the individual and the group level to maintain some co-ordination between these multiple and ever changing factors.

2: Mental Health, Spatiality and the Socio-Technical System

Classical models of mental health and much of "common knowledge" focus on an intrapsychic view and explanation of what are commonly called mental health problems. A more systems-oriented view offers a set of alternative explanations (Maxwell Jones (1968), Edelson (1970), Devereux (1951, 1980), Minuchin

(1978), Colman and Geller (1985) etc. etc.). This section aims to expand upon the systems view by adding technological and spatial dimensions that are often absent from all of these formulations. The model of Emery and Trist (1965) integrates economic forces into the conceptualization of the social context but the effects on mental well-being and the relationship to technology are not explicitly spelled out.

Technology and its consequences are frequently used to explain changes in behavior and mental health in everyday speech. For example, people frequently refer to the impact of cell phone usage on interpersonal connectedness and to a certain extent the impact of the internet is referred to in its impact on politics. However no explicit extensive and inclusive model has been forwarded to explicate the connective chain between technology, spatiality, society and mental health. This lack is further expanded if we add to the aforementioned the theory of positive disintegration.

This section aims at filling in this gap by first utilizing the generic model of the socio-technical system described earlier. It will be argued that the functioning of this model can be understood as one of the important, frequently overlooked, drivers of history and shapers of the social context for the individual who is in the role of creating, participating in and, at the same time, being challenged by this very matrix. In addition, reference will be made to the ideas of Heidegger and psychodynamic systems theory.

The Articulation of the Individual with the Socio-Technical Surround

One may argue that the happiness and well-being of the individual relies, to a great extent, upon the degree to which that person is able to link up, to articulate, valued parts of their personality with the socio-technical system in which they find themselves "thrown," to use Heidegger's (2008) term. These socio-technical systems are nested in one another and change through time and over space, thus introducing historical and geographical elements to the narratives of deterritorialization and adaptation. To render this complex situation even more complex, we add that this adaptation occurs not only on levels of consciousness, preconsciousness and unconsciousness but also on the different Dabrowskian levels of development at both individual and systemic levels.

Wells' (1985) categorization is useful, and it encourages us to cast our explanatory net wider when trying to explain behavior, affect, cognition, imagination and ideation. The net, however, is far wider. We may explain mental illness by reference to historical factors. Erikson does this admirably in his studies of Luther, Gandhi and Hitler (1993a, 1993c). We see that behavior is driven powerfully by intergenerational trauma or by secondary and tertiary trauma, the effects of which reverberate through generations and ripple out in shock waves through communities and cultures. The mathematics of these forces is daunting. If intergenerational trauma is active across up to ten generations and tertiary trauma can act across multiple years, each individual carries in their unconscious the registration of the trauma of thousands upon thousands of individuals across time and space.

Devereux, Roheim, Erikson, Kardiner and related writers provide vivid demonstrations of the cultural dimensions that contribute to factors associated with mental health as do the sociologists Berger and Luckman (1967). In so doing they provide yet another template for the explanation of mental health. Volisinov (2013) in his Marxist critique of Freud imports the dimension of class as an *explanans* of mental health and its vicissitudes.

There are also attempts to explain mental illness through recourse to technology. Such texts will attempt to explain violence, isolation, narcissism and other constructs through recourse to technological innovations and their deployment (Grossman, 2009). Unfortunately, many of these do not make vigorous attempts to make use of the multiple other explanatory frameworks outlined here.

This section is an attempt to expand and integrate this set

of paradigms. The expansion involves the introduction of a spatial dimension to the concept of mental illness. In doing this, it is an attempt to integrate geography and psychology. Such an attempt has been made in the establishment of the discipline of psychogeography (Self 2017, Debord 2002). We also find attempts in this direction in the work of Soja (2011). This attempt differs from that insofar as it engages the structuralist theories of the social and behavioral sciences. We also find useful contributions from Deleuze and Guattari (1986, 1987, 2009) who use the concept of "deterritorialization" to explain the many disruptive effects seen at the individual and social level. In many ways, each of the individuals described in the following section suffer from deterritorialization. In these cases it results from movements through space but it could have equally well have been seen as a deterritorialization resulting from the innovations and deployments of technology through time, for, as we have argued, such innovations rumble through the "PIBSCREAM" creating a new cultural milieu and, with it, a new spatiality which the individual and the group must negotiate in some way.

The individual inhabits a complex of social systems. These range from relatively small scale interpersonal interactions such as we might find in a nuclear family arrangement, through moderately sized communities, to regions, nations and ultimately what might be "civilizations." Each of these social networks occur in space and involve interactions and motion through space. Each is internalized as a "mental map" by the individual. We might assume that this mental map operates in a fashion similar to that outlined by Piaget (1969), insofar as it is a dynamic structure, open to the environment to a greater or lesser extent and maintaining a dynamic equilibrium through actions of accommodation and assimilation.

The maps or models are nested as in Russian dolls but are also interactive insofar as accommodations and assimilations in one section of the map tend to bring about adjustments in other domains. For example an experience that causes one to readjust one's conception of one's community will bring about pressures for adjustments in one's internalized models of oneself, family, community, nation and so on. All the other aspects of systems theory as outlined by Bertalanffy (1969), Laszlo (1969) and Hazell (2006) apply to the operation of these internalized representations. Further, all the principles of development of cognition, outlined by Piaget apply to the operations upon these systems. That is to say, the cognitive operations applied to these internalized systems will depend on the age/level of development of the individual such that they will be characterized by sensori-motor, pre-operational, concrete operational and formal operational cognitive procedures.

Concurrently, the internalized models of self-other-community-world will be subject to the dynamics described by Klein (1975) Fairbairn (1952) and Bion (1978, 1997), namely projective identification and splitting. These dynamics might lead to a stasis in the dynamics of the internalized models since there will be far less, perhaps no, oscillation between the paranoid schizoid and depressive positions which is essential if the mind or, as it is called here, the internalized system of representation, is to grow in complexity and differentiation. Since it seems that the outside world is dynamic, complex and ever-changing this stasis will result in a serious dislocation between the individual's representations of the world and the realities of the world itself.

Such dislocations can occur for a variety of reasons. The individual might find they are unable to articulate with the social world as a result of a trauma which has seriously modified their self-other-world model such that they find it difficult to elaborate one that functions well for them. Early unpleasant childhood experiences in their family might, for example, make it hard for them to create a positive notion of community.

Migration might also bring about a situation where the individual finds they are in a new community or country and that their old models do not articulate well with their new environment. As some of the cases below show, sometimes these are easily anticipated, for example where the move is from one continent to another. In other cases the move can be quite a small distance. In highly segregated cities, the move of a block or two can dramatically change the "feel" of a place. The psychogeography can change very dramatically as one walks down a city block, crosses a street or moves from one small town to another only a few miles away.

These narratives show the utility of taking not only a "history", but also a "geohistory" by taking a "spatial turn" (Tally, 2013, Bachmann-Medick, 2016). They also demonstrate the articulation between the Dabroskian levels as they interact with socio-systemic, technological and spatial factors.

3: Case Illustrations

"Every story is a travel story—a spatial practice."
Michel de Certeau, *The Practice of Everyday Life*, 1988, P 115.

"Narration created humanity."
Pierre Janet, *L'Evolution de la memoire et
la notion de temps*, 1928, p261.

These cases and vignettes are aimed at demonstrating that the paradigm that explains mental illness as mostly arising from within the individual are erroneous and often harmful. It also suggests that mental health practitioners would do well to move even beyond the interpersonal analysis of behavioral difficulties to a model that includes not only group-as-whole approaches as suggested in previous works (Semmelhack *et al*, 2013, 2015), but also to include models of community functioning. Further, insofar as there is a spatial dimension to groups, institutions and communities, geographical factors have a profound bearing on mental health. The acknowledgment of the operation of factors on this large scale is quite uncommon in the field of counseling or psychotherapy but, as the following cases demonstrate, such features can contribute quite powerfully to the genesis of what might be labeled as mental illness. It is also argued that only by addressing explicitly these larger-scale factors and acknowledging their power is the counselor able to bring about a positive change in the life of the client. Such findings are echoed in the work of Seikkula and Arnkil (2006) where the differences in labeling, treatment, prognosis and outcome for "schizophrenia" strongly depend, for example, on whether one is living in Nigeria, India or the USA.

Case studies do not "prove" a theory. However they do illustrate that in at least some cases the theory at hand does provide a framework of analysis, an explanation that organizes a plethora of otherwise confusing data. In addition, if there is clinical improvement in the clients, this suggests that the theory is worthy of further examination, elaboration and verification.

Case 1: Ted

Ted was a 55 year-old man who worked as an electronics repairman and field service technician. His job involved travelling on the outskirts of a large Midwestern city in the USA. He was white and lived in a small town, mostly inhabited by white individuals, in what he described as "the most corrupt county" in his state. He was about 5 feet 9 inches tall and weighed about 200 pounds. He walked with a pronounced stoop and limp owing to severe back and knee pain. He was referred to me by a physical therapist who suggested counseling since there was such a pressure of speech during the physical therapy session and a very high level of distress.

At the very first meeting, Ted handed me a slip of paper, informing me that on it was the diagnosis given to him by his counselor back in his home town. On it was handwritten, in capitals, "DELUSIONAL DISORDER, EXPLOSIVE ANGER DISORDER."

This certainly caught my interest. My meetings with Ted took place in the inner city, in another state from the one he lived in, so at this macro or meso-level, we were inhabiting different cultural and socio-economic contexts in our encounters than the one he inhabited at home. This turned out to be very significant as our work together progressed.

The diagnosis interested me and I inquired as to its origin. It was given by a counselor whom he was seeing with his soon-to-be ex-wife as they worked through their divorce. This topic stimulated some intense feelings of anger in Ted and it led to him expounding upon his theory of what was going on. This theory had been labeled his delusion and had prompted the outbursts of rage. Ted continued for many weeks to describe the harassment he had been receiving at the hands of a large and powerful sector of his community.

It turned out that the counselor was perhaps only a counselor in name since Ted could point to no certifications, licenses or ways of contacting her. The counselor had, in Ted's opinion, connections with what he called the "911 club," which was his term for the closed society of police, paramedics, firemen and all others connected to this social network in his community. This network extended, by virtue of family ties and the "favor mill" to all arms of the community—sports coaches, nurses, teachers, neighbors, lawyers, judges and counselors. They were knit together by an unspoken oath of mutual support, allegiance and code of silence. Woe betide any individual who should fall afoul of them because they possessed enormous power to sabotage, disrupt and even ruin not only the "miscreant's" life, but also the lives of those he or she held dear. This network, the 911 club, which occupied his home town and its environs, was out to get him, especially since his estranged wife was a member of this selfsame tight knit social network.

Ted could provide a litany of examples of such attempts to

disrupt and damage his personal life. For example, the police could use their Global Positioning Satellite technologies to locate his telephone and thus his whereabouts at any time. This meant that he was frequently pulled over in traffic stops and was always encountering police cars wherever he went. Even when he took evasive action and went to odd places, they would show up. Ted deduced that this tracking of him was being done "off the record" by the police who were using their personal cell phones, which would not be monitored, and texting each other as to his whereabouts. Thus they could circumvent the requirement to register the search for locations of someone who had done nothing wrong, other than divorcing his wife who had allegedly had an affair with a police officer, thus making himself a target for the 911 club and its connected networks. Ted had to be extremely careful if he went to the bar because, given his assumption that he was being located, or "GPS'd", he could be sure that he would be pulled over for a breathalyzer test within a block or two of departing for home.

Members of the 911 club and their cohorts or family members also occupied other positions of power and influence in the community. Thus Ted claimed that the coach of the football team de-selected Ted's son from more advanced teams even though he was the team's highest scorer.

Ted felt that his reputation had been besmirched in several places he patronized by virtue of the police simply going to those places and asking questions about him and his behavior. This aroused suspicion in those who were thus questioned and had a cooling effect on what had previously been warm and cordial relationships. The inquiries and expressions of interest in his whereabouts stamped Ted with the label *"persona non grata"*.

Since it was a small community, Ted would often find himself at events where there were purported members of the 911 club. Frequently these encounters would become extremely tense as Ted felt slyly teased and provoked, almost as if a trap was being laid for him, as if they wished for him to lose his temper, take a swing at someone and get himself in more trouble, thereby "proving" to one and all what a bad lot he was.

Ted felt that the only lawyers available to him were connected to the 911 club. The same went for the judges. Thus he could not expect, in most cases, a fair resolution to his divorce. In addition, when his car went off the road and he was taken to the emergency room, he felt he was given unnecessary treatments by the staff (who were also held to be members of the 911 club) and some of his possessions, including his wallet, mysteriously disappeared.

All of this resulted in Ted feeling terrific rage and isolation and this had resulted in him having an angry outburst in the presence of his wife and a police officer. This angry outburst, combined with his chronic fury over his situation contributed to the diagnosis on the scrap of paper having to do with "explosive disorder." The narrative he held of being persecuted by the 911 club contributed significantly to the diagnosis of "delusional disorder." In my initial judgment, if it was indeed a delusional disorder, then it would be of the type that is constituted from an elaboration of everyday events and phenomena that are commonly found in consensual reality. This would lead naturally enough to the explosions of helpless, frustrated, rage.

My beginning approach was not to challenge the "delusion." This approach of "going along" and showing curiosity about the phenomena is generally advised since to do otherwise creates a defensive rupture in the therapeutic alliance. I listened and clarified and attempted to empathically resonate. Much of the counseling would be categorized as "expressive" with the hope that if Ted ventilated his feelings with a listening other he might not respond to the provocations that seemed to beset him and get him into deeper trouble. This seemed to go well and Ted seemed to benefit from having someone outside the social network in which he was enmeshed who could listen and attempt to understand.

Often delusions are ways of memorializing or manifesting a past trauma, so at opportune moments, when there was something of a lull in Ted's pressured description of his painful situation, I would try to gather a history. His father had died when he was 17. Perhaps this could be linked in some way. Perhaps the "delusion" of being followed by the police was a disguised longing for the lost father. He had grown up in a rough neighborhood in the city and had a violent adolescence. He had brushes with gang members and several conflicts with employers and unions. However, attempts at drawing links between these and his current situation did not seem to be very meaningful to him. Forays into these areas were not intensely emotionally charged. I was puzzled and continued with my "Rogerian" (2003) listening to Ted's tales of persecution in his small town and neighboring towns by the highly interconnected, powerful 911 club.

One fine day, out of the blue, I was reading a local newspaper and there, on page four, was a story of a suburban policeman who had been indicted for harassing the new boyfriend of his ex-girlfriend and had been using GPS technology and his cell phone to track him and cause him problems--traffic stops, questioning and threatening behavior. The officer had also used his tracking technology and off-the-books use of his own cell phone to keep tabs on his girlfriend. The parallels between this story, which occurred some 150 miles from where Ted lived, and Ted's narrative were stunning. It shifted the balance in my mind. Ted's delusion now shifted closer to possibly being an accurate perception of reality. I decided to share the newspaper article with Ted at our next session and from then on there was a visible reduction in his frustration and rage for now our relationship had shifted from one where I was not sure of whether or not he was in touch with social reality to one where we together explored the dynamics of this psychotoxic community. We examined other examples to see how they applied to his current situation—the tactics of the Stasi in Poland, Stalin's designation of dissidents as mentally ill, the movie "Mississippi Burning," the story of the Emperor's absent clothes.

This approach had a very calming effect on Ted since now he had someone who believed him, someone with whom he could grapple with the problems and issues generated from living in such an unhealthy, closed social matrix. The possibility of generating explanatory frameworks to anticipate and contain the feelings he would have in this social situation seemed to be a tremendous relief. I came to regard Ted's issues as being similar to those of Jimmy P (Devereux, 1951), namely that of cultural dislocation or deterritorialization. An important question to ask in such instances is the extent to which the individual is able to adapt to the several cultures he or she faces and the extent to which those cultures are themselves adapted to a relatively functional macroculture. With Ted, it seemed that his capacity and willingness to adapt to his local culture, dominated, as it was by the 911 club was nil and the desirability of such an adaptation was minimal. We thus proceeded with the notion that he was located in a culture that was for him, psychotoxic and that the best course of action would be to relocate in a more health-promoting culture and social network where he would be better able to take up a more satisfying role. This, utilizing the terminology of Deleuze and Guattari (1986,1987, 2009) could be seen as a "reterritorialization."

Many problems remained. His divorce proceeded. He lost his house. He had to have long conversations with his children in order to explain the predicament they all found themselves in. Ultimately, he moved into a more populous suburb, outside of the reaches of the 911 club of his original community. The "delusion" or "perception" lost much of its compelling power and his mood calmed. A year later, Ted had relocated into a larger, more open community where he enjoyed some of the benefits of anonymity. He had changed his job and his concerns had shifted to more "generative" ones. He was motivated by a strong desire to maintain his positive relations with his two youngest children. He also regained contact with his older son from a previous marriage and made sincere efforts to help him.

Sometimes old adages are to be examined critically. The case of Ted shows that the old saw of "You cannot run away from your problems," might not always be true. Ted's story also demonstrates the impact of the spatial, or geographical, dimension in mental health. Social systems and all they entail, occupy areas. In addition we see illustrations in Ted's narrative, of the impact of technology (GPS and cell phones, for example). This impact is not only enabling in the traditional understanding of technology. It is also revelatory or "enframing" insofar as that which was concealed as a potential is now revealed. In this instance the revelation is of a very dark nature, involving persecution, jealousy, envy, revenge and spoiling. Dabrowski's template may be integrated into this story insofar as the 911 club is operating as a Level 1 group (somewhat reminiscent of Golding's "Lord of the Flies" (2013)) while Ted can be characterized as a conventional Level 2—a "regular guy," albeit a regular guy under duress.

Case 2: Bien

Bien was referred to me by her husband. She was about 5 feet three inches tall and weighed about 100 pounds. She was of Vietnamese descent, having been brought to the USA by her parents when she was nine. She had recently converted to the religion of her husband (Sunni Islam) and was dressed from head to toe in hijab and robe. She had just left the hospital where she had been confined for several days. She had been committed to the hospital for standing in the middle of a busy highway and loudly proclaiming the importance of Christian love, quoting from the Bible. The first sessions involved her having me listen to recordings she had made of very passionate love songs. In addition, she would speak at length of her love for her mother. These would reduce her to tears and we would discuss the beauty and moving power of the songs. She was quite heavily sedated and spent most of her day building imaginary farms in a game on her computer. Slowly we were able to piece together her story. Both her parents were living and in their sixties. Her mother was a housekeeper and her father was a janitor. She had three sisters, two older, one younger and one brother. All worked, including herself, in the family's nail salon. Apparently the culture of this enterprise was very intense. There was much emotionally charged sharing amongst the family and the clients. The feeling was of an enmeshed social system, where taking an individual action without oversight by many others was very difficult. The level of monitoring and social control in this quite closed network was high.

As to trauma, Bien herself had suffered the move from Vietnam to the USA at the age of nine and this was extremely challenging. Beyond this, however, there was no evidence of acute trauma. The father had been involved in the Vietnam war and had been in a concentration camp and suffered torture. Thus, there was a considerable chance of Bien suffering from inter-generational trauma.

Early in the counseling, strong cultural influences were apparent to the white, Anglo-Saxon culture of the counselor. Among these was a very strong feeling of esteem for older persons and especially respect for one's parents. In addition there was a very high value placed on family cohesiveness. These strong cultural values, however, were complicated by the several religious transitions that the parents and Bien had undergone. Back in Vietnam, they were, in her words, "ancestor worshippers and Buddhists." They were also regarded with some suspicion as their surname was Chinese-sounding, not Vietnamese and this fed into ancient tensions between the two nations and cultures. In the USA, the parents had become quite devoted Christians (Baptists). Bien had become a Muslim after meeting her husband, and was spending a good deal of her time studying this faith, its precepts and its practices.

It thus seemed that Bien was confronted with the complex problem of constructing a cohesive, coherent narrative for herself that spanned different geographies, epochs and cultures that were themselves very dynamic. In addition, she faced the task of integrating at least three religious identities. At the same time, the construction of such a narrative would entail her adopting a unique identity that would be in violation of the key values of her original culture, namely respect for the elders. She would be implicitly challenging the tenets of her parents, and family cohesiveness, since she would again, in formulating her own narrative, be differentiating herself from the enmeshed matrix of her family, clients and community. Bien was thus caught in the horns of a multidimensional dilemma, a cultural dilemma that was found in the family and wider community. As an example of this dilemma occurring in a different guise, Bien had managed to graduate with a degree in finance from a well-respected university. However, she did not use her diploma and the associated skills in her work at the nail salon. She went back to work in the intensely charged family business. The intensity was not only emotional, it was also physical; the fumes of the nail salon were physically overwhelming.

Bien was caught between at least two cultures and her outbursts, which were labeled "manic," could be seen as upwellings of deep feelings occurring at the boundaries of the two "tectonic plates" of these cultures. Her talents and development led out of the "nail salon" culture and into the "macro culture" of the USA. If she left the nail salon she would be betraying her parents, family and roots. If she entered the macro culture, she found it contained many values and norms that were counter to her deeply held beliefs. In addition, although she spoke very good English with a only a slight accent, she felt inadequate. She used some of the counseling, by her own admission, as conversational sessions to help her language skills and interpersonal confidence.

The metaphor of geological "hot spot" was an organizing one in our early conversations. In the analogy, she was in a position similar to that of Hawai'i, which lies on a tectonic hotspot. There, the thinning of the earth's crust leads to the continuous upsurging of magma from deep below the surface. She found herself between analogous cultural and historical tectonic plates. The ordinary containing and organizing function of these cultural matrices was not as available to her and she was thus subject to upwellings deep from the group mentality and even, we may surmise, the Jungian, "collective unconscious." These would inundate and overwhelm her ego and consciousness leading to these outbursts of so-called mania that lead to her hospitalization.

Given this formulation, which bears some similarity to the formulation Devereux uses in his work with "Jimmy P" (1951), the counselor followed Devereux's idea in proceeding with the plan of helping Bien formulate her situation along community/cultural lines. Once this was done she could proceed and articulate her individuality with whatever community cultural matrix seemed to work best for her. Bearing in mind, as Devereux points out, that it is very helpful for the individual if they articulate themselves with a culture, be it micro, meso or macro, that has something of a future, or, to use Winnicott's felicitous term (1992) is a "going concern."

Devereux's parting words with Jimmy P are "I enjoyed our conversations." And we see in Devereux's report (Devereux, 1951) that his style is very "conversational," similar to "psychodynamic interpersonal therapy" (Barkham *et al*, 2017). Devereux's approach is relaxed and informal, involving sharing of cigarettes and excursions on horseback. This general approach (minus cigarettes and horses) seemed to work well with Bien, perhaps in several ways.

First, the egalitarianism involved in the conversational, collaborative style countered in a potentially useful way some of the "patriarchal" assumptions she carried from her culture of origin. Admittedly this had to be done sensitively as sometimes Bien would feel that she had been disrespectful and apologized profusely for some remark she had made that might have offended me, as an older white male. Examination of the different cultural assumptions regarding male authority from our different backgrounds was very interesting and helpful for both of us.

Second, the conversational style enabled sharing of the type just mentioned and thus paved the way for full throated exploration of our different cultural traditions. For example, a very emotionally laden concern for Bien at the outset of counseling was that she had been unable to visit the sick parents of a friend. This concern was connected not only with her very deep empathy for others, for she was very emotionally sensitive but also to her cultural traditions of concern for the community and deep respect for elders. Absent awareness of these cultural imperatives, Bien's concern may have seemed quite odd. However, viewed from a cultural perspective, one could see and empathize with her plight, especially since it was at odds with the macro culture in which she was embedded. By sharing my culture, in which the old were accorded far less respect and there was a strong emphasis on individualism and through further critical examination of the plusses and minuses of both positions we were able to view the situation in a far more complex light.

Third, the sharing involved in a more conversational mode enabled transparency on the part of the counselor, who was an immigrant and, though (coming from England) this transition was comparatively easy, it was still very stressful. Thus the counselor was able to identify with and share, albeit in muted form, some of his work of acculturation to the culture of the USA. This seemed to help universalize and "normalize" some of the issues Bien was struggling with. These conversations were always interesting and often amusing.

Finally, as previously mentioned, the conversational style served to increase Bien's linguistic confidence, thus increasing her ability to link up with the macro culture in which she was embedded.

Bien worked hard on learning the religion and ways of Islam and this, in turn, led to an increasing integration into the Islamic community. She found that there was a very strong emphasis on community life, concerns and service in her new religion. She found that it was more than a religion for her, it was a way of life. She found herself exploring the roles of women in her new culture and found a certain comfort and stability in the prescribed roles. She found the experience a calming one and, at the same time, she started new hobbies of reading, studying nutrition, and gardening.

These changes led to a distancing of herself from her family. This distancing was not hostile, for she was simply more selective regarding the nature of the contacts and felt less obligated to spend so much time with them. This change in the boundary relation with her family of origin, involving committing herself to her husband and her new way of life, helped calm her down considerably. Small things were significant for her in this process. She found as she went about her business at stores and walking that she would be frequently greeted by others with "Salam." This made her feel very connected with a huge community of like others. She noted further, that while they could clearly identify her as Muslim by her garb, she often did not know they were Muslim until they greeted her. This seemed to show her that they could "fit in" with the macro culture.

As Bien's mood stabilized and as she connected more with her new culture so she started to consider getting off the major psychotropic drugs she was on. This led her into conflict because she accorded her psychiatrist with an enormous amount of power and was fearful of going against her wishes or making her feel bad. These sentiments seemed to be in line with the cultural belief that professionals be held in high regard. Again, these values were examined and she eventually was able to tell the doctor that she wanted to reduce her dosage, that she felt that she would not have a recurrence of her "mania." She ceased taking the drug and her calm state held.

At this time Bien came up with the idea of a family get-together. It was to be a late celebration of her marriage. She aimed at bringing together her own family and that of her husband. In terms of systemic therapy, this was a brilliant move. From a practical viewpoint, it was very functional since they, as a couple, would be surrounded by a more integrated social/familial network. From an intercultural perspective it would expose all participants to the diversity that existed not only between the two families (Vietnamese and Indian) but also within the families for on Bien's side there was considerable diversity since her siblings manifested varying degrees of adoption of American culture and had also married and had children of mixed ethnicities and race. She decided to have this intergroup event at a buffet, deliberately chosen as a low pressure public space to allow for intermingling and somewhat fuzzy boundaries around the two families.

At the level of separation and individuation from her family of origin, this event was of significance for Bien in that it offered a solution to one of her key problems, namely, how to be separate from and yet still in contact with her family of origin. Given that the event went smoothly and there were some channels of communication established across the two families, these objectives were secured and Bien continued to improve. She became calmer, less anxious and her interest in hobbies such as nutrition and flowers grew.

This ushered in a new phase in the work where Bien once again went through her life story, retelling it from a different perspective, namely that of a calm person, relatively secure in their personal boundaries and relatively secure in their linkage to a culture that is a "going concern". Part of this involved retelling the story of her family. This time the story was more like a culturally informed movie (say, like, "My Big Fat Greek Wedding" (2002) or "The Joy Luck Club"(1993)). The narrative was thus more stable, had an aesthetic form to it and generated new insights in the context of a cohesive, coherent narrative flow.

The literature on inter-cultural counseling is quite extensive and usually part of counselor training is devoted to increasing cultural awareness. Bien's narrative, however demonstrates that there is nevertheless a strong tendency to medicalize mental health issues, as evidenced by her diagnosis of "bipolar disorder" and to ignore the spatial, geographic, cultural, historical and technological factors that are, especially in her story, so very prominent. The next story illustrates that these spatial factors, associated as they are with shifts in culture and related factors, are prominent even within shorter distances, within a nation. In a later case study, we will see that these spatial factors play a prominent role even over distances of a few blocks, especially if the city concerned is a highly segregated one. We also note that Bien had a good deal of what Dabrowski would call "emotional overexcitability," this being evidenced by her strong concern for others and spirituality.

Case 3: Derek

Derek was a thirty-three-year-old white male, married, with one daughter aged three. I previously counseled him for several months regarding writing difficulties he was having in graduate school. This part of his narrative occurs some six months after he moved to a small town in the southwest of the USA. He contacted me asking for telephone sessions since he had encountered serious difficulties in his new job and was at risk of being terminated. His anxiety was extremely high and he was taking an anxiolytic.

He was being severely criticized at work for being too slow in writing reports and, as a result, not seeing enough clients. In our previous work we established that he felt insecure about his writing skills and that he tended to overcompensate by writing very long, detailed reports. Apparently, in his current context, such detail was not needed. It also seemed, from his description, that the institution in which he was working, which did neurological testing, operated under very high pressure. There was a considerable emphasis on making a profit and little emphasis on fully understanding the clients. The boss was quite autocratic and unempathic and the colleagues were uncommunicative and unsupportive. Derek was unsure of the overall "ethical feel" of the place. The organization faced some legal problems and this seemed to add further pressure to the overall situation by rendering many topics undiscussable.

I shared with Derek that if I was to use his description as reliable data (and I had no reason not to) and I utilized Levinson's scheme for organizational diagnosis, that the organization in which he was functioning was an unhealthy one (Levinson, 1972). It seemed, furthermore, that there was a particularly bad fit between Derek, with his conscientiousness and detail-mindedness, and this "sick" or "ailing" organization. Derek seemed not to take in this idea and persisted in the notion that there must be something wrong with him.

This situation persisted and worsened for several weeks. Pressure on Derek to change his ways increased and he became more anxious and depressed. Eventually, he felt that further intervention was needed so he saw a psychiatrist, who prescribed Seroquel and advised that he go to a therapy group. The psychiatrist diagnosed Derek as having a major depression, this diagnosis was accepted by the therapy group leaders who subscribed to there being something the matter with Derek—an attitudinal problem of some sort that could be corrected through cognitive behavioral treatment. Derek became angry at these interventions and his anger was taken as a sign that his problems were indeed serious.

Derek had worked on his life history when we met earlier regarding his writing difficulties in graduate school, so I had experience of Derek's capacity for work on his issues. One item in his history that was of importance was the sudden loss of his father at age nine to a heart attack. We were able to link this childhood trauma to many of his issues, including his difficulty writing. Thus, my image of Derek was of a thoughtful, careful, relatively undefended individual—a version considerably at odds with the narrative being generated for him in the American Southwestern desert.

Derek's plight was exacerbated by the fact that, due to his recent move to that area, his social network there was very small— his wife, his child and superficial and sporadic contact with some neighbors and colleagues. His wife worked from home over the phone, so this did not offer much opportunity for the expansion of his social contacts—social contacts that might provide him with a different version of himself. Since his version of self that was currently under construction was a pathological one and was becoming more pathological by the week, this absence was crucial.

Further, the town Derek lived in and the entire region had no other places where he could work in his profession. He had even tried to work in jobs outside his profession and considerably below his level of education and skills, but to no avail. The seriousness of this deterioration was dramatically highlighted when Derek shared with me that his psychiatrist had recommended electro convulsive therapy (ECT).

At this, I set aside the unwritten code that one only hesitatingly and tactfully call into question the judgment of one's fellow professionals and once again laid forth my interpretation of Derek's situation, namely that he was in a sick organization to which he was having troubles adapting. There was nothing "wrong" with him. The fact that he found it difficult to fit in with a toxic organizational matrix showed that there must be something "right" with him. In addition, the community he was in did not provide other institutions in which he could generate a more positive self-description supported by others.

Finally, and fortunately, this idea held. The idea of ECT had tipped the scales (even though Derek did consider it as a possibility). Derek started to examine the possibility of returning to his home, a large Midwestern city. That was where his friends were. He had a large, multicultural supportive network there, as did his wife. The families of both he and his wife were there. There were many institutions for whom he could work. As he explored these, I suggested he vet them for their organizational health, and gave him a few ideas from Levinson (1972) and others (Hazell and Kiel, 2017). His version of his story started to shift. True, it was a pain to have to move again. He felt bad for "dragging" his family across the country twice, but these costs were minimal compared to the health concerns derived from attempting to fit into a context—organizational, cultural and geographical that was not matched to his personality.

Derek moved. He found a new job in which the pace was more humane and the collegial relations more supportive. He did have to work on the boundaries between his family unit and his mother and mother in law, but these were manageable and much more suffused with caring than the issues he had just left behind him. Derek contacted me several months after the move and was off the medication. His wife was content. Her work could be relocated easily since it was on the phone. He had regained contact with his friends and his quality of life had improved markedly.

Mobility of the labor force is essential in a well-functioning modern to post-modern economy. Organizations often provide relocation benefits when they ask workers to move. This tends to perhaps overlook the sometimes profound psychological costs of the move. The "cultural competence" of the individual may not match the new host environment and considerable effort may need to be expended in order to achieve this new articulation of self with the socio-technical surround. During this period of adaptation which will vary greatly from individual to individual, the person may become "symptomatic". These "signs and symptoms" may be then interpreted not as emanating from the process of migration and attempts at adaptation but as "mysterious" psychological disorders which are then "treated", the treatment then giving issue to a cascade of iatrogenic "disorders" and so on as the individual takes up a career of "chronic mental illness".

Applying the Dabrowskian (1970, 1977) framework to this narrative, we see how a change in institutional culture or in location might precipitate a "negative disintegration" and how this might be, if adequate and appropriate supports are not provided, a first step towards serious and chronic problems of adaptation. Similarly, one might argue, that such changes could stimulate a Dabrowskian "positive disintegration" which itself places the individual at risk of being pathologized if it is not recognized as a sort of growth spurt.

The next vignette provides an illustration, alluded to before, of how movement patterns of the individual on a smaller time and space scale are impacted by the spatial arrangements of culture and socio-technical systems.

Case 4: M

M, a young Muslim man suffering from severe allergies was planning a road trip. It was a quest for a better environment, one that had fewer pollutants and one where he would be able to grow his own healthy food. We discussed the geography and ecology of a suitable area and arrived at some interesting possibilities. M wanted somewhere warm and not too dry. It seemed that a karst landscape in a subtropical zone might suit him well—warmth, subtropical humidity, with the underlying limestone rendering the soils light and dry and the vegetation sparse, even zerophytic. We felt that in connecting the total environment to his needs we were breaking new ground in counseling psychology. As the day for his departure approached he became more and more concerned about dangers he might face on the road and in the wilderness areas he might explore. He thought of buying a gun. That, however, could be problematic. He finally settled on a crossbow, which would be legal and also would serve to protect him. He ruminated on what he might do if he was followed in the forest or if he was pulled over in an isolated spot. As he spoke of these issues, he started to sound quite paranoid. I rarely considered such eventualities when I traveled. Of course, I am an old white man and am rarely pulled over or bothered by anyone. M, on the other hand, is young, brown and sports the tonsorial markers of being a Muslim—short cropped hair and a long free-flowing beard. Sometimes this is topped with a knit skull-cap. In addition, this journey was through states historically associated with the Ku Klux Klan and white supremacist groups. At the same time, we found ourselves only days away from the inauguration of a president who had spoken of the potential threats emanating from the Muslim community. I wondered aloud on these observations with M and they seemed to strike home. He opened up as to how, even in informal situations in bars, people might turn, see him and start in fright, as if they had seen the "boogeyman." Dramatically and importantly, his concerns which had seemed somewhat odd and paranoid at first, became sensible appreciations of social reality. As long as he stayed within the relatively multicultural spatial confines of his neighborhood he felt ok, reasonably adapted, albeit at the cost of painful allergic reactions. As soon as he considered explorations beyond these confines, anxieties surfaced, anxieties that could easily be labeled as intrapsychic but that were predominantly geographical, socio-technical and cultural in their origin.

Case 5: Retreat to the countryside

When I taught at L University, there was a retreat each year that was held at a camp in the countryside just across the boundary line of an adjacent state. Some 100 students would live in summer camp conditions for several days and explore themselves, the groups they inhabited and the community as a whole. Most of the time people seemed to find it a rewarding, if stressful, experience. After a few years, however, I noticed a pattern. I had no statistics to back it up, but it seemed that the African American students were concerned more frequently about the insects and bugs that might be found at the camp and were worried about what precautions might need to be taken. At first, I explained this by relating to the wonder and amazement many inner-city children would show upon seeing an earthworm, so removed were they from everyday encounters with nature. However, some reading on "Sundown Towns" or "Gray Towns" lead me to form another hypothesis. There were practices in many rural towns in the USA where all white towns would ring a curfew at sunset to let persons of color know that it was time for them to leave town and return to their own residences. Woe betide those who did not return. The African American students would have had grandparents and parents who would have living memory of these practices and it is highly likely that although these practices have been formally outlawed they still continue informally and the fear they evoked was still alive. However, the memory of such practices is repressed, both consciously and unconsciously, as would be characteristic of any traumatic and shameful experience. The repressed memory must manifest somehow, since that which is repressed in the real will emerge in the symbolic—and emerge it does, in the disguised form of concern over insects, bugs and beetles that might bite you. The underlying fear is a geographic one, "Will I be venturing into a forbidden space, where, if I am found, I will be unprotected and severely punished?"

This notion was reinforced when I was conducting a group with mixed races and ethnicities. During several of the sessions, one member, a white older man, moved from seat to seat so as to offer support and to get a "different perspective" on the group. When this was consulted to, one of the Asian men remarked, "White men can go where they want." This comment seemed to capture a vital theme underpinning the group. In addition this enforced immobility of under-privileged groups perhaps joins with the high degree of family cohesiveness found in many cultures and becomes a powerful force amplifying enmeshment of social systems creating difficulties in the separation-individuation process of the individual. This is all played out in the spatial dimension.

Case 6: S

S, a forty year old divorcee, has no children and has a history of hospitalizations for a range of diagnoses—bipolar disorder, delusional disorder, schizophrenia. For a year she was doing much better with fewer interpersonal conflicts and very few psychotic symptoms. She belonged to Alcoholics Anonymous (AA) and Emotions Anonymous (EA) and she really enjoyed the latter, attending several meetings a week. Through these meetings she had met and moved in with a sensitive, gentle man, who himself was recovering from alcoholism. She felt calmed by this relationship, referring to him as "her Clonazepam" since his very presence could calm her down. She suffered from multiple physical ailments and was on Social Security Disability since she was unable to work. Later, after breaking up with the calming man and suffering from straitened circumstances she was evicted from her house subsequent to a foreclosure. In response she moved in with her brother and his wife who lived in exurbia.

This geographic shift disrupted her social network. The AA and EA meetings were very far away owing to the significantly lower population density. Also distant were her friends and her boyfriend. Her relationship with her boyfriend ended and she found herself, "in the middle of nowhere, in the boonies." A week or so after this geographic shift she started to hear the neighbors talking about her. She started to believe that an assailant from twenty years before had moved in the neighborhood and was out to get her. She also felt that her brother and his wife "hated her" and were bugging her, recording her phone calls with special applications on their phones. Despite an increased frequency of sessions with the therapist, including telephone calls, the situation worsened even in the face of interpretations as to the importance of a supportive social network to her sense of well-being. Eventually, amidst conflicts and accusations, the police were called and she was admitted to a hospital where she was again diagnosed with schizophrenia. Upon discharge from the hospital she had the goal of moving in with an old friend, back in the city, with whom she had had a long term, supportive and warm relationship.

The vignette of S serves to illustrate the systemic interconnectedness of the developmental history of the individual, in this case involving severe chronic trauma, and the surrounding interpersonal, social, economic and geographic context. In this narrative we see multiple chains of causality bearing down upon the individual who is equipped with varying degrees of internal and social capital or coping skills to deal with them. We also see the spatial impact on S's well-being insofar as there is a severe deterioration subsequent to the move to the boonies where she is cut off from a social network that seemed to serve the purpose of acting as a container for her projective identifications. Absent this safety valve, she becomes quite delusional as her inner world fills with bad objects and the pressure of these exceeds her containing and metabolizing function. In addition, we see the Dabrowskian concept of negative disintegration at work in a very distressing form as S "goes to pieces" when her social network is severely disrupted by a relocation of about twenty miles. The deterritorialization has a devastating effect.

Case 7: Helena

Helena had grown up in a rural coal-mining area. She was, literally, a "coal miner's daughter." As such, she had arisen amongst rural poverty and the culture associated with it. From an early age, as far back as she could remember, she had wanted to escape. Finally, with a good deal of struggle, she managed to enroll in a nearby state college and gain a degree in business. This was especially difficult insofar as she had, following the cultural mores of her setting, become pregnant and moved into a trailer camp with her boyfriend who was not supportive of her upwardly mobile endeavours. She finally succeeded, gained her degree and moved to a distant city where she became self-supporting. In later life, she is beset with a depression and chronic fatigue and seeks counseling. The causes of the malaise are deep and complex, involving trauma, family dynamics, stress and issues related to gender. One causal factor, however, is geographic in origin. When uncovering her early childhood anger and disgust at her surroundings she feels guilty and ashamed in several ways—ashamed for deriding her parents and friends and their way of life, shame at perhaps coming off as "superior;" guilty for having left her original place of residence and yet, conflictually, proud and happy at her accomplishments and at the comfortable, interesting lifestyle she has managed to construct, mostly on her own initiative. This conflict seemed to interfere with her feelings of pride and enjoyment and contributed to a chronic feeling of low self-esteem and lack of exuberance when these were, to all intents and purposes, justified. Closer examination revealed that, in several ways, Helena was appreciating the situation in the highly-charged emotional way we might find in a child who was furious at their surroundings and vowing to escape them. When her life structure and narrative was looked at in this fashion it did lead, indeed, into irreconcilable polarities such as those just enumerated. Looked at in the relatively clearer light of adulthood, however, she could see that there was little to be conflicted about, regarding her migration. Her parents were happy for her and proud of her. Others could have decided to do as she did and leave. In fact, perhaps some of them were helped by the example she set of independence and achievement. It was as if the migration she had initiated and carried out was processed on the one level at Piaget's pre-operational stage and at the other level on a formal operational or even post formal operational level. The emotional experiences and self-states arising from these dual processings were radically different. One (formal and post-formal operational) seemed obviously preferable and more functional than the other and this was the one she opted for.

From the Dabrowskian viewpoint we see Helena moving forward in emotional development with signs of Level 3, namely; guilt, shame, concern for others and affective memory making their appearance. These aspects of her personality were enabled to some degree, for her, by a move from one place to another, by a reterritorialization.

In Helena's story we see the inside, as it were, of the dynamics of migration, for not only does the migrant have to generate new articulations with the new culture they find themselves in and even though these adjustments can be considerable even if, as is the case with Helena, the distance covered is only two hundred miles, the individual also may have to make considerable emotional and cognitive adjustments as they deal with the leaving behind of their social network and the depressive anxieties this may bring about.

Case 8: Leona

The following client narrative illustrates how an individual may find themselves in a painful emotional situation occasioned by their being in a region and culture where the practices in their socio-technical surround do not articulate sufficiently well with their psychological needs.

Leona was a 50 year-old woman who presented with a profound depression. She had recently been released from hospital where she had been given a sequence of electro-convulsive therapies. She had found these to be quite distressing, not to say traumatic, especially since they had no effect on her depression which was profound. She was emaciated, anorexic and almost mute. In sessions she would utter only the occasional monosyllabic response to the counselor, who felt under a good deal of pressure to establish some sort of emotional contact. In fact, she saw no point in counseling and was only there because her family deemed it essential and drove her to sessions. She saw no point in living, although she was not considering suicide. She seemed committed to a sort of half-life of passively watching television reruns and getting angry if anyone suggested anything different for her life.

When we inquired more deeply into Leona's history, the depression seemed quite explicable. Her husband had died in the previous year after a protracted and painful illness that was punctuated by multiple seizures. He had been the love of her life. Prior to this she had felt that her vocational world had collapsed as she discovered that the institution she was working for was operating illegally. When she blew the whistle on this, she was fired. This had a tremendously demoralizing effect on her.

All of this took place in the Midwest of the USA where there are frequently very few structures or other cultural practices to support mourning. The time from death to burial is typically a few days and one is generally expected to recover from the loss quickly and get back to work. These practices are quite consistent with the practices of less-regulated capitalistic economies and cultures emphasizing uninterrupted production and consumption. In other, more agrarian cultures we find cultural practices around mourning to be quite extensive. Even in Great Britain, a capitalist economy, several weeks might elapse between death and burial as the family and friends make funeral arrangements. When we look further afield, we find rituals for extended periods. In Bali, for example, where on an annual basis, the entire village goes through a ritual to mark the passing of everyone in the village the previous year. In Mexico the celebration of the "day of the dead" where various practices are seen that support the working through in a family, group or community context, the loss of loved ones.

Viewed from this geographic/cultural perspective we may reformulate Leona's "major depression" as her having the misfortune of enduring a traumatic loss in an area where there were little or no cultural practices to recognize and work through such an event. Instead, it is seen as a "chemical imbalance," or as if there is something wrong with her, rather than there being something lacking in the ensconcing culture which is failing to provide an adequate holding/containing/metabolizing function. In addition, the idea that traumatic demoralization might eventuate from participating in an organization that is corrupt is not widespread or held with much conviction or understanding. However, if we subscribe to the notion of the institution serving as an internalized object and perhaps as a form of narcissistic guardian, we may quickly arrive at the conclusion that such a setback could have very serious and deleterious consequences.

Once this was pointed out to Leona as a possible explanation for her malaise (along with other causal factors) and once the counselor attempted to pick up where the culture left off, there seemed to be a marked improvement. This was not the only factor in the work together, which was captured by much of what may described as an expansion of "Psychodynamic Interpersonal Therapy" (Barkham, 2017), but it did provide a useful explanatory template for the situation in which Leona found herself. In addition, it helped normalize and universalize her experience. In this way she could see her story as being one that many others would have, as something communicable. In this, it moves from being something that has her to something she has a hold of.

We see, from the preceding vignette that geographic factors

can enter into the explanatory equation even if the individual has not moved through space. One's personality might be reasonably well adjusted to one's geographic cultural surround for much of one's life, only to be jarred into disarticulation as a trauma or a new life-developmental stage arises. We saw some of these dynamics exemplified in the previous case of Helena, for whom her geographic/cultural surround "worked" quite well until late adolescence/young adulthood. Again, we note how serious the negative disintegration might be as these phenomena are visited upon the individual and how at risk they are at being pathologized.

Case 9: R

The story of R illustrates how a move that is seen by the parents as essentially a positive one and that only covers a few miles can make a drastic difference, especially if the region is segregated. R, a second generation Indian immigrant to the United States of America was born in a neighbourhood that contained a very high proportion of people from India. The streets were filled with sari shops, Indian restaurants and various community organizations. It was here that R grew up for the first few years of his life. All around him, at school and in the streets were people with whom he felt in common. When he reached fourth grade, however, his parents' fortunes improved and they decided to move to a different neighbourhood, only a few miles away. This involved changing schools and community. R went from being one of many to being one-of-a-kind. Unfortunately this was not a positive experience for him. He was bullied and found it hard to make friends. He became exceptionally isolated and this, according to Sullivan (1953) at a crucial stage, the "chum" stage of preadolescence when out of the "gangs" of the juvenile stage the child selects a close friend with whom they learn all the skills and challenges of an intimate relationship. These skills are then carried forward into adolescence and beyond where they form the bedrock of later intimacy, so vital to psycho-social wellbeing. Sadly, R did not get to experience this stage to its fullest. There were no chums, no sleepovers, no shared community activities, no teams to be joined. R was the lonely kid on the edge of the playground. This dynamic of ostracism brought on by the move to a neighbourhood where he was one of a kind, to a neighbourhood in a city where racism was a way of life, was accentuated by the enmeshment of his family. This continued throughout his childhood, adolescence and extended into his young adulthood and had devastating effects on his social network which was sparse and somewhat unselective due to his not having had a lot of interpersonal experiences that might inform his choices.

In a highly mobile society, where there is such a premium placed on upward mobility, such changes in location are frequently overlooked by parents who are unaware of the devastating impact a move can be on a child's developing interpersonal world. The parents will often see the move as an improvement as they move into a "better" neighbourhood, a larger house or a more highly-achieving school district. For the child, however, it can be an unacknowledged catastrophe. Important to note, however, is that it might also work in the opposite direction. A child who has garnered a negative social label in one social network might benefit from a "fresh start" in a new social matrix. However, the strain of the shift should be acknowledged and the appropriate supports put in place to assist the child, or even adult, in that transition.

We see also the other paradigms at work. For example, R's isolation and singleton status sets him up for the repository role in the group, destined to be a target for unwanted projective identifications, especially as the group, community or society undergoes stress. In fact, each of the stories above involves just such vulnerability. We also note how the factors of spatiality, group dynamics, technology and emotional development interact crucially with other developmental lines (A. Freud, 1965) thus rendering the situation enormously complex and subtle.

Conclusion

In these examples we can see several "causal pathways" through which community, technological, developmental and geographic factors might generate "mental illness." In each instance the individual concerned seemed to be significantly impacted by factors operating in these registers. This is not to imply that the intrapsychic, individual or familial factors were not involved. It aims, however, at establishing that much improvement in individual's lots can be achieved by addressing these layers. Organizing concepts for these interventions can be found in Hazell and Kiel (2016) and Hazell (2006).

When we examine the causal matrices in each case we can see that Ted's plight was brought on by a closed, powerfully connected social network that extended to a wide array of community functions. There was a persecutory element in this network that resembled that of a police state even though it was located in a western democracy. The functioning of this network was heavily reliant on the introduction of cell phone and global positioning technology.

The case of Bien involves migration and the difficulties involved in cultural difference and change. These tensions existed within the family with the older generation adhering more to the "old ways" and the younger members being more "American" and they also existed between the family and the meso and macro cultural surround. Thus Bien confronted difficulties in finding a sustaining and sustainable micro, meso and macro culture with which she could find meaningful articultations.

The case of Derek illustrates how a seemingly straightforward move across the country can result in significant cultural dislocations that can, if not properly identified, place the individual at considerable risk, especially of iatrogenic illness. We may also see how issues of career development interface in complex ways with the individual's articulation of valued parts of the self with vectors of the micro, meso and macro culture all of which have spatial dimensions.

These cases and vignettes are intended to demonstrate that there is a much-ignored aspect of psychological counseling— the spatial aspect of the relationship of the individual to the community—the dimension of cultural geography, broadly conceived. This connection is routinely underestimated in its power over the individual and may lead to the misidentification of multiple, supposedly "psychogenic illnesses." These cases are all adults exposed to pressures emanating from the community at large. Of especial interest is how these pressures, considerable as they are, might impact those who are young, ill, or otherwise vulnerable and lacking in access to facilitative resources.

Seikkula *et al* (2006) demonstrate how psychosis can be effectively treated through "dialogical meetings in social networks". This work occurs in Western Lappland, Finland, and there schizophrenia is not looked upon as a chronic mental illness treatable mainly through pharmacological interventions. It is viewed as an acute, short-lived phenomenon which, for the most part, can be effectively treated through integration of the individual in the community. In this we see a clear relation of spatiality to serious mental illness. If one is diagnosed with such severe mental illness in the United States, or, for that matter in most wealthy countries, one is much more likely to be seen as having a chronic condition that can only be managed with medicine (Saha *et al*, 2005). If, on the other hand, one is diagnosed with a psychoticlike disorder in Western Lappland, one will be treated as if the condition is relatively short lived and can be corrected through "dialogical meetings in social networks". In addition, as is pointed out by (Saha *et al*, 2005) if one is diagnosed as "schizophrenic" (the inverted commas are to emphasize the variability of the construct) in a poorer country where finances for even medicine are relatively unavailable, one will be seen as having a condition of short duration that can be dealt with through re-integration into the matrix of one's community. Again, geography, from a mental health standpoint, can be destiny. In the late 1970's in the USA there was a policy of disestablishing the large state mental hospitals towards "community-based treatment." This is, however a far cry from what we see in the set-up forwarded by Seikkulla *et al* in that these programs in the USA did not provide, by and large, the type of intensive re-integration into the life of the community carried out in Western Lappland. Too often, while the client would visit the Community Mental Health Center, perhaps once a week, the rest of the time, they would be left to their own devices, socially disconnected and prone thus to chronic isolation, with a consequent lack of reality testing that occurs in the mix of a social network. This led to a consequent sense of anomie and meaninglessness. These differences in diagnosis, prognosis and treatment are driven by factors in the socio-technical environment, and these vary over space, or geographically. Thus, the wealth of the regional economy plays a role, in that a poor region will not be able to fund long hospital stays or prolonged medication. Even if two regions are economically similar as, say Western Lappland is similar to many reasonably well-off regions, cultural factors-(such as the value placed on individualism, family, community), political factors (having to do with how decisions are made with regard to the deployment of resources), religious, and ideational factors will all come into play. When we consider this variability, many of our systems of diagnosis, prognosis and care which are seen to be "scientific" turn out perhaps to be "scientistic" insofar as they are based on horizons that are too narrow, perhaps to be assessed in the way we would assess scholastics arguing over the number of angels on the head of a pin. Just as we might suggest that these "monastic philosophers" open up their theoretical systems to new inputs to better approximate a range of realities, so we might suggest that many psychologists might benefit from broadening their horizons to include other paradigms, or to entertain the notion shared by Kuhn (1962) that the "normal science" of psychology is need of a "scientific revolution"—a paradigm shift.

The flow chart (Figure 8) inspired by Wisner *et al* (2005) helps provide a framework of analysis since what is being proposed here is that the processes they describe in explaining the distribution of opportunities and hazards may be conjoined with a psychodynamic model to assist in explaining the high degree of irrationality found in these dynamics. By adding the concept of a dynamic social unconscious (item 9 on the figure) which powerfully affects items 5, 6, 7 and 8 we may explain many of the "irrationalities" found in such systems.

V

The Discourse of the Clown

The purpose of this section is to describe the discourse of the clown. In a previous text (Hazell and Kiel, 2018) the Lacanian concepts of discourse ore described and related to the conversation found in groups. Lacan identifies four discourses (five if we include the discourse of the Capitalist). The discourse of the Clown is seen as a sixth discourse, namely one that cannot be included in any of the four primary Lacanian discourses (2007 a) and which has sufficient internal integrity to be labeled as a discourse in and of itself. In addition to defining this discourse, we will place it in relation to the four discourses of Lacan, namely those of the Master, University, Hysteric and Analyst. This relationship is a dynamic one. It is also a revelatory one insofar as the discourse of the Clown, when it makes contact with any of the other discourses, uncovers those elements in the discourse that are usually hidden from view. This is especially the case, as we hope to demonstrate, with the revelation of that which is "barred" in the discourse (to use Lacan's term), namely the Truth and the Product of the discourse. Finally, examples from group life will be used to illustrate the interaction of the discourse of the clown with the four Lacanian discourses.

Definition of Discourse of the Clown:

Freud (1905) shows how wit (or jokes, or humour) is closely allied to his conception of the dream by providing examples of how the same dynamics of the dream—condensation, displacement, reversal, rebus, homophony, suspension of logic, metonymy, the representation of a repressed wish, regression—are to be found in the multiple forms of humour in its many forms. At several points Freud refers to the "work of wit" or "wit work" as if to imply that humour involves a form of working with the unconscious that is parallel to the "dream work" discussed in his earlier treatise on dreams (1900). We may thus locate humour as an intermediary step, although perhaps not an essential one, in the evolution of thinking. Referring to Bion's theory of thinking (1978) we may see humour (or the discourse of the clown) as a working over of "dream thoughts" into a more manageable form, a form involving concepts that might be organized into theories or proto-theories. This working over described by Bion and represented on his grid can be seen as parallel to the linking of the imaginary, symbolic and real of the Borromean knot. As we saw in the previous discussion of the *sinthome*, this linking is sometimes carried out by the function of the addition of a fourth ring, namely, the selfsame *sinthome*. Thus, the discourse of the clown can serve in the manner of a *sinthome* insofar as it links the three registers of symbolic, imaginary and real, thus preventing the separation of one register from the others or, more seriously, total disintegration. Perhaps part of the laughter is evoked by the anxieties aroused in the mating of ideas necessary for the processes of conception, and the drastic consequences of this not occurring.

Freud develops a detailed typology of the different forms of wit, categories covering humour, caricature, irony, wit, punning and so on. In the current conceptualization of the discourse of the Clown, we lump all of these forms together, seeing them as different techniques deployed in the overarching, inclusive discourse. We accept also the tantalizing vision of humour offered by Koestler (1945), which sees humour as arising from the "bisociation" of two frames of reference, and see this as included in the array of procedures used in the discourse of the clown.

The discourse of the Clown at times might seem very close to two of the Lacanian discourses; the Analyst and the Hysteric. It is however different from both. While the Clown discourse has the revelatory function of the Analyst, such a function is not its primary operation and usually much of the revelation of humour is done unawares. A Clown discourse in its gaiety and other features might seem like that of the discourse of the Hysteric, but the clown discourse involves more work on the part of the protagonist. There has been some working through of the ideas and impressions that potentiate the discourse. Thus the discourse of the Clown is not to be confused with Ganser Syndrome or hysterical escapism. Again, sometimes the Clown discourse can be seen as "educational" and thus resembling the discourse of the University but if it becomes too much so, it is usually not amusing and drifts off into the realms of disguised indoctrination. It then falls flat.

The Relationship and interaction of the Discourse of the Clown to Lacan's Four Discourses

In what follows, a series of hypothetical relationships between the discourse of the clown and the four discourses of the Lacanian system will be explored. It is hypothesized that when the discourse of the clown is deployed and encounters one of the Lacanian discourses that a sequence of events takes place. This sequence is funny but can be mapped out using Lacan's fourfold framework. Exploring this offers alternative explanatory frameworks for the functioning of humor and, in addition, offers those who wish to understand human interaction at all levels—intrapersonal, interpersonal, group, societal and cultural—new frameworks of analysis.

The application of the four Lacanian discourses to the analysis of group dynamics has been described by Hazell and Kiel (2017). The four discourses (Master, University, Hysteric and Analyst) are created by the placement of four elements (S1, S2, $,a; corresponding to Master signifier, Signifying chain, Split subject, Desire or Jouissance) in rotation through four positions corresponding to Agent, Object, Product and Truth. Thus, in the discourse of the Master, for example, the arrangement is such:

$$\underline{S1} \longrightarrow \underline{S2}$$
$$\$ \qquad\qquad a$$

This signifies that in this discourse the agent of the discourse is seen to possess the master signifier, is oriented towards a signifying chain, creating desire and, in truth, is a divided subject.

Each new discourse is created by rotating each element through each of the positions, resulting in the four discourses. As the diagram below attempts to show, the discourse of the Clown (let us signify it with a C) can be deployed so as to make contact with each of the four Lacanian discourses. When it does so, we hypothesize the following to occur:

a) That which was in the position of Truth moves so that it becomes a Product. (In this, we see the wisdom in the old saying, "It is funny because it is true.")

b) That which was in the position of the Product is barred, temporarily annulled. It is assimilated into that which was the Agent prior to contact with the Clown.

Thus, the discourse of the Master, when exposed to the discourse of the Clown shifts in this way:

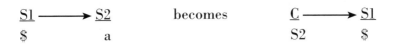

$$\underline{S1} \longrightarrow \underline{S2} \qquad \text{becomes} \qquad \underline{C} \longrightarrow \underline{S1}$$
$$\$ \qquad\qquad a \qquad\qquad\qquad\qquad\quad S2 \qquad\quad \$$$

What this means, in the everyday experience of humor, is that the Clown addresses the Master Signifier, reveals the erstwhile hidden Truth of its split, divided nature and that the concealed Truth of the Clown is that, despite its seeming irrationality, the discourse rests upon a signifying chain which involves some form of rationality. The Desire that was being created in the discourse of the master has been annulled, probably because the hidden split has been revealed and its accompanying desire placed back into the would-be Master.

An example of this would be Chaplin's "masterful" depiction of the "Great Dictator" (1940) who bounces the globe on his butt in gleeful anticipation of world domination. The Chaplinesque discourse is aimed at the master signifier. The megalomania is revealed. The splits, the neurosis, even psychosis, of the dictator are on full display, saturated as they are with unquenchable desire, with jouissance. The Truth is revealed and that which was the product is assimilated into what was the Agent. Meanwhile, Chaplin, who looks superficially "silly," has, beneath the surface, his Truth, the fact that this clowning is founded on a signifying chain, an ideology. (Interestingly Chaplin was blacklisted for this ideology by the powers-that-be only a few years later.) Examples of this form of the Discourse of the Clown are quite common since it can form as a counter-power in situations of oppression. Lear's Clown performs the function of trimming the sails of power, and this was part of the function of the court jester. While not formally present in the modern era, the comedy "roast" of those in power ritualizes this discourse, perhaps robbing it of some of its "blind" power. In addition, forms of "Guerilla Theatre" as popularized in the revolts of the late 1960's exemplify this structured discourse.

When we take the discourse of the University, which is structured as follows:

$$\frac{S2}{S1} \longrightarrow \frac{a}{\$}$$

It becomes, when we have it subjected to the discourse of the Clown the following:

$$\frac{C}{a} \longrightarrow \frac{S2}{S1}$$

In this discourse, we see that the Agent, the Clown, addresses the object of the signifying chain. The product is the master signifier and the truth becomes desire. Examples of this would include the comic discourse by a "clown professor" such as the Ted Talk "lecture" given by Sam Hyde (2013) or Sacha Baron Cohen at Harvard (2015). A textual example of this discourse would be "1066 and All That" (Sellars and Yeatman, 2010) which is a delightful compendium of schoolboy howlers charting the course of British History. A further example in a movie would be that of Will Ferrell in "Land of the Lost" (2009), who incessantly propounds theories and explanations that turn out to be false with comically disastrous consequences.

In each of these examples the discourse of the Clown takes aim at the signifying chain of the would-be educator. Part of the presentation is the undeniable certainty with which the errors, malapropisms and falsehoods are delivered, as if they are the Gospel, as if, in other words, they are the master signifier. Revealed is the truth of the desire to be omniscient, to be wise, to be admired, even held in awe. Thus the application of the discourse of the Clown to the discourse of the University reveals and unravels another truth of the discourse, the wish of the Agent for admiration and splendor. In addition we may note that Lacan, in his presentation at the Catholic University of Louvain (Evers, 2010), where he is wearing something that looks like a blouse and seems to be smoking a broken cigar, seems to undermine the authority of his speech with something resembling a cross between Groucho and Chico Marx. I cannot help but feel this is intentional and anticipates the ideas in this section. In addition, we note that there is a vibrantly comic aspect to the entire performance when a student interrupts him, pours water over his notes and delivers a meandering speech on the absurdity of the enterprise at hand.

We also see this deployment of humor, insofar as a pun is involved in "A Story from Lacan's Practice" (Miller, 2011) when Lacan, upon hearing that a client wakens every morning at five a.m. because that was when the Gestapo would come and take the Jews away, walks across to her and touches her gently on the cheek, uttering that this is a *"geste a peau"* (a gesture upon the skin). In French the two sound the same; Gestapo and *geste a peau.* It seems like a grim joke, but the client reported that it forever changed the experience of her five a.m. awakenings since now these experiences were accompanied by Lacan's gesture. From a theoretical standpoint the language, the pun, the play on words had moved the experience into a different symbolic register, thus loosening its grip on the person.

The discourse of the Hysteric is structured as follows:

$$\underline{\$} \longrightarrow \underline{S1}$$
$$a \qquad\quad S2$$

The divided subject addresses the Master Signifier, produces a signifying chain and "sits on" the Truth of desire, of jouissance. When we apply the discourse of clown according to the rules we have generated it becomes the following:

$$\underline{C} \longrightarrow \underline{\$}$$
$$S1 \qquad\quad a$$

The agent, the clown, addresses the divided subject, produces desire, and sits on the truth of a master signifier. In this last situation, the discourse of the clown is similar to that of the Analyst who addresses the split subject.

Examples of this structure and dynamic are common. Cervantes depiction of Don Quixote (2018) has, as its object, the deluded knight, attempting to live out the dream of rescuing the oppressed and of righting wrongs in the noblest possible way while wearing ludicrous armor, riding a broken-down nag and creating more problems than he solves. We see, in this, a comic split between the ideals and the reality of the man of la Mancha. In addition, this split is accentuated by the commentary offered by his manservant, Sancho Panza. The product is desire, in this case desire for fame, romance, honor, justice. The truth lying beneath the discourse of the clown is S1, a master signifier—sentences having to do with the unavoidable tensions between dreams and reality, between vaulting ambition and the mundane, the down-to-earth.

Another, more recent example is that of George Costanza in the situation comedy "Seinfeld" (1984-1998). This structure is made manifest in multiple episodes. For example, when George is teased for eating too many shrimp he spends hours developing a snappy comeback so as to even the score. He even, in his obsessional drive to get back at the man who teased him, drives many miles to another social engagement where he will be able to get back at the perpetrator with a carefully planned and rehearsed riposte. The split subject is George who has lost face in public and is driven obsessively to regain his self-image as a competent, suave and effectual person. The desire is just that, the narcissistic wish to be seen as perfect; smooth, sophisticated, debonair. The signifying chain is a commentary on the hopelessness, sadness and futile emptiness of this enterprise of saving face through acts of petty vengeance. George's efforts fail miserably and he wastes much precious time and energy in his attempt at self-affirmation. In this example the S1 (master signifier) has a decidedly psycho-educational, moralistic tone.

The discourse of the Analyst has the following arrangement:

$$a \longrightarrow \$$$
$$S2 \qquad S1$$

Jouissance or desire, addresses the divided subject, the one who is at war with themselves or of two minds. The product is a master signifier, perhaps something of the order of what Hazell (2009) terms a "phallic organizer," a starting or origin point in a discourse, and the truth is that the analyst, who seems to stand for untamed jouissance, actually rests upon an organized signifying chain.

When it encounters the discourse of the Clown it has this form:

$$\underline{C} \longrightarrow \underline{a}$$
$$\$ \qquad S2$$

The discourse of the Clown is directed towards desire, the product is a signifying chain and the truth the clown sits upon is the divided subject. This type of discourse structure is a fairly common form in the well-worn "analyst with an impossible patient" trope. The movie "What About Bob?" (1991) provides an excellent example. Bob is an adoring, compliant but clingy patient of the analyst, Dr. Leo Marvin, who is played to obsessive-compulsive-with-narcissistic-features perfection by Richard Dreyfuss. Marvin's desire is made manifest by various means, among them his naming his son "Sigmund." The signifying chain created in the comedy involves Marvin's treatment technique which rests heavily on the concept of "baby steps." Marvin seems driven to be seen as possessing the master signifier as is made manifest by his twitterings about his upcoming interview on television. However, Bob's inability to recognize or observe the usual therapeutic boundaries (he follows Dr. Marvin on vacation and charms his family) results in the manifestation of the splits in discourse of the analyst who is repeatedly caught off guard.

Another example of this structure is found in this old joke:

> *Two mothers are talking to each other. "How is your son doing?" asks one. "Oh, not so well. He is seeing a psychiatrist." "Really!" replies the other, "What is the matter?" "Well, apparently the psychiatrist says he has an Oedipus complex." To which the other mother replies, "Oedipus complex! Why can't he just be a good boy and love his mother!"*

This joke demonstrates the subversion of the logic inherent to and necessary for the signifying chain. It therefore makes contact at one and the same time with discourse of the University (which produces a signifying chain) and the discourse of the Analyst, which rests upon a barred signifying chain. At the same time, the second mother in adopting the discourse of the master in her authoritative claim that the son should be a good boy and just love his mother makes manifest the curlicue, Mobius-strip-like circularity of her tautological logic, while all the time the joke rests upon Hysteria and its split desires. We see, in this example, the discourse of the Clown make subversive contact with each of the four Lacanian discourses, rendering each more adventitious, conditional, subject to reformulation, criticism and thus, more supple.

Lacan (Contri, 1972) delineates, in addition a discourse of Capitalism, which he diagrams thus:

$$\frac{\$}{S1} \longrightarrow \frac{S2}{a}$$

In this discourse, the split subject addresses the signifying chain, produces desire and bars the truth of the master signifier. An example of this would be advertising which creates desire while concealing its true aims. When we interpose the discourse of the Clown we arrive at the following:

$$\frac{C}{S2} \longrightarrow \frac{\$}{S1}$$

Here, the Clown function addresses the split subject (much in the manner of an analyst), produces, or unveils, the master signifier while having the barred truth of a signifying chain. Thus in this context, the clown addresses the split nature of the capitalist agent (\$) and uncovers the erstwhile latent organizing principle (S1). While the Clown/agent appears somewhat scattered in their free flowing "riffs," their discourse is, however, based on an organized signifying chain.

Examples of this type of Clown discourse are to be found

in comics who criticize socio-economic and political conventions and culture in a humorous fashion. Ricky Gervais in his opening speech at the Golden Globes in 2020 (Fire Films, 2020) provides an example among many others. Another example would George Carlin's diatribes concerning advertising, economics, politics and culture (2008). Examining the reactions to these discourse, which are frequently intense and mixed, even vitriolic, we may form the hypothesis that this intervention of the clown discourse is perhaps the most provocative and thus the one that creates the most anxiety.

Examples from the Community Meetings:

To further "flesh out" these ideas and to demonstrate their application in a group setting, we will now select four vignettes having a comic element from the tavistock-influenced large groups documented in chapter VIII. While none of these vignettes can claim to be side-splittingly funny, they did bring a smile into the proceedings and contain elements of the comic such that they may illustrate the useful dynamics of the discourse of the Clown.

Vignette 1:

This short interaction occurs at the end of group two. The process notes are as follows:

> *"Subsequently the man in his forties (let us call him Lionel) addressed the visiting consultant as "Dr. Hazelton." This was consulted to as giving the older male consultant (Dr. Hazell) extra weight. This was followed by laughter. The feelings at the end were warm and convivial."*

This "joke" bears a striking resemblance, in its structure, to one given by Freud (1905), namely the play on the word "familiar" and "millionaire" to create the new word, "famillionaire" which captures the irony of a newly wealthy person meeting an established rich person of the upper classes and feeling treated as an equal. The neologism contains a split meaning. This split and this new word can be regarded as the "product" function in Lacan's diagram. Thus, we may diagram this witticism as follows:

$$\underline{C \longrightarrow S1}$$
$$S2 \qquad \$$$

Which may be summarized as follows: the Clown discourse addresses the Master Signifier (Dr. Hazelton is Dr. Hazelton and nothing else), produces a split in the meaning (a compression of Dr. Hazell, the person, and the added "ton," a heavy weight), reveals the potentially troubling truth that the signifying chain (S2) is riddled with problems, some of which cause confusion, some of which can be put to good use, and causes the cognitive stir of undecidability which results in laughter.

Vignette 2:

The following vignette occurs in group 4, towards the end. The comedy in this vignette is just below the surface. It lies in the play of the "clang associations" of hook, cook, book, look and the multiple meanings of these words, book being slang for "to leave," for example.

At this, someone mentioned that some hobbies were extremely expensive, like horse-riding. Then the lady sitting next to me who has a terrifically disabling disease stated that she could ride horses. The interpretive possibilities of these statements again were not fully explored. However a lady broke in after a brief pause in the group's discourse and asked (it felt out of the blue) if anyone had a crochet hook. She had been looking for one and the summer had been hard for her, because of the heat. A member responded that she had been looking for a book in the library, but could not find it.

At this the following consultation was offered. "The group feels like it is drifting, it cannot find anything to hook on to nor a book or words that will help. Was it just the heat this summer that was difficult or was it difficult in other ways?" The last question was offered as the consultant was aware that several changes in personnel had occurred in the home over the summer.

Members started talking about difficulties outside the home, in their families for example—brothers who had run out of cash, sicknesses and so on. There was a brief discussion of Bob Marley, who apparently,"never went to see a doctor." And some small exploration of the anxiety of being nothing or expanding and growing. Finally they homed in on the disruption caused by the psychiatrist leaving the home and several members voiced feelings of anger, even rage and helplessness and fear in response to this. This led to a discussion of the missing of a staff social worker who had left. This seemed to be the most affectively charged sequence in the group and it seemed to be manifested in three individuals leaving the room to get water. These people returned and some consultations were made to acknowledge the strength of feeling around these departures.

The group ended and in the discussion group immediately following there was a fair amount of enthusiastic talk and questions by some of the more talkative members, one of whom, a middle aged man who also serves as the representative to NAMI (National Association for Mental Illness), asked if Dr. H. had written any books. Three more members asked for the name of Dr. H., who is the oldest male consultant.

This humorous interlude in which the consultation provides a vital link may be diagrammed as follows:

$$\underline{C} \longrightarrow \underline{S2}$$
$$a \qquad\quad S1$$

where the discourse of the Clown addresses the signifying chain (S2) which seems to be superficially dispersed and unrelated, creates, through its play, a Master Signifier (S1) insofar as it offers one meaning for the dispersed meanings of the chain. The truth is the jouissance of the clang associations, words created in any way that rhymes, according to one's whim and the desire for the lost objects (the psychiatrist and social worker, hooks, books and maybe crooks) and what they symbolize.

Vignette 3:

This vignette occurs in group 6 and involves a member sharing an element of the "Peanuts" cartoon (1950-2000) wherein Lucy promises Charlie Brown that this time she will not remove the football he is about to kick at the last instant and cause him to fall down. Of course, she does move it and he falls on his rear end. Something in the group had stimulated a member to recall this trope and to share it. In a very significant way, this lighthearted sharing of a joke (which is almost a cultural artifact) leads to the revelation of something very serious in the community; someone was considering suicide.

In response to this, it seemed, the member to the left of the consultant said she was thinking of "trust falls" she did in camp as a teenager, and how the group was kind of like that at times, or kind of like the "Peanuts" cartoon where Lucy tricked Charlie Brown with the football, each time promising she wouldn't take it away at the very last instant but then, of course taking it away leaving him ending up on his butt, tricked and dismayed. The group seemed to "get" this set of metaphors.

There was then talk of God and trust in God and Jesus and at this point an elderly lady admonished the group not to have a nervous breakdown and expressed the desire to sing a song. The group assented and she sang a poignant hymn. Then the lady who had shared the Charlie Brown image sang a hymn-like song. A consultant shared that the tone of these songs contained a longing for companionship, support and love.

Then another elderly lady stated that someone in the institution had told her of her intentions to commit suicide that day. The consultant stated that he was responding to that on multiple levels; first that this was a concrete problem that should be addressed (Who was this and where were they now?) and secondly that this was related to feelings of deep despair and disconnectedness that might need to be addressed. At this, one of the consultants went aside with this lady and gathered the data on this person and left the room to attend to the problem.

This episode can be diagrammed as follows; it seems to have exactly the same structure of the preceding example:

$$\underline{C} \longrightarrow \underline{S2}$$
$$a \qquad\quad S1$$

The discourse of the Clown addresses the narrative of the signifying chain (S2), positing its fundamental structure, namely trust betrayed, falling and the ensuing despair. This narrative is then applied to the group in the here and now as a Master signifier (S1), in effect, this turns the joke "inside out" stripping it of its comedy, rendering it deadly serious for the Truth position is revealed, the hidden truth of someone who had given up hope was being tempted, taunted perhaps by the desire for death. This last, is not to hypothesize, along with Freud, a "death wish" but to agree with Porges (2011) that there is an emotional position beyond the fight-flight-freeze response, a place where the traumatized individual simply wishes to die painlessly and to put an end to their suffering--a wish for a shut-down.

Vignette 4:

This episode occurs in week 18. It serves as an example of the form of the discourse of the clown that involves irony, the amusing statement of the opposite of what is the case, combined with teasing, which might be understood as the playful demonstration of power not fully utilized leading to a paradoxical stimulation. The group had been on a three-month hiatus and it was hypothesized that there were some feelings about this, especially given the sensitivity of the group on prior occasions to the departures of staff from the institution. A member asks, with a smile on his face and in a friendly tone, "Where were you, Dr. Hazell?" and, after inducing some anxiety with this question, brings relief by saying it was not a problem. A little later the same member tells Dr. Hazell that they have their ways of dealing with people they do not like, quickly reassuring the wayward doctor that he is safe from their vengeful predations. This, however, is followed by the recounting of several stories of past professional miscreants in the institution who did not fare so well. The raising and lowering of emotional tension in this way had a humorous effect. The following set of process notes captures some of the vicissitudes of this discourse.

This was consulted to as referring to the three month break in the meetings of this group. It was nice to be close to one's family, but if they were not available then one relied on this group more and the satisfactions it might have to offer.

At this a member turned to Consultant H and said, "Yes, where were you Dr. H?" And then very quickly helped out by saying, "It's OK. I know people need to take a break." It felt as though there was an emotion of resentment and hurt that was immediately patched over by understanding.

However, the group continued on the theme of gratitude for the group, even citing C's frequent reference to "We need each other" in his perorations.

This was consulted to with, "It is as though the group did have some feelings about the gap in the meetings but that the consultant has been forgiven for leaving, even welcomed back."

This lead to a series of stories. G said, "Oh don't worry, Dr. H. We have managed to get rid of some bad people." Then there was a series of stories of bad people, nurses, administrators, psychiatrists who had been mean and who had left, often with the feeling that the group had had something to do with their departure.

This was not consulted to.

However, it was followed by a series of members sharing very sad and painful stories of disruptions in their lives extending often over decades. These involved being forced from homes and placed in various institutions, some very bad, some not so bad and ending up in this one which they experienced as good.

This was consulted to as relating to the group's concerns about continuity and breaks in the continuity of one's relationships and the resulting sense of instability, of insecurity.

At this, an older male suffering from PD mumbled incoherently. The student leaned forward to hear what was said and translated. "He said, 'Thank you for coming.' This led to a few more comments on gratitude for the group and the institution. Then the group, in the midst of these feelings, ended.

This episode may be diagrammed as follows:

$$\underline{C} \longrightarrow \underline{S2}$$
$$a \qquad\quad S1$$

In taking up the ironic position, namely saying everything is ok when in reality, there are some negative feelings, the Clown discourse is talking to the position of the split subject ($) and addressing the signifying chain (S2). The product (S1) is the point that there are two feelings at one and the same time and the truth is that there is desire that the object never leave, or that it be under the control of the subject. In this way, the departures are "made light of" while at the same time being taken seriously._

We see, in these examples, that the discourse of the Clown may be applied to the other four discourses according to the following rules:

It moves the Truth to the Product position in the discourse. For example the Truth of the discourse of the Master, the split subject, becomes that which is produced through the application of the discourse of the Clown.

It temporarily negates, or brackets, the Product of the discourse to which it is applied. Thus the split subject ($) of the discourse of the University is suspended when the Clown discourse shows up.

It moves the Object of the discourse to the Truth position. Thus, in the discourse of the University, jouissance, or desire becomes the Truth. It is as if the desire of the professor has been revealed.

These rotations, with their jarring, surprising effect, besides being comic or amusing, assist in the rotation of the discourses. This rotation, as has been argued elsewhere (Hazell and Kiel, 2017), is essential to the functioning group. When a group gets stuck in one of the discourses, we tend to see problems arise. It is as if each discourse represents a different mode of information processing and to disable one or more prevents the effective adaptation of the group to its internal and external realities. Groups can become too autocratic and rigid (Master discourse), too "teachy" (University), too conflicted and neurotic (Hysteric) and too speculative regarding the unconscious (Analyst). They can also become overwhelmed with buffoonery and silliness (Clown), as we might see in Ganser syndrome or as depicted in multiple Monty Python sketches (1969-1974). While being locked in the Clown discourse might be undone by a dose of the Real or another discourse, the four Lacanian discourses might, at times of group "stuckness," benefit from a loosening bump from the Clown discourse.

However, humour does not always loosen up the discourse in the manner just outlined. Certain forms of the Clown discourse can lock up communication. For example, sarcasm is a form of humour that induces shame. In this, it acts as a form of social control. Shame has a paralyzing effect on the subject, or is aimed at so doing. It freezes the person in their tracks, if it is effective, and blocks their discourse by causing them to doubt themselves, to think they are an object of ridicule. How might one differentiate the types of Clown discourse that free up the discourses from those that cause them to shut down? One clue might be the degree of aggressiveness involved in the humour. It is as if there is a spectrum. At one end we find the playful humor of puns. Toward the other end we find the angry humor of satire, where a mirror is held up to folly. At the far extreme we find bitter sarcasm, or *schadenfreude,* which can be saturated with hatred. Also to be found on this spectrum would be the type of humor that is self-deprecating, which directs aggression towards the protagonist. This too can be mild, as in a gentle philosophical self-observation through to medium, where the Clown reveals their own inner contradictions or their amusing struggles with life and on through to an extreme where an individual harms themselves and laughs at their pain. As the discourse of the Clown becomes more tinged with aggression, so it starts to resemble more the discourse of the Hysteric or the Master insofar as, respectively, it may become itself a symptom, a behavior carried out more unconsciously (as in the Hysteric) or as a means of controlling the object (as in the case of the Master). We find, on closer inspection, that any of the discourses can immobilize conversation if too heavily imbued with aggression. One can have an assaultive Analyst, Master, Hysteric or University. Each can serve to freeze dialogue and each may be unlocked by the less aggressively tinged ministrations of the discourse of the Clown.

Relation to Authenticity and Consistency:

When we juxtapose the discourse of the Clown with the two-by-two table shown in Zizek (1993) and below in Figure 9, we are lead to question the relationship of this discourse to the twin concepts of authenticity and consistency. As we see in the diagram, the discourse of the analyst is both authentic and consistent, that of the Master neither authentic nor inconsistent, the Hysteric is authentic but inconsistent and the University is consistent but inauthentic.

	Consistent	Inconsistent
Authentic	Analyst	Hysteric
Inauthentic	University	Master

Figure 10: Relationship between Discourses, Authenticity and Consistency

Where is the discourse of the Clown located on this quadrant? It is indeterminate in all of these respects, being neither consistent nor inconsistent; neither authentic nor inauthentic. It is only a joke, while at the same time it is very serious about something. In fact, if the discourse of the Clown settles in one of these other spaces/discourses for even a short period of time it becomes that discourse with its complexion of authenticity/inauthenticity-consistency/inconsistency and it is no longer comic. The discourse of the Clown must therefore be seen as a floating point above this matrix, occasionally making fleeting contact with each square, only to fly off at once if it is to retain its comedic impact.

When we juxtapose the notion of the discourse of the clown with the oscillation between the paranoid-schizoid and depressive positions posited by Bion (1978), we arrive at the idea that this communicational form plays an important role insofar as it facilitates that very oscillation which is itself a vital aspect of mental health. There are several possibilities that can play out: without the discourse of the Clown the flow can become locked in so that it becomes deadly serious as it loses its lightness; on the other hand if there is a locking into the discourse of the Clown, the response might be, "It's no joke!" as there will appear to be a departure from the gravity of the situation. The discourse of the Clown, since it provides new linkages and associations through its very workings may provide new ideas and spark creativity on the other hand old, established and perhaps "sacred" linkages might be felt to be attacked by the discourse of the Clown and the disruption of the stability of the depressive position is felt to be under too much of a threat. Thus, the vicissitudes of the discourse of the Clown can alert one to the adaptive dynamisms of the group or individual.

The idea of the discourse of the Clown may be linked with Bion's theory of thinking. Freud (1905) writes of "wit work" in a fashion that is analogous to the "dream work" he describes in "The Interpretation of Dreams." Bion sees the dream as an essential early step in the process of thinking. It is in the dream that the bits and pieces of the beta elements and alpha bits are linked together in the warp and weft of the dream. This fabric forms the cloth, as it were, out of which cognitions and, later, theories may be formed. Thus dream work is an essential step in the work of thinking. Yet Freud talks of wit work, thus suggesting to us that wit, or the discourse of the Clown is likewise an important, perhaps essential, step in the thinking process. If we shut off dreams, we shut off thinking. Likewise, if we shut off the Clown discourse, we retard the thinking process, both in individuals and in groups.

When we examine Koestler's theory of humor (1945), Erikson's thoughts on "toys and reasons" (1977), Huizinga's disquisition on "Homo Ludens" (2014) and integrate the previous linkages of the Clown and the oscillation between the P/S and D (Paranoid/Schizoid and Depressive) positions of Klein (1975), this idea seems to hold some water. We may thus come to some assessment of the openness or closedness of a system, be it an individual or a social one, by noting its deployment of the discourse of the Clown. It is of note that Vaillant (1998) places humor as one of the more sophisticated defense mechanisms insofar as it is, for the most part, relatively inexpensive in terms of loss of contact with reality.

Further, integrating the ideas of technological innovation and deterritorialization and the stresses and traumata these visit upon social systems, we may argue that the importance of the discourse of the Clown increases during the periods when such impacts are being experienced throughout a social system. Again, this hypothesis might be of help in understanding the adaptive dynamics in systems.

Integrating the discourse of Clown with the Lacanian notion of the *sinthome* (2018), we posit, along with Lacan, that it is used to stitch together the realms of the Real, Imaginary and Symbolic. This stitching together can be understood as preventing the total falling apart of the registers, or in more commonplace terms, preventing complete and utter madness. Thus, for example, the discourse of Clown might be used to hold the Symbolic register fast and connect it to the Imaginary and the Real, thus preventing psychosis where the Imaginary and the Real are left on their own as it were—the Imaginary playing fast and loose with the Real, unhampered by the rules and regulations of the Symbolic register. Thus in Ganser Syndrome, an example of which would be the compulsive joking of Hawkeye Pierce on the TV series "Mash" (1972-1983) or hebephrenia or attacks of "hysterical laughter," can be seen as desperate attempts to "hold it together" with the discourse of the Clown being utilized as a *sinthome*. Milder examples are captured in moments in everyday life where one might utter, *"I'l faut q'on rit"*, or "You have to laugh".

The discourse of the Clown is very close to the magician insofar as an illusion is created. One expects to find the card in one's pocket, yet it shows up in a cup across the room. A set of expectations is framed and suddenly those expectations are cast asunder and one is left momentarily helpless as to how to explain the two contradictory events. This is much akin to the mechanisms of humor as described by Koestler, namely in the bisociation of two matrices of meaning or understanding. The resultant helpless feeling is experienced and then mastered as we realize, it's only a trick, or a joke, and we laugh. Koestler also points out that it is this very bisociation of previously unrelated matrices that is part of the process of creation. It is, at were, the secret of the functioning of the muse.

The concept of magic and the related notion of illusionist is connected to Langs' (1971) notion of the space of illusion in psychotherapy, or as is our current concern and application, the consulting to groups. This "space of illusion" is the space in which the "trick", the magic, the mistake, the *"trompe loeil"* the *"meconnaissance"* of the transference occurs.

Resistances to Humor:

Given that the mechanism of the discourse of the Clown is often that which dislodges the smooth running of the other discourses, the resistances to its operation are reasonably clear-cut. On the one hand, one of the other discourses may be aligned with the task at hand and such a disruption may be off task. In this case, the operation of the discourse of the Clown can be seen as a defense against the anxieties induced by the task and that which it stimulates. On the other hand, the discourse being disrupted might be holding a grip on the discourses in the group such that the machinery of group discussion has seized up. In this case the discourse of the Clown will operate as something of a lubricant, in the manner described above. In this case the extent to which the locked-in discourse is defended and the Clown discourse excluded will be an indicator of the defenses being mobilized in the group or individual.

Practical Implications:

The concept of the discourse of the Clown might have several practical implications. It is an old psychotherapeutic saw that by finding out the client's favvrourite joke, one gains dynamic insight into their unconscious conflicts. This model, namely that of interpreting the content of the joke much as one would interpret a dream or a symptom, can be applied at all levels of analysis.

In addition, as being forwarded here, one may simply register the operation of the discourses at a fairly abstract level, along Lacanian lines (Hazell and Kiel, 2017) and, in addition note the usage of the discourse of the Clown. One will often find, in all likelihood, that certain individuals or subgroups will take up the role of expounding the discourse of the Clown. This, in and of itself is interpretable. Again the model can be scaled down, to the level of the individual and up, to include cultural analysis.

VI

Spaces of Differance

It is the purpose in this section to delineate the concept of differance, as described by Derrida (1985, pp. 1-27) and explore ways in which this idea might be applied to the theory and practice of group work and, in addition to connect it to spatiality and the theory of positive disintegration.

Definition of the concept

Those familiar with the concept of differance will see immediately that we have started with a paradox, for "difference," "is literally neither a word or a concept." (Derrida, 1985, p3) It eludes the senses of both hearing and seeing. When we hear it we might mistake it for the word "difference," when we read it we see a "sheaf" (as in a sheaf of papers), or perhaps a "sheath," which contains and conceals, that has "different threads and lines of meaning." Derrida invites us to associate freely to the "a" that is hidden in the spoken word but revealed in the printed—it is like a tomb, a family. It reminds him of Antigone, of fraternity, of burial, laws and suicide.

But, "differance is not." "It derives from no category of being" and, "it has neither existence nor essence." However, it seems Derrida is not positing the now-familiar nihilistic position. Differance is not nothingness. It represents, insofar as it may represent, "the quest for a rightful beginning, an absolute point of departure." In this there are echoes of the "Master Signifier" of Lacan (2007a) or of "O" of Bion(1978). Perhaps this is closely allied to Winnicott's (1965) experience of patients looking for a fresh start.

The neologism "differance" may also be seen as a collapsing together of two meanings—"defer" and "differ"—to defer differing, to put off categorization, "to suspend the accomplishment or fulfillment of 'desire' or 'will' (Derrida, 1985, p 8).The word "defer" implies time, insofar as there will be lapse between the wish and its fulfillment. The word "differ" implies space insofar as differing implies distancing and boundaries that are part and parcel of categorization. Could it be that we are close here to the concept of the pleroma from Gnostic thought as expounded upon by Jung (Hoeller, 1992)? In this exercise of "differance" we are exploring the "originary constitution of time and space," (1985, p 8). This exercise quickly returns us, however, to a Mobius-like paradox, for differance "defers differing and differs from deferring in and of itself" (1985, p 8).

Derrida informs us that differance is not to be confused with the unknown or with the drives insofar as he points out that differance is neither active nor passive. It has neither the activity of the drive nor the passivity of the unknown, which seems to await discovery. Differance thus takes up a "middle voice" between activity and passivity (1985, p. 9).

Differance seems to lie between the thing in itself and the sign. The substitution of the sign for the thing in itself is seen as both "secondary" and "provisional" (1985, p.9). By this Derrida locates differance in the symbolizing process itself, in the very formation of categories that undergird language. For "in language there are only differences." (1985, p10-11). This location is essentially a playful region, a region of possibilities.

"Such play, differance, is thus no longer a concept, but rather the possibility of conceptuality, of a conceptual process and system in general." (1985, p11) This playful process itself creates differences. We seem close here to the ideas contained in Bion's theory of thinking (1978) where a concept is created through the "alpha function" which then leads on to a conception, a meeting of thought and thinker in a mating process that leads to a cognitive frame or, to use Quine's term, a "web of belief" (1970).

Differance, thus, "is the movement according to which language…is constituted historically, as a weave of differences." (1985, p11) "In language there are only differences"…in a signifying chain there is the "play of differences." (1985, p. 11). The signifying chain involves spacing and timing. One element in the chain is differed from the next by an interval, which is both spatial and temporal. For example it is not helpful if words or sounds run into each other too much. In addition the chain itself takes time to deliver. We cannot be really sure of the meaning of a chain until it is seen as complete. (Perhaps it is never complete.)

In addition, the subject becomes a speaking subject only by making its speech conform to the system of rules of language as a system of differences, or at the very least, by conforming to the general law of difference (1985, p. 15). Additionally, the act of speaking renders the subject present and tends to give the subject self-consciousness. Thus an effect of differance is the emergence of consciousness. Thus, differance, this "moving discord of different forces" (1985, p 18) which acts as a disruptor of stable categories could undergird and potentiate consciousness.

The subject, in becoming a speaking subject and entering the realm of difference and language is adapting to reality. In addition to the introduction of time and space that is part and parcel of the deferment (which is temporal) and the differing (which is spatial) involves the deferment of the pleasures of immediacy, the delaying of gratification. This, too, is an aspect of the reality principle of Freud (1927) and is an active function in Bion's theory of thinking.

However, "Differance is not. It is not a present being, however excellent, unique, principal or transcendent. It governs nothing, reigns over nothing, and nowhere exercises any authority." (1985, pp. 20-21) On the other hand it wields power insofar as "differance instigates the subversion of every kingdom", and is, "a bottomless chessboard on which Being is put into play."(1985, p21) It is "the trace of that which can never be presented, the trace which itself can never be presented." (1985, p. 23) Differance is thus that which is unnamable. It is ineffable, undecidable and still, unendingly defies even these labels. One is reminded of Quantum theory, of Schrodinger's cat which sits and yet does not sit, either alive or dead until the box is opened. The state of things is determined by the very act of inspection, of measurement, calibration, notation. This notation determines all that follows. Thus, to anticipate the application of this concept to group dynamics, the group consultant, in addressing the differance of the group mentality, in labeling it, is determining the reality of and for the group, wrenching somethingness out of the indeterminacy of differance, with radical consequences.

Differance is, "the trace of that which can never be presented, the trace which itself which can never be presented." (1985, p 23) Here Derrida suggests chimes of Zen and this resonance is amplified when he continues, linking differance with being. Citing Heidegger, he asserts that being is bounded all around by oblivion. This oblivion, however, is bounded by differance. (1985, p 25) This "being speaks always and everywhere throughout language." (1985, p27) This language is made possible through differance, and "this, unnamable is the play which makes possible nominal effects…" It is this differance which enables the process of categorization undergirding language and, thus, being. Differance is prior to name and form.

Finally, Derrida connects differance, with its play, with the idea of hope. This connection is not fully spelled out, but it would seem that the possibility of generating new concepts and thus new understandings along with the generation of a more robust sense of being and its contingencies would be cause for hope. One is reminded of the centrality of "hope" as a concept for Rorty (2000,2009) in his writings on democracy and of the "virtue" of hope that is developed in the very first of Erikson's stages (1993), "Trust versus Mistrust."

Viewed this way, we may see differance as occupying the space prior to the four Lacanian discourses (Master, University,

Hysteric, Analyst) and prior to the additional discourse posited herein by Hazell, namely, the discourse of the Clown. In figure 10 below we see it located at the outer edges of discourse. It is not for nothing that Derrida's text, in which the first chapter is on differance, is entitled, "The Margins of Philosophy." Differance places us in the hinterlands of the possibility of discourse, where we might envision a "Brownian motion" of preconcepts (Bion, 1978).

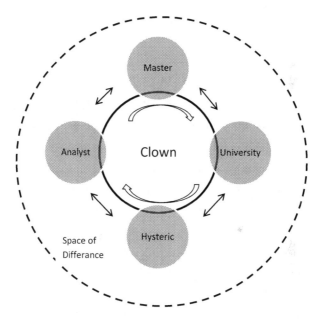

Figure 10: The Relationship of the Space of Difference to the Five Discourses

Attributes of Spaces of Differance in Groups

We may now move on to connect this "concept which is not" to groups, consulting, group therapy, sociotherapy and therapy in general. As a point of departure we may link the notion of deferral and the deferral of meaning to the theory of discourses. When meaning is deferred it implies that "the last word" is left unsaid, meaning that meaning is in a state of suspension. This playful state is an attribute of the space of differance. Each of the five discourses above will invoke, at some point, the last word. In the discourse of the Master, the last word is the law or rule of the master signifier. In the discourse of the University, the last word is the conclusion, arrived at through some form of reasoning. In the discourse of the Hysteric, the last word is the certitude of the reality of the symptom, the assurance that the "cigar is just a cigar" and not symbolic of anything else. In the discourse of the analyst, the last word is the interpretation that speaks to the split subject in the hope of stitching it back together again. The discourse of the Clown offers us the final word of the punch line, which paradoxically and because it is the discourse closest to differance, oscillates between the multiple meanings in the narrative—in the form of the *double entendre* or the pun or the sudden switches of frames of reference from a play on words or in an unexpected outcome, for example.

The space of differance defers the final word. It forestalls the foreclosure of the last word in the signifying chain, creating a never-ending play of meanings—meanings that lie in the space before meaning. We are close here, perhaps to the "primal space" of Aulagnier (2001)—a primal space out of which, she argues, a proto-language of pictograms emerges—pictograms that feed and inform discourse. We are perhaps also close to Sullivan's concept of *prototaxic* language, language before it has been socialized, before it has entered the realm of laws—rules that govern language, discourse and, ultimately, meaning. We are also linked to the idea of "primary maternal seduction" (Laplanche, 1999) where we imagine the infant leaving this primal zone as it is drawn into the interpersonal realm with its languages, codes and categories through the "seduction" of the mother.

A space of differance thus would have the quality of deferral, of negative capability (Bion, 1978), of not irritably reaching out for meaning, of the sustaining of provisionality in meaning. Often there will be resistance to this. This resistance will perhaps take the form of a shift into one of the five discourses (Master, University, Hysteric, Analyst, Clown). This resistance can perhaps be met by a recourse to differance. It is likely that someone will take up the role of promoter of differance. We might see Derrida (1985) or Socrates as taking up this role. In a group, and the group could be of any size from small to societal, this might be taken up by an individual or a subgroup. If their role is not formally recognized, or if it does not carry the prestige of, say, a Derrida, this individual is in a vulnerable position, despite the fact that they are arguably performing a social service, for they are likely to be labeled as a troublemaker, as crazy or, perhaps a visionary or an artist. Perhaps, as in the case of Socrates, they will be killed off. Conversely, one might also have an individual who resists leaving this zone of differance.

Another fairly straightforward attribute of a space of differance involves the deferral of the formation of categories. Any discourse is a sort of rut, a guided, trammeled form of thinking based on the prefigured meanings assigned to categories. Differance abjures these. It returns us to the *chora*, as delineated by Kristeva (1984) and related to community dynamics by Hazell and Kiel (2017). In so doing the space of differance disrupts these categories and, further interrupts, defers, the formation of new ones. If those in the group, in the space, can tolerate this experience of unknowing, new meanings can emerge, and with this, new categories, new solutions and novel discourse.

Derrida points out, early in the paper (1985) that differance is to be found especially in the spoken word, despite the slippages we find in a text such as "Finnegan's Wake" (Joyce, 1999). The slippage of meanings can be created very readily in speech through, for example, homonyms, puns, mis-hearings, and even slurred speech which feed the inchoate, the miasmic experience of differance. Joyce himself suggested that if one had trouble following Finnegan's Wake, one should simply read it aloud in an Irish accent. Of interest also is that Joyce's text has an end that wraps around to the beginning, with a "riverrun past Eve and

Adam's".... There is no last word, just as differance has no "last word." Thus while many aspects of group life may be captured, for example, in online groups that rely on the written word, much will be missed when the spoken word is left out. Much can be accomplished in these groups but if the ideas constellated around the notion of differance hold any sway, much more will be achieved in a group utilizing the spoken word. Perhaps both together would offer multiple advantages, much in the way online teaching can supplement the "traditional" "chalk and talk" classroom lecture and discussion format.

Another attribute of a space of differance has to do with time and space. The phenomena of time and space have their origins in deferment, which has to do with waiting for a duration of time, and differentiation, which implies a gap existing between phenomena. This gap has a spatial quality. Thus, if we enter into a space of differance we will experience alterations in our conventional experiences of space and time. While the space of differance might occur within a well bounded place and within clear time boundaries, the experiences within that space may involve all the varied experiences of time and space with which one becomes familiar in everyday life, clinical work or, say, aesthetic or religious experiences. The way in which one might experience the sequencing of events might alter, such that precedents become antecedents or sequential events are seen as occurring simultaneously. Events of long ago are experienced as here and now, time flashes by, slows down or stands still. These experiences can radically alter the phenomenology of the experience, and this can lead to re-categorization of phenomena and, at a "deeper" level, alterations in one's experience of being.

As one ponders the preceding paragraph one might see connections between these ways of experiencing and the psychotic process, where conventional experiencing of time, place and person are suspended. This idea perhaps gives us insight as to how the space of differance contributes to increased cognitive and affective complexity, because, as Bion (1997) argues, it is in the oscillation between the Paranoid-Schizoid position and the Depressive position that the growth of the personality occurs. If this dialectic is not engaged, growth in the personality comes to a standstill. We may apply systems theory-- information processing theory--to this model of the mind. The Depressive Position operates with whole objects and is linked to reality. It can be seen as a network of ideas about the world. However, it is in constant need of updating. Some of this occurs through inputs of new information from the world but the rest comes from within, from the network of unconscious ideas. These internal ideas, both conscious and unconscious are in constant need of reformatting and this can be seen to take place along the lines suggested by Piaget, namely through accommodation and assimilation, such that higher degrees of complexity are achieved in the internal representations. This higher degree of complexity better adapts the organism to the internal world and external reality. The space of differance enables this processing. It offers an opportunity to re-categorize and to reformulate. It also offers opportunities to rethink causal chains and, thus, causality, for causality depends on the concept of time and categories' relationships through time. In differance all this is thrown into playful question. Given the transformative power of the space of differance, we might predict that there will be individuals, groups and institutions that will resist it. Such resistance, however, runs the risk of causing stagnation in the individual, group or institution.

Examples of the Space of Differance

Fortunately it is not too difficult to find examples of spaces of differance. We believe that the group described in Czochara, Hazell and Semmelhack (2016) provided such a space. This group is described in the form of process notes and comments in the Chapter VIII of this text. As we read this description, we can find examples of what occurs in the space of differance and how the events thus created can be of tremendous use in group consultation, especially insofar as they enable deeper empathic contact with the group as a whole and its members. In what follows, we will highlight a few of the examples of differance as they manifested in the first few groups of these sessions.

In Group 1, for example, we witness a member who had a debilitating disease that made it very difficult for her to speak. It required a trained ear and much patience to glean a sense of her meaning. This task was rendered all the more challenging since her speeches were usually very impassioned. However, from a group-as-a-whole perspective she would be understood as speaking on behalf of the group and the inchoate nature of her communications point towards it being an example of a space of differance, calling for a patient deferral of meaning and a melding and morphing of categories. The subsequent consultations were built upon the passionate, pained words of this member and it seemed that the group "latched on" to these possible meanings.

In Group 2, we see a member start to say something and then lose their train of thought, only to be helped complete the sentence by another member. Rather than write this off as a neurological event, as something coming from the Real alone, we see it as a momentary irruption of the space of difference, an excursion into the realm Derrida describes, an excursion curtailed as the member is brought back into the group's routine discourse. In this co-operation between members we see something potentially crucial insofar as it represents teamwork, collaboration in the deft process of oscillating between the space of differance, and the more conventional discourse of the group.

In Group 3, a member spontaneously performs a hymn for the group (and indeed, the very "sacredness" can be viewed as an aspect of differance) only to find that, as she starts to talk afterwards, she loses her train of thought. Her thoughts become scrambled and she loses her way. It is as if she has been dipped in the waters of differance and this has upset the linear signifying chain upon which she was embarking. The consultants attempt to pick up on this interruption in remarks that contain possibilities for further meanings, further ideas.

In Group 4, we have a member blurt out, out of the blue, "Don't believe a word they say!" This interrupts the signifying chain in the group quite dramatically, ushering in the indeterminacy of understanding the discourse that is going on. The consultants struggle with this event and do not quite piece the bits together. Later, someone else says, again, out of the blue, (and this "out of the blueness" seems to be a part of the space of differance) "Does anybody have a crochet hook?" Right after this, another person says, almost with a clang association, perhaps, "I couldn't find the book I wanted in the library." These two "out of nowhere" comments, seemingly with all the randomness of the space of differance, feed into the consultations that follow which seem to capture some of what is going on in the group-as-a-whole.

Each group in the series contains at least one example of the space of differance. It is our hope that these preliminary examples are of help in identifying them and folding it into the mix of the group. The results of the group were positive. (Czochara, Hazell and Semmelhack, 2017)

Establishing a Space of Differance

There are structures that can assist in the establishment of a space of differance. We believe that the structures we established for groups that we report on below and in Semmelhack *et al* (2013,2015) illustrate some of the possibilities. Following is an enumeration and description of some of the ways in which a space of differance might be established.

Preparation of the participants is helpful. This preparation can take the form of psycho-education, this to follow roughly the theory outlined herein and elsewhere, for example Wells (1985). Also of help is the experience of small groups in the tavistock tradition. We believe that the success of the large community group meetings described in chapter VII and reported in Czchohara *et al* (2017) owes in large part to the fact that many of the members had had at least several months of experience in such groups, were aware of the underlying theory and the interpretive orientation as well as the role definition of members and consultants. There are many other social arrangements and structures that facilitate the creation of a space of differance; psychoanalysis, tavistock-style groups, non-directive counseling, social dreaming, open space activities and listening posts, to name but a few.

The space of differance should probably have well defined boundaries, both temporally and spatially. This is probably the case since the experience of differance involves novel experiences of time and space. While this clarity of time and space boundaries is not always possible, those responsible for their management ought to be aware of the operations at the boundaries and ready to weave these into their consultations to the group. Related to this is the importance of acknowledging the nesting of social systems, that the space of difference is nested, like the proverbial "Russian dolls" (only interactive and dynamic dolls) in a host of other systems that have their own force fields impinging upon it.

As to guidelines when operating as consultant (or in any related role, such as facilitator or convener) of a space of differance, these are harvested from the familiar. Patience is a virtue in these circumstances. This is related to Bion's description of "negative capability,' the capacity to sustain ambiguity and not "irritably" reach out for certainty or closure. It also involves the capacity to let things happen, as opposed to obsessively making things happen. We operate here, in the space of differance, in the top left hand corner of Bion's grid, where the beta bits are combined, recombined, rent asunder and joined. This is the realm of the preconcept of Bion's grid, the space before thinking, as conventionally recognized, becomes possible. It is, as Derrida reminds us, the zone of play. This play can be delightful but it can also be awe-inspiring, terrible and dreadful, for truths may be revealed.

Another factor to be aware of in the establishment of a space of differance is that it involves the discourse of the Analyst, if we invoke Lacan's theory of the discourses. It also will involve the discourse of the Clown, as described earlier in this text. In these, it stands in opposition to the discourse of the Master. For this reason it will serve as disruptive contents to whatsoever institution should contain it. This disruption will more likely than not require some management. This will involve education of other sectors of the institution in the purposes, practice and utility of the space of differance. This work will also require some preparation on the part of all in the institution and linking the practitioners of the space of differance with centers of power and authority in the organization. Frequently participants or observers will ask questions like, "What is being achieved here?" as if it is a managerial meeting. The answer, unfortunately, is that conventional metrics of achievement do not apply. Achievement is in the process of experiencing the space of differance and then integrating it into other realms of discourse and action.

Relationship of Differance to Hill's Interaction Matrix and Bion's Grid

The Hill interaction matrix and its relation to group-as-a-whole work is discussed in Hazell and Kiel (2017). When we attempt to link the idea of differance with Hill's interaction matrix (1965), we arrive at the notion that it does not fit onto it in any way. It cannot be placed in any one of the twenty cells. This makes sense since the very idea of differance lies outside of categories. The relationship of differance to the Hill matrix can be seen as it lying in the space outside of the matrix itself. However, when differance makes contact with the discourse, immediately the possibility for its migration to the discourses at the bottom and to the right of the matrix is increased. This is to say that the therapeutic potency of the discourse has the potential for increasing once the space of differance emerges into the ongoing exchange. (We note, however, that Hazell and Kiel (2017) propose a re-ranking of this therapeutic impact such that the therapeutic potency of confrontations of the group as a whole be recognized as being more powerful than hypothesized by Hill.) Put in everyday language, it seems that the differance, "shakes up" the prevailing discourse, creating a re-categorization of its meaning systems and a reorientation of the cognitive systems and their underlying "webs of belief" (Quine, 1970). In this an increased flow of information is enabled between systems at all levels—individual, interpersonal, group, intergroup, institutional and inter-institutional. Needless to say, there will be resistances to such an increase in information flow and these resistances will take the well-worn forms outlined by Freud, S. (1916 -17), and Freud, A. (1965, 1993) along with the overt and covert social defense mechanisms described in many of the texts on the psychodynamics of social systems (Menzies-Lyth, 1960). Given this connection, through discourses, cognitions and webs of belief, we argue that the space of differance is a key element of what is called cognitive behavioral therapy.

As intimated earlier, the link with Bion's theory of thinking can be found in the step from *Beta Elements*, which may be visualized as granules of experience through the *Alpha Function*, which links the Beta Elements such that they may form the elements that go to form "Dream Thoughts." These last, in turn, may then be transformed, through "Preconception" and "Conception" into a "Concept" which may then be integrated into a "Scientific-Deductive System" which may then, possibly, be mathematized. It seems that the clearest linkage between Derrida's notion of differance and Bion's theory of thinking is in the stages running from Beta Elements through to preconception. And, correspondingly, it is in the first of these three phases that the proto-thinking of Beta Elements is liable to jump across to "Action" (Cell A6 of Bion's Grid). In other words, it is here that we find acting out in its least cognitively elaborate form where scattered beta elements are translated into action without accompanying alpha function, and certainly without concepts. This is the realm of "severe mental disturbance." One way to counteract such A6 activity is to build supports of various kinds for the alpha function and its operation upon the beta elements of experience. Such work is prior to dream-work, which is itself built upon alpha elements. If this line of thinking is correct, then the establishment of spaces of differance would serve to buttress thought. It is a form of "cognitive psychology," but a form that operates, as it were, at the level of "machine language " of the biocomputer, machine language in computer parlance being the first generation language, the language that is but one step above the zero's and one's of digital electronic systems.

As an example, a local school has built into its daily schedule small spaces of time devoted to quiet contemplation. Admittedly this is done individually and it may or may not tap into the beta elements and alpha functions of participants in that system, but it seems to be a step in that direction. In other parlances this might be called moments of mindfulness or "here-and-now-experiencing." Such structures, among the others mentioned above, help increase the "deferment of difference" that Derrida refers to (1985). It also increases, insofar as new ideas emerge from the space of differance, new interpretations. Hazell (2003) has argued that a vigorous "hermeneutic function" that maintains the individual's interpretive matrix as an open system, with all that implies, is a key feature of emotional, spiritual and cognitive well-being (Hazell, 2003). The success of this "quiet space" as a means of metabolizing thoughts that might otherwise be unthinkable will be increased if a group mechanism is established to enable these to be processed in the wider community. In this, one might follow the ideas of de Mare (2011) for example.

Referring again to Bion's grid, we notice that column two, the Psi column, denotes resistance. It stands as a membrane between "Definitory Hypotheses" and Notation, Attention, Inquiry and Action. At the level of Beta Elements it prevents all but Action. If, for example, an experience is not even "Notated" or, as it were, inscribed upon the metaphorical "Mystic Writing Pad" (Freud, 1925) then it cannot be thought about. This is the equivalent of the defense mechanism of denial, which, to use a computer metaphor would be like typing on the screen, not saving the words, turning the computer off for a while, and then turning the computer back on again. Nothing remains of what was written. It is like it never happened. As in Freud's explanation of the Mystic Writing Pad metaphor, this Psi function serves a dual purpose, to act as a means of inscription of the experience, but also to protect the inflow of too much or undesirable, overwhelming, traumatizing information. This same dynamic can be seen to exist around the space of differance. On the one hand there will be an inscription of it, but on the other hand there will be a denial of it. This ambivalence will manifest itself in all levels of the system's organization—in the individual, in the small group, the institution and the society. We may expect, therefore that while it might be possible to introduce a space of differance into an institution, there will also be arrayed against it significant defenses, these organized around key institutional conflicts. An example of this may be found in Hazell (2005) where a group in the Tavistock tradition was established in a county jail. While it had positive results, it ran counter to the predominant culture of "discipline and punish" (Foucault, 1995) in the institution, and, once a sponsoring psychiatrist left the jail, the group was terminated by the powers that be. A similar example may be imputed to the Northfield experiment and its somewhat hasty demise (Harrison, 2000). However, "the truth will out" or stated dynamically, "That which is not represented in the Symbolic emerges in the real" (Lacan, 2007a) The unconscious will express itself in some form or another if it is not symbolized. Not infrequently, it will manifest in social symptoms, sometimes, in the discourse of the Clown.

We may thus envision the space of differance as located prior to the space of the paranoid-schizoid position, for this relies on the existence of concepts and boundaries and is established upon categories that have to some extent been settled upon. The space of differance is prior to even this form of thinking. It is this fact that separates it from being simply another form of "creative thinking" or "thinking out of the box," or free association. It is this placement as prior to proto-thinking that also separates it from sheer randomness. For example, we might, in error, see the activity/passivity of difference being accessed in the practice of the indigenous hunters of Labrador (cited in McGinn, 1990) of heating the scapula of an elk and reading the resultant cracks as a means of improving their hunting. Some anthropologists argue that the method is effective because it introduces randomness into the behavior of the hunters and this allows them to take their prey, who have long-since figured out their predators' patterns, by surprise. No, difference is none of these for each relies on a codification system, upon ways of reading that, to a greater or lesser extent, are pre-determined. The space of difference has deferred the employment of such meanings and suspended the application of these categories.

However, the role of difference in creativity, in the generation of new ideas, and thus behavioral routines, remains. It is simply that the intervention in the chain of thinking, especially as outlined by Bion, occurs at an earlier stage, namely at the level of Beta elements, or, to utilize the terminology of Aulagnier (2001), in a space prior to the Primal Space, prior to the pictograms even, of her theory. The space of difference is also analogous to the "Chora" of Kristeva (1984) and to its application in the thinking on community dynamics expounded by Hazell and Kiel (2017). The work of Joyce, especially "Finnegan's Wake," takes us to the very brink of the space of difference . As Joyce notes (Bristow, 2018) only the thinnest transparent sheet separated his later works from madness itself. We may also note, in passing, how artistic products may be effective in mobilizing the space of difference . This idea is further elucidated by Blanchot (1988) and Astruc (2015).

Just as the dialectic between the Ps and D positions, as is posited by Bion (1997) is an essential aspect of psychological development, we may posit that the space of difference is a third essential element and argue that for psychological complexity to grow there must be a migration in mental processes, at all levels (individual, group, institutional, societal) between the tripole of the spaces of Differance-Ps-D. We would therefore argue that the establishment of spaces of differance at all levels can be seen as a vital aspect of development in each of these realms. In addition we hypothesize that the space of difference induces receptivity to *transformations in O* as described by Bion (1978). This encounter we regard as vital to all transformations of any lasting significance.

Summary

So far, a complex field has been traversed. In addition, it is a field in depth insofar as throughout, unconscious dynamics are at work. We will here recap the major domains that we argue should be brought to bear upon social problems as they might occur at all levels from individual through to social.

At the outset, we used the diagram below to sketch the overall design of this book:

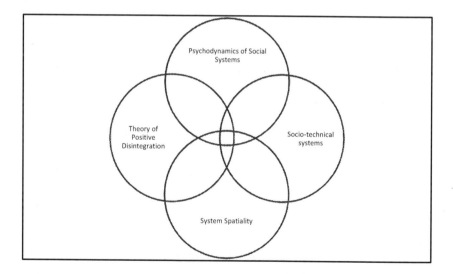

Figure 11: Socio-technical systems, Psychodynamics, Spatiality and Positive Disintegration

Thus far we have traversed these domains arguing that it is at the intersection of these four domains, fully conceived, that we find the individual and his or her travails.

In the domain of system psychodynamics we find powerful unconscious forces at work at all levels of organization. This include the forces of splitting and projective identification, along with the developmental drives towards increased complexity. Dabrowski's theory of Positive Disintegration places development in a hierarchical sequence (1970, 1977) and here we argue that a similar sequence can be seen in groups and larger social systems.

In the domain of socio-technical systems, we find the individual impacted by the manifest effects of technology as explicated by the model of McGinn (1990) and the elaboration of that model posited here. In addition we see the releasing effect of technology as described by Heidegger (2013). We emphasize that these dynamics interact in complex ways with both of the other domains in that they have unconscious meanings and that they are expressed differently in different regions of the world.

Finally, there is the domain of spatiality or, more commonly, geography. Socio technical systems occupy space—space ranging in dimensions from the chair one sits in at a dinner table through to the continent one inhabits. All the dynamics of the other two domains are subject to spatial laws. This text goes only a small distance in exploring some of those dimensions in that it skirts the many theories to be found in theoretical geography. What it has accomplished, we hope, is to alert practitioners to the spatial component of psychological issues ranging from individual through group, community, region, nation and civilization.

Social and personal problems abound—addictions, hatred, violence, lack of dialogue, poverty, climate change, public health—the list goes on *ad infinitum*. Too frequently the approach to these issues is through a single discipline—politics, individual psychology, economics, and so on. What is required is a multi-disciplinary approach at all levels, not only between the "grand labels" of disciplines but within the disciplines themselves for each discipline tends (and this is especially true of psychology) to not only sequester itself from other disciplines but also to adopt as creed one particular explanatory paradigm as being the one and only way to solve problems. Psychology is still a pre-paradigmatic science, to use Kuhn's (1962) terminology. The best path is to admit this and proceed accordingly, with an open mind and a consequent inter-disciplinarity within the science itself.

The text suggests some possible procedures or technologies that might assist in this regard. Following is a list of them, each with one exemplary reference. Given the tragic events that are unfortunately ubiquitous across space and time and given that these can be attributed to failures of leadership systems and group dynamics, it is hard to underestimate the potential importance of interventions like these.

- Group Relations Conferences

These, and other groups conducted in the Tavistock tradition are aimed at uncovering and working with and through the unconscious dynamics of groups and organizations.(Colman and Geller,1985)

- Social Dreaming Matrices

These involve groups assembling, sharing their dreams and then using the material thus created to interpret not the individual dynamics of the dreamer but the group-as-a-whole unconscious. (Lawrence, 2003)

- Open Space Activities

These are activities, somewhat similar to those described in the "Northfield Experiment" (Harrison,2000) involving community meetings out of which form interest groups based on members' suggestions.(Harrison,2008)

- Listening Posts

In these, groups assemble and form lists and descriptions of what seems to be "on the mind" of the community. The format is free form, somewhat free associational and groups might convene in different departments, neighborhoods or regions. As an end product, a summary report is distributed. This report can then be used to inform political and managerial activities.

- Psychodynamic Ethnography

This type of work involves the application of psychodynamic concepts and procedures to cultural anthropology. The focus can be wide ranging or focused. Erikson, Devereux, Roheim and Gregor (1987) provide good examples of this type of analysis.

- Dialogical Meetings in Social Networks

This work relies upon the work of social network theory and social-community driven theory of mental health. In it, each individual is seen as belonging to a social network, usually of two hundred or so individuals. Thus any meeting is an "intergroup event" between two social networks. The idea involves the creation of a "dialogical" meeting at this boundary. The term "dialogue" is infused with the meanings derived from Buber, and Bakhtin, to name but two. Seikkula and Arnkil (2006) give an account of this type of work in practice.

- Spaces of Differance

This concept is based on the description in the foregoing text. It is an extremely subtle "space" in which meanings and differences are deferred by the group so as to create a "playful" discourse, a conversation which enables discursive flexibility. (Derrida, 1985)

- Discursive Flexibility (Master, University, Hysteric, Analyst, Clown)

In this the group determines that it will, through the efforts of leadership or consultation, maintain a flexible rotation through the discourses, becoming aware of occasions where it gets stuck in a given discourse and analyzing the defensive reasons for this stuckness. The discourse of the Clown is described in a foregoing chapter of this text. (Lacan, 2007a : Hazell and Kiel, 2017)

- Koinonia

This set of procedures is based on the work of de Mare (2011) and his work with median groups. His discovery was that in groups of this size (20-45 members) there is an initial outpouring of hatred but that if this is worked through dialogically, one finds underneath, as it were, "koinonia" a sense of community, or, as he terms it, "impersonal fellowship." (de Mare,2011)

- Spatial Analysis

In this, the individual group or institution is analyzed from a geographical standpoint. This analysis is necessarily both spatial and historical. One asks, "What geographic, locational factors have been brought to bear on this issue?" To what extent can some of the phenomena at hand be explained by looking at not only classic geographical factors (climate, economy, geology, landforms, culture) but also at the unconscious dynamics associated with these spatial differences, dynamics we find elaborated in group-as-a-whole work, for example? (Soja, 2011)

- Psychogeography

In this a more "free form" reflexive approach is taken to the spatial factors that might be involved in explaining individuals in social systems. One might, for example carry out a *"derive"* (following Self and Debord) where one takes a "random walk" across a city or region, noting one's subjective impressions as one does so. This works as a sort of spatial free association which perhaps opens up unconscious dynamics of the socio-technical-spatial context.

- Political ecology

The domain of political ecology includes, but is not limited to the study of the differential impacts of spatial events on different groups in society. For example Blaikie et al (2003,2018) show how disasters, both acute, as in hurricanes and in chronic, as in soil erosion, impact different socio-economic groups differentially. This model can be scaled up to involve continents or down so that it explains "office space." Again these models may be integrated with the group-as-a-whole model to unravel some of the unconscious dynamics both powering these differences and leading to resistances to change.

- Sociosomatics

Much as an individual will at times manifest an unconscious conflict or an unworked trauma in their bodies, so will groups at all scales manifest their unconscious issues in illnesses, epidemics, aches and pains. To posit this is not to deny germs, infection, stress, strain, sanitation and so on as causal factors. Just as is the case in individuals, the real of these will intrude on well-being. However, as argued by Reich (1980a, 1980b); Hazell and Perez (2011) ; Hazell and Kiel,(2017) there can be, at times an unconscious vector in some of these conditions. This is probably most evident in the geography, sociology and epidemiology of addictions. Such a symptom, along with others, may be used as a means of reading the unconscious of the individual, group or society.

- Community Art Projects

These projects, usually accomplished in a public space can take on many forms. The sponsorship of these projects is of key importance insofar as it is important that they be articulated with what is on the mind of the community at hand. An example of these can be found in Semmelhack *et al* (2013).

In addition, some of these approaches are described, and explained in Hazell and Kiel (2017). Work in these contexts is not easy, for each involves an encounter with the unconscious which is no walk down a daisy-lined pathway. However, given the stakes and the failure of so many previous efforts some acceptance of these strains seems apposite.

VIII

Tavistock Large Group for Adults with Diagnoses of Severe Mental Illness

The following is a set of process notes with discussion of 21 sessions of large group sessions run in the Tavistock tradition in a nursing home in a Midwestern suburb. These notes constitute the content of the study published by Czochara, Semmelhack and Hazell (2016). The study provided some evidence that such a group was both possible and beneficial for participants. These notes are offered in the hope that they might provide practitioners with further insight and ideas on the running of these groups.

Assumptions about large groups are biased towards the negative. Kreeger (1975) and Czochara *et al* (2016) enumerate several of the reasons that large and median groups, that is, groups of over 12 members, are liable to dynamics that are inimical to psychotherapy. De Mare, on the other hand (2011) points out that median groups (that is, groups ranging in size from about 12 to 45 members) can be used for the development of community feeling (or as he terms it, "koinonia") if the correct approach is used and one is willing to work through the initial phase of "hatred." Encouraged by previous research on small groups (Semmelhack *et al*, 2013, 2015) in the above-mentioned nursing home, bolstered by the belief that residents would be able to make use of the large group experience and desirous of developing large group interventions, we embarked on a series of large group sessions, on a roughly once-a-month basis with residents at a nursing home who carried diagnoses of "severe mental illness." The parameters of this study are described more fully in Czochara, Semmelhack and Hazell (2016). We monitored the groups with surveys, questionnaires, interviews, group discussions and process notes.

This study demonstrates that such a group is feasible and beneficial for such a population. It is important to note that this population is stigmatized and gets little treatment in traditional nursing homes outside of medication management. We also describethemes that emerged in the group and managerial issues involved in conducting such a group. These might be of use to other practitioners. At the end we will posit several hypotheses and formats for future research.

The groups were conducted on Sunday afternoons at a nursing home in the suburbs of a metropolitan center in the Midwest of the USA. Attendance was entirely voluntary. The membership ranged from 12- to 30. Members and consultants sat in a large circle. This deviation from usual Tavistock procedure, where members sit in concentric circles or spirals, for example, was done for two reasons. First, we believed that the circular arrangement was less intimidating, since it allowed for more face to face contact and did not, by virtue of spatial arrangement, stimulate issues of "front seat/ back seat" or "in group/out group." Since we were experimenting we wanted to introduce such novelties in a stepped or titrated fashion. We anticipate using other structures in upcoming groups. Second, several members in this group used wheelchairs and walkers and access to chairs was greatly facilitated with the circle arrangement. At the end of each session, there would frequently occur an informal discussion which sometimes took the form of a discussion group similar to Tavistock-style discussion groups.

The groups were conducted in an open space, the home's lunchroom and were initiated and ended with the ringing of a chime. It is important to note that most of the members had had several months, at the very least, of experience in small tavistock style groups (reported in Semmelhack *et al* (2013)) and were thus conversant with the style of operation and the role relations involved in this type of group.

In what follows we have the process notes of 20 of the first groups which were noted down by one of the (usually three) group consultants. Each set of notes is followed by commentary by the consultants added at a somewhat later date to add depth and multiple perspectives on the dynamics of the situation.

Group Process: First Group

The first group consisted of 28 members and they started speaking almost immediately after the ringing of the chime. A female member of the group who was suffering from Tay-Sachs disease and seemed to have considerable difficulty, as a result of this in clearly enunciating her words spoke at some length and with moving eloquence on the theme of the problems of communicating clearly with others. Some members then pointed out that it was a concern to them that people take turns in speaking. Others spoke of the fact that they knew most people in the group, but not others. Some people were strangers.

This was consulted to as relating to a dread in the group about not being able to make contact with others, that while there were some previous relationships existing in the room, it was a large group and there was a fear of a free-for-all and a fear of loss of emotional contact with others.

These and similar consultations were seemingly accepted and then certain members spoke to the importance of co-operation, kindness and empathy. While these speeches did not sound particularly sermon-like, the consultants commented on the possibility that the group was attempting, out of anxiety at being in such a large group, to establish firm norms, so as to set rules against cruelty and meanness.

Again, these remarks seemed to be accepted as reasonably accurate and the group continued, this time with a middle-aged male member pointing out that he was to act as a representative to an outside mental health advocacy group (NAMI) and that should people have concerns, they should address them to him. This was understood by the consultant team as an early emergence of leadership in the group and the overt taking up by a member of a role in the group.

These consultations led to a discussion of roles and some of the risks of taking up roles. Many members in the group had been cast in unpleasant roles elsewhere in the past and the consultants remarked that there might be a concern as to what roles members might end up with in this group. There seemed, again, to be assent to this idea especially since roles could be very sticky; once you had been assigned a role by a group, it would often stick and could be hard to shake off.

Comments on Group 1:

Clive: As we reflected on this group, we noticed that the response had been quite "positive." There was little of the hostility and high levels of anxiety we have noticed in large group-as-a whole settings elsewhere. We explained this as being due partially to the fact that many of the members had been in Tavistock style groups for many months and so were "old hands" at this type of group. Also the circle arrangement, which was also familiar to members from previous in-house group experiences, perhaps did not stimulate so many paranoid thoughts and feelings. In addition, we hypothesize that such community experiences are longed for and that there was a protectiveness in the group so as to preserve a good experience. This was strikingly similar to the experiences we had conducting a similarly structured group in a large county jail (Hazell 2005).

In addition, the institutional context of W (the hospital in which the group was conducted) is very positive, so the transference and working alliance between patients, institute and staff is quite positive.

Di: The group ran very smoothly. While some trepidation was expressed by some members, there was not the ambivalence of being in a large group that might be characteristic of a large group of the "worried well." Members exhibited more curiosity about the group process. Periodically members who were not sitting solidly in the circle would come into the room and briefly observe the work going on. It was as if these members sought some emotional nourishment from the experience but were not 100% committed to the experience. Symbolically these visiting members represented the fact that the 28 people in the circle were processing on behalf of the entire institution.

Second Group:

This group was attended by 21 members, eight of whom were male. There were six student observers. The group started off with a period of silence and one member stated that this signified gratitude. Another member voiced a wish for Dr. Di to read from the "good book" (a book of inspiring quotations often read in other contexts). A consultation was made that this indicated an anxious wish that the group be a good one.

At this a female member spoke at some length of her experiences of being kidnapped as a child, her struggles with alcoholism and her experiences in a "dual diagnosis group." This led to her expressing deep feelings of remorse and a gratitude for this group. This was followed by remarks alluding to the healing influence of a "greater power" and talk of god.

This lead to a consultation that this was a large and powerful group. Perhaps it too was a "greater power." At this there was a comment that some individuals in the group had greater powers, and there was a wish that this power be used for the good of the group and the institution as a whole.

Several members spoke of their membership in other groups. One of the younger males (in his forties) stated that he, as a representative to NAMI, would like to hear of any concerns other members might want him to share. This led into a consultation that while this was one group, members clearly belonged to other groups as well.

At this several members spoke of encounters with negative people and how these must be coped with and avoided. Again this was consulted to as a concern in the group that it be a "good" group. This was followed by an event where a member lost their train of thought half way through a sentence and another member helped the person complete their thought and locution. This short event was consulted to as evidencing the group's wish and capacity to co-operate, especially to help each other think (and link) with and for one another.

In the ensuing discussion a lady, probably in her seventies spoke for quite some time in a very emotionally charged way about the traumas she had experienced. The lead consultant eventually gently interrupted her. (This seems in retrospect to anticipate a later theme of trauma and other experiences that are seen as uncontainable in the group and thus occur outside of the group boundaries.)

Subsequently the man in his forties addressed the visiting consultant as "Dr. Hazelton." This was consulted to as giving the older male consultant, Dr. Hazell, extra weight. This was followed by laughter. The feelings at the end were warm and convivial.

Comments on Group 2:

Clive: In reflecting on this group we felt that the issue of trauma of unspeakable proportions being uncontainable in the boundaries of the group was quite salient. We also were struck by the strong references to a higher power which we felt had dual references, namely, to the higher powers that be and to the power experienced in a large group. This was linked with a good deal of anxiety that this power be used for the good, not for the bad.

In a more speculative mode we wondered if the "sacredness" mentioned in the group might relate to basic assumption oneness

(Hopper, 2003) which is often found in groups where there is a significant amount of trauma. Certainly most of the members in this group had experiences of severe trauma. If this is the case then this sense of sacredness would be serving a defensive function. On the other hand, there was evident in the group a related sense of benign symbiosis and this reminded us of the healing impact of a positive symbiosis discovered by Searles (1960, 1979, 1986) in his work with schizophrenic patients. Could it not be that the large group, with all of its power of dissolving individual boundaries, could provide such a healing experience?

We also found ourselves wondering about the neuropsychology of such an event. Social neuroscience as documented by Harmon-Jones and Winkelman (2007) shows us that social situations have significant impacts on a wide array of neurohormones. This large group is a powerfully charged social situation. Could it not be that it is having powerful impacts on members' neuropsychology? In this case, we would hope that, and indications seemed to indicate that, these impacts were positive.

Di: The reference to a higher power might also have been indirectly linked to fantasies of the abusers who many of the group members had fell victim to (and who had perhaps felt all powerful at some point in the members' lives). It was therefore imperative for the group to see itself as benevolent for the fantasies that it would be a malevolent (abusive group—a reenactment of the abuser in their lives) would be too painful to bear. Likewise, the consultant team could turn out to be abusive rather than benevolent.

Brad: From a neuropsychological perspective, it is interesting to hypothesize that the attachment being experienced in the group is related to the secretion of related hormones such as oxytocin, dopamine and serotonin which are related to feelings of well-being. Additionally we might hypothesize that the group, while activating "flashbulb" type re-experiencing of trauma, also allows for the symbolic and narrative usage of language in a community setting to help mitigate the overload that might otherwise occur.

The power of the large group is sufficient to manage this flooding which is similar to that encountered in PTSD.

Third Group:

This group commenced with an older white man speaking in a sermonic manner on the importance of faith and truth. He spoke with his eyes closed as if in deep thought or as if "channeling" wisdom. These comments were followed by a long silence which was interrupted by a consultation pointing out that often people got anxious when approaching the truth. At this a man sitting two seats to the left of the consultant gave the consultant a congratulatory "high-five" (to which the consultant responded). Then the man left the room. At this, an older woman commented on the struggles she had in overcoming her alcoholism. This was followed by several group members speaking about how difficult life was and how important it was not to let negative thoughts get in the way. Then a consultation was delivered to the effect that the taking of a step involved faith and then when life was difficult (when "life sucks" as the members worded it) it was often necessary to take a step. What was the next step for this group?

By this time the man who left the room had returned and he was similarly congratulatory in response to this comment. (He seemed to be containing a lot of anxiety for the group, and in retrospect, this could have been addressed in the consultations.) This was followed by an energized discussion involving the ideas that god was on the side of group members and that there was a great hope for the group insofar as there was a give and take, mutuality, reciprocity. There was talk of the bonds existing between those who resided on the first and second floors of the institution and that there were strong feelings of friendship across these two groups. There were also comments aimed at helping people overcome hard times.

This was consulted to by mentioning that the underside of hope was despair and that the group seemed to have developed procedures for allaying this, especially through sharing. However, there seemed to be a carefulness in the group in approaching the experience of despair, the opposite of faith.

This was responded to by the group embarking on a discussion of the all-powerful nature of god and the importance of faith. This was addressed with the consultation that while god was all-powerful and the individual had little power, this large group had considerable power and the problem for the group was, "How to cope with the power of this group?"

This was followed by a late middle-aged music composition teacher announcing that she has picked a small bunch of flowers that symbolized hope for the group and that she wished to sing a hymn for the group. She closed her eyes and sang a hymn. This was an affecting moment. As she spoke about the meaning of the hymn afterward she once again lost her track. The silent consultation to this was that this was a sociosomatic incident because of the emotional power of the experience of hope being so delicate in the face of despair.

Comments on Group 3:

Clive: In reflecting on this group we were impressed once again by the religiosity of the themes and of the recurrence of the themes of divine power. Also evident was the theme of anxiety and other experiences that seemed to be uncontainable within the group and the physical contact (the high-five) of the member containing this anxiety and a member of the consultant team. We were also aware of the several blind-spots in the consultations, that is, of significant issues that were not addressed (the high-five for example, the absenting of a member from the group) and we felt that this was perhaps just part and parcel of large group life (there is just too much going on for it all to be consulted to) and to the contents of this group. There is a terrific amount of unprocessed trauma that cannot be fully addressed, that is, "beyond words."

Di: The amount of trauma in the group when approached

head-on could be overwhelming. The composition teacher's song and the small bunch of flowers picked for the group represented the hope that something new could spring from and flow from the group, something unexpected and healing to the trauma in the group. The sermon-like nature of the middle aged man's comments earlier in the group contributed to the spiritual nature attributed to the group by many of its members. Ironically, the group overlapped with a religious service in the facility. Many members chose to participate in the group rather than the religious service. This suggests that to some group members the group was an alternative spiritual service/a transcendent experience.

Fourth Group:

While the group was fully assembled, but before the official beginning of the group (marked by the ringing of a chime) Dr S. (one of the consultants) gave a reading on honesty in relationships and its life-giving qualities. This book is apparently part of the ritual-life of the community as it is often read from prior to the small groups held over the past few years.

The group, which was comprised of 21 members (there were a few empty seats) embarked on a discussion of the importance of hobbies, especially as a coping mechanism and as a pathway to health. During this discussion, one older lady, sitting in the corner was heard to speak out quite loudly, "Don't believe a word they say." After a few minutes, she departed. This was later felt to be quite significant by the consultants but at the time was left unaddressed, responded to in the thinking of the consultants in a more "managerial" fashion, that is, as a disruption rather than as an interpretable event. We will return to this later. Also an old black man was perambulating about the periphery of the group with a walker and very squeaky shoes. This also was not interpreted. Eventually this man left the room.

The discussion was responded to in a fairly manifest fashion as the group attempted to find ways to cope with difficult life situations. This led to a discussion of hopes for cure and recovery, from smoking, drinking and other addictions. This was responded to with a consultation incorporating the idea of people "blowing smoke" in the group and the difficulties of being honest because of fears of being judged.

At this point someone mentioned that some hobbies were extremely expensive, like horse-riding. Then the lady sitting next to me who has a terrifically disabling disease stated that she could ride horses. The interpretive possibilities of these statements again were not fully explored. However, a lady interjected after a brief pause in the group's discourse and asked (it felt out of the blue) if anyone had a crochet hook. She had been looking for one and the summer had been hard for her, because of the heat. A member responded that she had been looking for a book in the library, but could not find it.

At this the following consultation was offered. "The group feels like it is drifting, it cannot find anything to hook on to nor a book or words that will help. Was it just the heat this summer that was difficult or was it difficult in other ways?" The last question was offered as the consultant was aware that several changes in personnel had occurred in the home over the summer.

Members started talking about difficulties outside the home, in their families for example—brothers who had run out of cash, sicknesses and so on. There was a brief discussion of Bob Marley, who apparently "never went to see a doctor" and some small exploration of the anxiety of being nothing or expanding and growing. Finally,they homed in on the disruption caused by the psychiatrist leaving the home and several members voiced feelings of anger, even rage and helplessness and fear in response to this. This led to a discussion of the missing of a staff social worker who had left. This seemed to be the most affectively charged sequence in the group and it seemed to be manifested in three individuals leaving the room to get water. These people returned and some consultations were made to acknowledge the strength of feeling around these departures.

The group ended and in the discussion group immediately following there was a fair amount of enthusiastic talk and questions by some of the more talkative members, one of whom, a middle aged man who also serves as the representative to NAMI, asked if Dr. H had written any books. Three more members asked for the name of Dr. H, who is the oldest male consultant.

Comments on Group 4:

Di: The talk of the psychiatrist leaving and the social workers departure could also have been linked to unconscious fears that the consultants might leave and therefore the group would dissolve. The comings and goings of members in the group may have reflected on the fear of being a committed member who if the group ended would have to experience the deep pain of loss— loss that resonated with many traumatic losses experienced by group members. It was better to come and go than stay and risk becoming attached only to suffer great loss later. The notion of hobbies relates to the group—should the group be viewed as a hobby or is it something more serious than an activity that just fills in time. The comment made by the member regarding not to believe anything that is said may have been in reaction to the departure of several staff members including the psychiatrist— they (members) may have believed what they (authority figures) said only to have them abruptly depart from the facility. The black man with the walker and the noisy shoes may have been interpreted as the issue of race hovering around the periphery of the group but an issue ripe for interpretation. Was there something lurking around the periphery of the group that needed to be voiced related to the diversity of the group itself and the insidious racism that many members my experience or have experienced..

Clive: This group demonstrates the capacity of consultants to "miss" some important consultative opportunities and the fact that groups seem to survive these fairly well as long as the basic frame is maintained. The interpretations that were missed in this instance seemed to have to do with the themes of truth-telling ("Don't believe a word they say.") and the capacity of the group to include disruptive feelings, thoughts and fantasies. Eventually the group did seem to "get there" insofar as some potentially useful work was done addressing the loss of some central staff members and the consequent disruptions over the summer. One of the staff members to leave was an older male psychiatrist and this might be linked to the emergence of some admiration of the senior male consultant at the end.

Brad: Much of the process of this group could be regarded as attempts at self-regulation and/or behavior regulation from a neuropsychological approach. Many of the severe mental health diagnoses include impairments in self-monitoring, self-regulation and behavior regulation. In this case their self-monitoring and regulation is improving or, at the very least, maintaining.

Fifth Group:

This group occurred the day after a resident had died unexpectedly. In addition, another resident had died two weeks previously. We thus anticipated that death, dying, mourning, grief and loss would prove to be themes for the group this day. This in fact was the case.

A member mentioned that Halloween was over. Another said that it was a lovely day. Another averred that she missed her family. Then C, who often had the role of "orator/preacher," held forth for some time on the importance in life of setting goals. At this someone shared that A had died the day before. Another member, being careful to not appear "insensitive," shared that A had told him that she wanted to die, that she had had enough. The consultation was offered that the group was dealing with the very complex feelings related to this loss, having to do with life in the presence of death.

At this several members shared previous losses they had experienced, losses through death and departures of loved ones.

A consultant pointed out that this recent loss had stimulated awareness of other losses in the group and along with these complex and conflicting feelings centering around grief and sadness.

At this the lady who had been the roommate of A shared her deep sadness at her personal loss. Sharing that what was especially difficult for her to bear was the empty bed, previously occupied by A. Her deep sadness seemed difficult for the group and her to bear and she started to cry and left the room. The consultant offered that the feelings were difficult to cope with and this was manifested in people coming and going from the group. (Several other members had been leaving and returning thus far, presumably to go the bathroom.)

At this the group embarked on a discussion of the importance of completing tasks and of following through on things. This discussion was lead by C (the orator/preacher) and D, a member who frequently speaks of the importance of her AA group. This led to an assertion of the positive nature of heaven, the caring nature of God and finally the importance of coping with stress and strain. This was addressed with a consultation asserting the difficulty of the conflict between making a commitment to life and things to do with living, projects and so forth when we are all faced with loss and the fact that everything seems temporary.

At this C gave a fairly long detailed and vivid account of the loss of his fiancé to death four days before their intended wedding. This "left a hole in his heart" from which he never recovered, falling into a deep pit of depression. The consultant wondered if what C shared was a parable for the group, a story that contained so many elements that were true for the group as a whole.

At this a lady with an extremely debilitating neurological disorder who had arrived at the group late spoke on the theme of her hopes for change and growth, her need of a laptop computer and her desire to work. Her speech was very difficult to comprehend and was very impassioned. The group ended at this point leaving the consultants with half formulated interpretations around the incomprehensibility of death and the incommunicability of experience.

During the debriefing/discussion section after the group, consultants mentioned that members might notice some more feelings bubbling to the surface over the next few days. Members also pointed out that A, the departed member, had sung "Somewhere over the Rainbow" in the recent show. They also mentioned that her empty chair at the lunch table caused them to feel loss. A consultant pointed out that there was an empty chair in the room caused by A's roommate leaving and the empty bed made for empty spaces throughout the group's experience. These perhaps, along with the song, served as markers of their loss.

Afterwards the consultants met with A's roommate very briefly to check in with her and contract to work with her further on the upcoming weeks and to ensure that a new appropriate roommate be found for her.

Comments on Group 5:

Clive: This group seemed to serve as a powerful medium for members to "work through" their feelings about the death of one the members. This group put the consultants in mind of the work of Maurice Blanchot in "The Unavowable Community" (1988) and Jean-Luc Nancy in the "Inoperative Community" (1991) where they argue that the sense of community is established upon the death of one of the members, that death, perhaps only exists in and for the community. Viewed from this perspective, this meeting takes on a deeper significance, for not only is it a venue for the working through of mourning, it is also an opportunity to bind to a community.

Also of especial interest in this session is the reference to places, predominantly empty spaces (the deceased's chair, bed and seat) that carry additional meaning as a result of her departure through death. Nancy (1991) points out the significance of sacred spaces in the establishment of a sense of community. This, along with the flavor of ritual that the song the departed sang, all contribute to this meeting having a strong significance in the development of the sense of community.

Blanchot's work (1988, 1998) frequently asserts the unspeakability, the incomprehensibility, the radical alterity of death. Perhaps this is what is being hinted at in the barely decipherable words of the member afflicted with the debilitating nervous disorder at the end of the group.

Di: The flurry of members to the bathroom may have served an emotional regulatory function with the members removing physical waste from the group symbolic of painful feelings linked with loss. The patience with which members listened to the woman who spoke the barely decipherable words may have represented the strong desire to understand that which is nearly incomprehensible—death. In attempting to understand her words the group may have been suggesting that they have great patience in learning the emotional language of the group which is like another language. The passion in which the disabled woman spoke may have represented the deep passion the group has for learning the language that is unspeakable and uninterpretable at the present time. Her disabled speech may have also represented a disabled part of the group which longed to make contact with painful feelings linked with loss but struggling with the MO to do so. The references to empty beds and chairs where the deceased sat may have symbolically pointed toward holes or wounds in the group left from the deep levels of trauma experienced by group members over time and fears that these wounds scabbed over with time might reopen should the group touch upon the painful affect associated death.

Sixth Group:

This group consisted of 22 individuals, 15 were male. One male member, noting that Christmas was approaching, spoke of wishes, hope and resolutions for improvement. This theme was picked up by several other members, one of whom spoke of the importance of AA to her. At this a consultant suggested that this was a continuation of a theme from a previous group in which the taking of new steps and the attendant anxiety was discussed. He also mentioned that support was essential if one was to take new steps.

At this point the singleton African American woman spoke up stating that she was extremely interested in pursuing her musical interests and asked the consultant who had just spoken if he knew of any resources. The consultant wondered if there were perhaps resources available in this group here and now. At this several members offered some ideas and connections with people in the music field. The woman then spoke about the importance of communication, of understanding others and of being understood and this was addressed with a consultative idea on the importance of communication in exchanging material assistance that is often needed in taking the next step and also in establishing a sense of community.

Several members then complimented the African American lady, pointing out that she, in her role of providing water at mealtimes, was very cheerful and pleasant. A consultant formed the silent consultation that she had provided "water of life" for the group and the African American lady expressed gratitude for the thanks and shared further her use of humor in the sharing of water, namely that she would sometimes pretend she was serving alcoholic drinks. At this the lady who had spoken positively of the role of AA in her life mentioned that she did not mind a joke about alcohol, but it was no laughing matter for her. This potentiated some discussion and the consultation was offered that the group was perhaps unsure as to how to tell the difference between water which was life giving and other substances which could be potentially harmful.

In response to this, it seemed, the member to the left of the consultant said she was thinking of "trust falls" she did in camp as a teenager, and how the group was kind of like that at times, or kind of like the "Peanuts" cartoon where Lucy tricked Charlie Brown with the football, each time promising she wouldn't take it away at the very last instant but then, of course taking it away with him ending up on his butt, tricked and dismayed. The group seemed to "get" this set of metaphors.

There was then talk of God and trust in God and Jesus and at this point an elderly lady admonished the group not to have a nervous breakdown and expressed the desire to sing a song. The group assented and she sang a poignant hymn. Then the lady who had shared the Charlie Brown image sang a hymn-like song. A consultant shared that the tone of these songs contained a longing for companionship, support and love.

Then another elderly lady stated that someone in the institution had told her of her intentions to commit suicide that day. The consultant stated that he was responding to that on multiple levels; first that this was a concrete problem that should be addressed (Who was this and where were they now?) and secondly that this was related to feelings of deep despair and disconnectedness that might need to be addressed. At this, one of the consultants went aside with this lady and gathered the data on this person and left the room to attend to the problem.

The group then embarked on a discussion of the possibility of upcoming cuts to the Medicaid budget and what this might mean to the viability of the institution where they are living in now. This was led by the middle aged male who started the group off with messages of hope. There was discussion of political activity aimed at the state capitol especially in the form of letter writing. Again, two consultations were aimed at this. First it was pointed out that the group had covered managerial functions (offering of material assistance to the aspiring musician), community (the singing of songs) and, now, political matters (writing letters to the governor of the state). This consultation, for all its intellectualism, seemed to make some sense to several members. In addition, a consultation was made pointing out that the group itself was coming to an end and that issues of trust and connectedness had become more prominent in this group stimulating anxieties of sudden catastrophic loss. At this point the group ended. There was a ten minute debriefing after the here and now event of the group to check in and it seemed that everyone was in reasonable shape.

Comments on Group 6:

Clive: It was hard for the consultants to trace connections between the content of this group and the preceding group which had dealt with loss, although, upon reflection the suicide gesture of an absent member might have been related to this. The disclosure of the intent to commit suicide, however does occur close to the manifest concerns regarding the future of the institution so it is perhaps these that are related. The loss of security symbolized in a home, a safe place to live and be and the consequent loss of hope and faith could, in our opinion stimulate a suicidal despair. This was a significant missed consultation. One of the consultants did find out who was seen as suicidal and followed up on this, meeting with the person.

Di: On some level the talk of suicide might speak to the group itself, that on some level the group might run the risk of killing itself off or dying. The African American woman who asked for any assistance in boosting her musical career might speak to the fact that the group wanted to boost its career—to symbolically make music together and to therefore be "in-tune" with each other.

Group Seven:

Twenty-two members were present. Eight were male. In addition one male paced back and forth outside the circle of the group. One male consultant was absent due to sickness. This was announced prior to the start of the group.

The female member next to the remaining male consultant, who had stated that it was nice to have a "handsome man" sit next to her opined that it was warm inside. Several other members agreed and there was a discussion of heating in the home. To this the consultant responded that perhaps the group was discussing some emotional warmth in the room.

The group then launched into a discussion of their concerns over the possible closing of the nursing home, mentioning that they needed to activate themselves by sending letters to NAMI, the governor and senators, pointing out how good the home was for them, how much they relied upon it and how afraid they were of the consequences should the home be closed. The consultation to this was that the anxiety connected with losing one's home was indeed deep. (The consultant shared that he himself had come close to losing his own home over a property-tax error). In addition this potential loss of home was perhaps re-traumatizing for many in the group since they had previously experienced loss of home and hearth. In addition, there seemed to be a deep concern in the group that decision makers who might have serious influences on their well-being were not going to behave entirely rationally.

This consultation was met with a fairly general round of agreement which was followed by yet more voicing of concern and ideas and arguments for the utility of the nursing home that was their home and, for many, had been their home for many years. It appeared to the consultant that this part of the discussion seemed to result in more leaders emerging in the group, leaders that might take up the role of representing the group to other groups such as decision-makers and advocacy groups. It also seemed that there was an emerging concern over issues related to delegation and representation by the leaders. These consultations were made with the consultant noting to himself that at this point they seemed very much like consultations made to groups in the Institutional Event section of a Tavistock Study Group where issues of representation, boundaries, delegation of authority and role differentiation are prominent.

At this a female member reminded the group that they had, in fact, carried out a fairly large letter-writing campaign. Several members asked about this campaign and there was again a feeling of concern and disquiet in the room. At this the female consultant stated that it was as if the group wanted to be saved and that this issue had been alive in the home for about a year.

This was followed by several comments from members arguing that it would be crazy to close the home down. It served important needs. It was cost effective and the alternatives of homelessness and displacement were terribly bad. At this a consultant mentioned that his associations had been going to his memories of reading about tribes of Plains Indians as the white man moved in, and to groups of workers concerned that their factory or school was to be closed by head office. In both of these situations there was a lot of anxiety about the irrationality of the decision makers and the response to the poor decisions.

At this there seemed to be a renewed resolution in the group, especially amongst those who had emerged as tentative leaders, to write letters, and continue to push for the home's survival.

Comments on Group 7:

Clive: Most of this group was spent discussing the thoughts and feelings around the possible closing of the home. As such, the group had a distinctly "political" tone, as if action was about to be planned. While none was planned, some action had been taken in the past and perhaps the ground had been laid for some further mobilization. What is of particular interest is that the group did seem to be capable of thinking and feeling at roughly the same time. This was demonstrated by some members being able to acknowledge that this potential loss of home and hearth constituted a re-traumatization for many in the home. I was especially aware of Nancy's tripartite scheme of political, managerial and community and of the interaction between the three as I sat in this group. It seemed clear to me that such a "free floating" discussion served a very useful function in unearthing and allowing for the expression of wishes and concerns in the group, wishes and concerns that could potentially be organized through an alpha and other linking functions into clear thoughts and programs of action, programs of action that would be yoked to the interests of the group. It is here that we return to Dewey and his definition of freedom, "The capacity to frame one's purposes and carry them into effect." Could it be that such community meetings, by which we mean community meetings with an analytic discourse, are an essential ingredient for emancipation?

Di: Anxiety about closing the home seemed to link with fears of ending the group. The group had become a home of sorts--a cost effective community where thoughts could be freely exchanged. It was the free exchange of ideas in the group which made it a very different kind of place for the members. The group served as a place where members could be or feel emancipated from the constraints of leaders who perhaps did not have their best interests at heart. Closure of the home itself would signal the demolition of the group and the elimination of a place where members who were constrained by mental illness and other maladies could feel free.

Eighth Group:

The group was comprised of 11 women and 6 men seated, as usual, in a circle. It was an early day in Spring after a long and particularly snowy winter. Owing to consultant illness the last session had been postponed. Also significant is that one of the usual male consultants was absent this day and his place had been taken by a recently graduated doctoral student who had previously held the role of observer and logistics organizer of the meetings.

One member started sharing that as a child she had lived in a house that had to be knocked down because they were building a highway. As a consequence, she had to move to another house. This was followed by several other members sharing their experiences with having to relocate. The consultant opined that this talk of relocations was related to anxieties about the nursing home and its permanence and stability in the face of political moves to cut back on its financing. These concerns had been brought up in earlier sessions.

This consultation seemed to jibe with members' concerns as there followed a discussion on the types of political action they could take and that they had taken. After several minutes of this, there was a sudden flurry of comments and cross conversations in one "corner" of the group. This was followed by a discussion of tornadoes that had touched down in the southwest of the country. At this the consultation was offered that there had just been a "tornado" of conversation in this room that had not been remarked upon.

This was followed by talk of how it helped to talk about issues. One member recounted once again how thankful she was for the home and the staff and the way it supported her in her abstinence from alcohol. This was responded to with the consultation that the talk, although it was sometimes uncomfortable was rather like a series of small non-destructive earthquakes that relieved pressure a little at a time rather than everything looking peaceful only to be disrupted by a terrific shift in the earth in the form of a major earthquake.

At this point one of the older males stated that he would really like to hear what Dr. B. had to offer. (Dr. B. was the "new" consultant). Dr. B. smiled and stated with some surprise that he was just about to speak to the anxiety he was experiencing in the group regarding the vulnerability of the home. The members confirmed this observation and moved on to discuss their anxiety over the upcoming performance of their show, "The Sound of Music." There were mixed feelings voiced about the performance, feelings of excitement, pride and apprehension. The consultation was offered that one of the themes of the musical was "escape from the Nazis" and that this theme jibed with the concerns of the group and was connected with the individual histories in the group.

At this one member shared that she had been amazed at how supportive people in the home had been. For example, when she had hurt her wrist, people had been so supportive and understanding and she really appreciated this. On the other hand, there were people in the home who really annoyed her, people who asked for money, people who invaded her personal space and people who pushed in line at lunch time. At this the group came to an end.

Comments on Group 8:

Clive: Once again we see the recurrent theme of deterritorialization, of the uncertainty of their living situation emerging, at first in derivative form and then, with very little consultation, emerging as a manifest concern. The utility of airing these concerns is discussed with very interesting contact points with Nancy's theory (1991) of the three domains of "Political, Managerial and Community," the clear idea emerging that if the three do not move somewhat in step, then social convulsions can be the result. This in and of itself is a provocative and potentially useful set of ideas. The member's activation of Dr. B. is significant since it seems to represent a sort of tender caretaking of a staff member by one of the group and it passed quite unremarkably, that is, without the facilitating member getting attacked in any way. The theme of the Nazis may be related back to the uncertainty of the home's future and to the histories of the members of the group and the last comments may be an attempt to weld together the "good" and the "bad" elements of the community and institutional experience.

Di: The mention of the "Sound of Music" and the Nazi regime may have been a missed interpretative possibility. The Nazi's were like tornados. They attacked quickly unexpectedly and destroyed those who they viewed to be inferior. The stigma of mental illness and being institutionalized might symbolically resonate with the stigma of being Jewish during Nazi times. There was a great vulnerability about the label and a fear that one's home could be ripped away by the authorities and one could be put away. The government might act like a tornado that suddenly could rip away one's security—in fact all that one has.

Brad: The request and concern for the distressed members also demonstrated how the group's social cognition is beginning to improve in the reading of social cues and empathy for both other individuals and the group.

Ninth Group:

The group was comprised of 20 members, twelve female and one male. There were two consultants, one male and one female. The regular other male consultant was absent due to illness. In addition there were three young female graduate students, two of whom sat in the group circle and one who chose to locate themselves outside.

The group started, as it so frequently does with an older male member delivering a speech on the importance of the group and the ways in which the members needed each other. This was infused with a strong feeling of affection. At the end, the member turned to the older male consultant and asked for validation of his statements. The consultant responded that he did agree with the ideas expressed and that this was consistent with the ways in which several members of the group had mentioned with pleasure that family members had renewed or made contact with them recently. The consultant said that he thought that this was a way of describing some of the affectionate feelings in the group in the here and now. Members were making deeper contact with each other.

There then followed a discussion of safety concerns in the United States and the performance of the president and the government in protecting citizens from danger. To this was offered the interpretation that there was a concern for personal safety in the group in the here and now.

This was followed by a set of statements expressing gratitude for the group and the institution, with one member sharing, as she had done several times before, how she has recovered from addiction and is happy for it. There then followed a discussion about young people and how life can be risky for them in certain neighborhoods. This was interpreted as a reference to the two young members in the group with the observation that this was the first time that such young people had sat in the group circle. This was a change in demographics and there was some concern as to their safety.

At this a lady who had been quiet up until this point almost blurted out, "What are we doing here?" Several members, in a very kind and understanding way, explained that this was a group meeting, a place where one shared one's concerns and so on, but she still seemed puzzled. At this, the consultant offered that the member in question was giving voice to a confusion that was present in the group, namely, "What is the purpose of the group?" The member did not seem to register the consultation at all but continued, sharing that she had ridden an exercise bike for the first time yesterday and that it felt good but today she was very sore. She asked the consultant directly if that was normal. The consultant opined that yes, this was a normal physical reaction but that once again, she might be speaking on behalf of parts of the group that felt like they were doing something new and different in this group in the here and now. It felt good, but they also thought that maybe they should take it easy because it could make you sore. Again, there was no validation or otherwise to the consultation, but the emotional tone in the group seemed to relax.

Next, a middle aged male member, who often takes up a leadership role complimented the female member for working out, stating that having hobbies was a good thing and that the members should look for hobbies. Again, the member turned to the male consultant and asked if this was a good idea. The consultant responded that yes, indeed he did agree that hobbies were very good ways of achieving many results, among them coping with anxiety and depression. He continued wondering if the group-as-a-whole, here and now might be looking for a hobby, or something that might be called a "group culture."

This consultation was met with a nodding of a few heads and then the group member with a seriously disabling chronic illness asked what would happen if someone was prevented from engaging in their hobby. The speech of this member is very difficult to decode and her concern was not addressed. The group started to talk about the survivability of the institution, whether or not the state governor would renew funding. Then they turned to the female consultant, who works in the institution and asked her opinion. She responded that on a reality level there was little or no risk of a shut down, but that perhaps there was concern about the imminent ending of the group in a few minutes time.

At this, the male member sitting to the male consultant's left became quite activated, holding his hand up, as if wanting to speak. He did speak, sharing intense feelings of anxiety about the institute closure and how he had painted some pictures as a mural on the wall but they had been painted over and this upset him. He was somewhat cut off by the male to the right of the male consultant who asked if a list of motivations should be generated in the group. The male consultant then offered that this was not a bad idea but that the male on his left was holding a significant charge of feelings for the group that he would be left with if they were not shared. At this the male on the left shared some very moving aspects of his personal history of being left alone for long periods as a child and shuffled from one institution to another and how he finally had a home here and he was afraid he might lose it. The consultant shared that this anxiety of having found something good and then having it taken away had been touched upon frequently in the group and that it was a very common human concern. The female consultant, in announcing the end of the group, pointed out that while the group was ending, there was no intention of painting over his thoughts and feelings.

Comments on Group 9:

Clive: We see the continuation of the theme of cohesion and affection in the group. Even though it could be seen as a reaction formation against disavowed feelings of hostility in the group, this consultation is not made because of the strong concerns for safety and consistency that are discernible. In addition the issue of having found a good object and the ensuing anxiety of possibly losing it seems to be the overriding concern. Although the consultations are not explicitly validated, the affective tone and derivative content seems to indicate that they are not too far off target. There is considerable idealization of the consultants and something of a dependency culture as demonstrated by the repeated asking for the consultant's opinion. In some circles of Tavistock work these would not be responded to. We believe that a two track response which includes the answer along with an interpretation is just fine. It adheres to the notion of having "binocular vision" which we think is a useful social skill and we also think that this is what Bion did in his groups (see Lipgar and Pines, 2002).

There is a significant *unmade consultation*. The female member whose question, "What if you are prevented from doing your hobby?" was left dangling and unresponded to leaving the consultants (and probably the group) with an unfinished feeling. This was probably not responded to for a number of reasons, among them, countertransference. Such unmade consultations can provide fertile ideas as to where the group wishes to go next. Asking oneself, at the end of a group, "What were the unmade consultations?" is a useful way of preparing one's psyche for the next steps. In addition we see considerable concern regarding deterritorialization.

Di : The question of hobbies might have indicated that some of the consultants looked at the group as a hobby (less seriously) than as a therapeutic event. Or maybe thinking of the group as a hobby was a defense against just how serious the material being discussed during the session really was. The intense fear of institution closure was also prevalent. Not just simply closure of the institution but closure of the group—members had found a good object in the here and now and felt grateful for it. Underlying fears that it could be taken away as so many safe places may have been in the past may have resonated in the unconscious traumatized parts of the group.

Tenth Group:

This group was comprised of 20 individuals, 7 males, 13 females. The group was initiated by a middle-aged member who is usually active suggesting that the group talk about needs and what happens when needs are frustrated. This was followed by an older man, who is also usually quite active, delivering a speech on needs and how they might be frustrated by fears. At this the consultant offered that these fears might come from several sources—the physical environment, the community, the group, interpersonal relationships or from within oneself.

At this a woman quite clearly stated that what she wanted was attention. She knew that this sometimes created problems but that she was just being honest. This was followed by several other women agreeing and sharing that they wanted to be recognized. Since individuals seemed to feel that they had to ask for permission to talk by raising their hands, often referring to the oldest male consultant. The consultation was made that the group was quite in touch with the need for attention and recognition but that there was considerable anxiety in the room about "turn-taking." The consultant wondered aloud if there was a connection between the words "attention" and the French word "attendre" meaning to wait. Perhaps the group was concerned about waiting their turn for attention. Maybe their long histories of neglect and abuse pushed them not to expect anything but to wait their turn.

This consultation seemed to meet with some agreement. One of the ladies left the circle and one of the other female members asked her where she was going. "To the bathroom," she replied.

This was followed by several members talking on the theme of the importance of being remembered by others. It was also mentioned that while it was nice to be remembered, it was also nice not to be locked into a role forever by those memories. At this the consultation was made that one of the needs present in the group might be the need to be a part of the group, but also to be apart from the group. This was made with specific reference to the noticed departure of one of the members. It was hypothesized that this was an instance of caring in the group.

The lady who left for the bathroom then shared that she was often emotionally hurt by the treatment she got from the nursing assistants, that they would often speak in Spanish which she couldn't understand and seemed to ignore her. She cried and stated that she felt lonely. At this, the male who had started off the group said that the lady who was crying was new to the group and he invited her to play cards with their group. She accepted and the man pointed out that this was an example of "Intimacy versus Isolation, one of Erikson's ideas." Later, the consultants surmised that the woman's tears might have represented the deep sadness of being left out and how some many of the group members had experienced this form of neglect—and somehow feared that it would repeat itself in the here and now of the group.

The group continued talking about the poor treatment they got from the nursing aides and seemed to find that they would turn to each other for solace in response to the unempathic behavior of the aides. This cohesion and mutual caring was consulted to as perhaps being an effective coping mechanism, in the absence of any immediate institutional change.

This was followed by the lady with a seriously debilitating illness speaking of her isolation in the home. She was only in her fifties but, because of her illness, she was housed with the older people and felt cut off. She was responded to by G, who had been actively playing the role of "includer" in the group. The group seemed to watch their discussion with great interest. The consultant pointed out that it was perhaps significant that the individual who was in many ways the most "gregarious" (G's word for himself) was speaking to the person who was structurally set up to feel isolated. It was as if two parts of the group were meeting each other.

At this, C, who delivered the speech on needs at the beginning, gave a speech on playing the piano as a way of coping with stress. He played the piano himself and it gave pleasure both to himself and others. This was consulted to as perhaps being a metaphor of the group. Was this group like a piano? Were the members like keys that could be played together to create a cohesive, understandable and loving song?

Comments on Group 10:

Clive: The focal moments in this group seemed to revolve around the needs for recognition, the need to be noticed. What was particularly interesting is the clear and simple ways in which these needs were expressed and met. Exponents of large groups, especially those involving persons not designated as seriously mentally ill, will see this as very unusual, for, typically, far more paranoid ideation is to be found there.

Di: The group member's deep need for recognition speaks to the great shortage of it in their lives up until the here and now. The need for recognition also speaks to the need to be understood by others as a function that the group provides to a greater or lesser extent. The group was an instrument that could be played in such a way that acknowledgement and recognition could be acquired and a cohesive song could be played by the voices in the group. .

Eleventh Group:

Owing to illness of two of the male consultants, there had been a lapse of some six weeks since the prior meeting. Present were 17 members, 12 female, 5 male. Of note is that several members left the room and their places were taken up by several members who came into the group late. The number of members thus stayed at approximately seventeen throughout the one-hour session. Of note also is that C, the older male member who played a central role in many of the previous groups, operating as a "old wise man" who delivered sermon-like speeches that seemed to have a calming and organizing effect on the group, was absent owing to a fall he had taken that morning. It seemed that G, a middle aged white male was more activated in this session, as if he was filling in the gap left by C. This was commented on by a consultant towards the end of the group and seemed to be acceptable to the group as a hypothesis.

The group was started by a woman stating that she had just heard from her son who was in the military and stationed in Italy. Upon questioning by G, it emerged that although the son was safe, she was still concerned for his safety. At this another lady mentioned that she was looking forward to seeing her daughter at Thanksgiving. This was followed by another woman sharing that she missed her sister terribly and at this, she started to cry deeply sobbing in sadness. At this the consultant stated that it seemed the theme of the group thus far had to do with missing loved ones and how it hurts to love. This remark seemed to meet with agreement and was followed by a member expressing gratitude for the group and the institution and thanking God for her sobriety.

The discussion then switched to concerns about terrorism and Ebola at which a consultant wondered if there was some concern about safety in the group. This was not immediately confirmed or disavowed but the lady who had welled up with tears spilled her cup of water on the floor and a couple of members and the student observer quickly moved to help her. The group then talked about the importance of giving and taking and how some members had more money and yet were willing to share with those who were less well off. At this point the consultation was made that the accident of the spilled cup might have several symbolic meanings for the group. On the one hand the spilling might refer to concerns about feelings spilling over and making a mess. On the other hand, there was perhaps a feeling in the group of gratitude for the "cup runneth over".

This was followed by a discussion of the necessity amongst humans for exchange and sharing. Eventually one of the members turned to the older male consultant and asked for this theory to be validated by him. The consultant responded to the question by saying that indeed that did seem like a robust hypothesis and, in addition, it made him think of the first interpersonal situation humans are in when they are babies--how they need their mothers to give and how their survival depends on this. Perhaps the group was touching upon this sense of vulnerability.

This was followed by G asserting that he gained a sense of meaning in life from giving to others and that having a sense of meaning was essential for human contact. It then seemed that this idea was expanded to include the necessity for human contact and that this gave one a sense of meaning too. Again, G asked the consultant for his opinion. The consultant replied that this again seemed like a good idea but he was also wondering if this discussion was in any way connected to the absent member, C, who usually was an active member and for whom G seemed to be filling in.

At this a petite lady in a wheelchair who was new to the group spoke at some length on the topic of her physical problems of falling down inexplicably and how no doctors could seem to come up with an answer. The time for the group was almost up and the consultation was made that the group seemed to be ending on something of a mystery.

Comments on Group 11:

Clive: This group is interesting insofar as there was a seemingly unrelated patchwork of topics, addressed in sequence but without a unifying theme. In this way, it resembled other large groups which often have a fragmented "bitty" feel. The emotional tone, however, was not unpleasant. The major unmade consultation seems to belong at the end where the comments about doctors who do not understand could have been understood as a derivative aimed at the consultants, especially the older male visiting doctor.

Di: The cup spilling over and the swiftness with which members helped secure the situation might speak to the ability of the group to act effectively and quickly in cleaning up emotional spills. I agree that the unmade consultation about doctors not understanding may have been directed at the consultant team, that members would have to clean up their own spills lest the consultants miss them or ignore them.

Brad: Also, this group was relying on memory components and memories of past groups to remember what to discuss. The sequencing was important from a cognitive level, but they could not get beyond the abstract reasoning of a "unifying theme." However, this group shows that members integrate information into their long term memory, including social themes and topics.

Twelfth Group:

The group had two visitors from France, sisters of one of the members. This was announced prior to the group and all the members agreed that this was fine. The bell indicating the start of "group time" was rung and shortly thereafter a member spilled her coffee on the floor. Several members swiftly came to her aid and cleaned up the mess. This was consulted to as the group perhaps having some concern over spillage and what this might mean or bring about in the group—associations were made to cups running over, overflowing with feelings, making a mess of things—and a connection was made to the spilled water of last session, suggesting that these or other themes were ongoing concerns in the group.

At this a member expanded upon the theme of the true meanings of Thanksgiving (which was but a few days away) and Christmas. It was emphasized that too often people forget the true meanings of these festivities. This was consulted to with the ideas that Thanksgiving was about gratitude and Christmas was about giving and receiving. Perhaps these themes had something to do with the group.

At this, several members shared their concerns about their families. One member teared up at her love and concern for the well-being of her daughter. Another member shared that her brother had just had a heart attack and this worried her. Several members voiced consolation. This was followed by a consultation that this group was precious to members. This consultation was met with widespread agreement. The discussion then shifted back to talk of Thanksgiving and Christmas. This was consulted to with the notion that these festivals served also as markers of time, of time passing. They were anniversaries and as such they reminded people of past times, perhaps of childhood. There was also perhaps a connection to the fragility of life. Time was passing by. This group itself was close to its one-year anniversary.

This was followed by series of *homages* of gratitude to the lead female consultant with whom many of the participants had long-term relationships as a therapist both individually and in groups. Then a female member shared that she had a disturbing dream where there was a man poised to cut a turkey with a saw and a knife. This was followed by one member (the one who had shared her concern about her daughter) offering that she had stopped smoking for four months. After congratulating this lady, the group once again embarked on an avowal of the importance of the group to them and the necessity of a social life and sharing feelings. This was consulted to by sharing the idea that smoking was a way of avoiding feelings and that somehow the group was feeling more able to sustain, contain and express feelings.

Once again the group enlarged upon its deep admiration for and gratitude towards the lead female consultant. The lead female consultant wondered aloud why this was the case, beyond the fact that the gratitude was realistic, was some other end being served? The group continued in its praise and this was followed by a suggestion that perhaps the group was anxious about being in the role of helper and giver and was, for this reason, having all the helping and giving located in the lead female consultant. Although the anxiety that one might end up being carved up or eaten, like the turkey in the dream, was present in the consultants mind as a formulation, it was not included in the enunciation and was left as an unmade consultation. The bell was rung, indicating the end of the group.

Comments on Group 12:

Clive: One theme that seems to emerge is an anxiety about the intense emotions overflowing the group, either inundating it or leading to some unpleasant consequences. Some of these feelings seem to be gratitude and love. Even though groups frequently will form reactive feelings of love and gratitude as countercathexes to their hostility, this did not seem to be the case in this group. The almost unbearable countertransferential emotions of the consultants were of tenderness and love. The turkey dream perhaps offers an avenue of insights. Perhaps the anxiety is that if one becomes the object identified as the giver or helper, one might be eaten alive, carved up, torn to pieces. This would speak to a deep oral longing in the group. It is of potential interest that the brother of the two sisters who were visiting the group had, as his brother, a man who had murdered their father.

Di: Perhaps the group on some level held the fantasy that the group itself served as a kind of Thanksgiving and Christmas holiday. But this fantasy did not take away from the fact that things get eaten up (per the dream) and cut-up all over these holidays and that while on the surface thing seemed very festive— at any moment thing might go awry and get torn up and eaten away.

Thirteenth Group:

As usual, the consulting team met for thirty minutes before the start of the group to discuss their personal lives and relationships with a view to examining how this affected their approach to the task and the group of that day. Also this group discussed whatever contextual issues came to mind that might have an impact on the dynamics of the group that day. Among these were the following: C, one of the central members of the group had lost his mother two days previous. This was not part of general knowledge in the institution. Also there had been recent planning for the addition of a new 32 bed wing. This was deemed interesting given that a prominent theme in the group had been concern over the viability of the institution. In addition, one member, D, a female, had been suddenly and inaccurately "diagnosed" as "mentally retarded" by one of the staff who was not qualified to render such a decision. This had been very upsetting. A new show was also in the works, "Music Man."

The group commenced with 20 members, 10 male and 10 female. C initiated with the announcement of his mother's death. This was followed by an outpouring of condolences which C accepted. Then several other members shared their experiences of loss of family members. This was at times quite pained as the many aspects of grief were experienced in the group. Members wondered at the suffering of the last moments of their loved ones. They expressed remorse over things they felt they could have or should have done. There was confusion, loss, sadness and grief. The consultants offered up that the group was doing just this, namely examining the flood of mixed feelings that come with the experience of grief.

The group then seemed to veer toward ways in which they had attempted to overcome the grief. For some it was belief in God, for others it was happy images of loved ones that they treasured and used for comfort. A consultant pointed out that perhaps this group in and of itself was a source of comfort and healing. No member rejected this idea.

The group then focused its attention on Dr. Brad, the youngest male consultant and applauded him for his recent licensure and professional advancement. There was much tender smiling enjoyment of this. The other consultants wondered if there was a fantasy that Brad was a son who had been successful and if they felt some satisfaction in participating in this success. This set of thoughts and feelings instilled hope and purpose in the context of loss.

The group continued with members sharing experiences of hope and demoralization, of having faced challenges that crushed them and then others sharing methods they had found for overcoming hopelessness. This theme was reflected back by the consultants with the additional notion that perhaps this group played some role in hopefulness.

Comments on Group 13:

Clive: In many ways, this group could be seen as a "grief and loss group" and it seemed to serve that function for the members. As such, there is not much to distinguish it as a Tavistock style of group. Perhaps the only things that do this are the references to the group as a whole and the displacement of affect and fantasies onto Dr. Brad. These, while small differences, are believed to be very significant as they tie the concerns of group members to the here and now context of the group in which they are currently participating.

Di: Perhaps while members took joy in Dr. Brad's licensure there was also some envy. Perhaps this envy if it existed under the surface of the group dynamics stemmed from opportunities lost by other group members. Concurrently, Brad's licensure could be seen as an accomplishment of the group-as-a-whole--that his accomplishment had licensed the group to continue on the process of the work of the group. His licensure also offered hope (the birth of a new psychologist) in the face of so much loss. In some sense had the group midwifed Brad's birth although this consultation was not made.

Brad: I agree, since I was a "student" there before. It is as if the group moved from a "student" to being an "expert" on the group.

Fourteenth Group:

The group was comprised of 12 females and 8 males. There were three consultants; a younger male and a senior male and female. As soon as the group began, MB, a new member started singing quite loudly "Rockabye baby on the tree top..." While this was going on and the rest of the group seemed to ignore it, C started talking about the loss of his mother, sharing how he had begun to work through the loss and was utilizing an image of a woman he loved as a way of dealing with the loss. MB continued to sing, on and off, but vociferously, throughout this.

At this the consultant opined that the group-as-a-whole was coping with loss and that this was being talked about by C and sung about by MB. When one lost a loved one, it was as if one had been dropped from a great height. Perhaps there was a hope that the group would provide holding. The group seemed to accept this idea and continued to talk, offering more condolences to C. The feelings of kindness and empathy in the group seemed to mount.

At this point the male member seated next to the senior male consultant got up and walked out the room. At this MB said, "There he goes! He won't be back." and, "My! There are a lot of people in here!"

This sequence was consulted to with "The group seems to be anxious about making contact and loss." This was followed by several other members sharing how their mothers and others had died.

At this the senior male consultant noted that there were several individuals outside the periphery of the group. Two were wandering back and forth rhythmically and three were seated at some distance from the group circle. This was consulted to as manifesting the group-as-a-whole anxiety about belonging, about joining, about making contact because to make contact might entail loss.

At this one member who had been silent thus far shared that she had recently lost her mother to cancer. She cried and the group responded very kindly, especially when the female member shared that she felt alone and had no friends. This was followed by several offers of support and friendship. Then the conversation drifted off to other topics and it seemed as though the member had been abandoned.

At this there was a consultation that the group was full of kindness but perhaps there was an anxiety in accepting the kindness, since this would lead to close contact and dependency which opened up the risk of deepened loss of a valued relationship.

This was followed by two members, who frequently took up this role, "sermonizing," expounding on their recovery from alcoholism thanks to the intercession of the Almighty and sharing their ideas on the importance of sharing. The aim of these, it seemed, was to induce a calmer state in members.

Although this last was not consulted to, the female consultant shared that she found it interesting that the member who was talking about not having any friends did so while holding the hand of the member to her left. This was acknowledged by the group and the member further shared her feelings over the loss of her mother.

Comments on Group 14:

Clive: This group shows in an important way how the everyday discourse of the group can be integrated, in a consultation, with the "psychoticlike" discourse of a person with a diagnosis of severe mental illness. There are a number of interesting aspects of this phenomenon. First, it is seen that the member who was seeming to babble meaningless phrases and ditties was, when viewed from a binocular perspective (Bion, 1978), right on the money in her comments on the group. In fact, the very themes that she was speaking about formed the content of the rest of the group and led to a dramatic deepening of the feelings in the group and in specific members. Secondly, we see how the "patient with the severe diagnosis" calmed down almost as soon as the interpretation acknowledging her utterances was delivered. This phenomenon happened twice in the session. It suggests a way of listening to "psychotic" discourse such that it has the effect of joining the individual with the discourse of the group. This validation calms the patient.

Di: It's interesting that the group started with the song "Rock a Bye Baby". Perhaps there was the fantasy that the group was like a cradle holding painful feelings of grief and loss among other things—and the concern that it would fall. In the song the baby does fall out of the cradle But this group did not fall as the baby does in the song and solidly held the discourse both psychotic and other for the members of the group.

Fifteenth Group:

Twenty-one members were present, nine males and twelve females. In addition there were eight graduate student observers who sat outside the circle of the group. There were three consultants, two male and one female.

The discussion focused in the beginning on the warmer weather, approaching Easter and its meaning. It was also acknowledged that this was the fourteenth convening of this group. In response to this, a consultation was made regarding the rhythm of time, of renewal, of time markers and of hopes for rebirth.

In response to this, a female African American member spoke about her visions and visits she had received from the spirits. At the same time an announcement came over the loudspeaker that the church meeting would be held in the small dining room. This was consulted to with the observation that although the church meeting was elsewhere it felt as though a church meeting was taking place here.

Following this the group discussed anxiety over future funding of the institution. The African American member announced that she had invented the cell phone and franchising. This was followed by a member sharing her experiences in battling her alcoholism.

Then a male member asked the older male consultant, "Isn't it sometimes good to give things up?"

All of this was consulted to as if the group was attempting to cope with helplessness and powerlessness—powerlessness inside the self, in the group and in the wider world.

After this a middle aged white male, G, said that he had finally been able to piece together his thoughts. He had been feeling quite scattered thus far in the session. He went on to talk about the importance of hope and how he managed to achieve a sense of hope in the small pleasurable anticipations he felt, in addition to the medications. Another member added that it was also a matter of will—of setting one's mind to doing things.

The consultation was made that G had helped lift a sense of depression in the group through his speech and that talk could have an effect on moods just as powerful as medications.

This was followed by a younger male who had never spoken in the group raising his hand and speaking for the first time. He spoke about the importance in life of taking a small risk every now and then, that this was very important to do if you wanted to feel better. At this another member agreed and said it was also important to make plans. At this a male member got up off his chair and moved it so a female member could leave the group. As he did so he made quite a noise and the top of his butt showed above his beltline. G said out loud that this was very rude to make that much noise while someone else was talking. At this the group ended.

Comments on Group 15:

Clive: The last exchange is significant insofar as it is the first outright statement involving some degree of hostility. Even though it was not followed through on, it probably will manifest itself in some form of content or other in upcoming groups. We also see in this group an example of "psychoticlike" utterances being quite connected to the manifest content.

Di: I ponder if the angry outburst at the woman leaving by the man in the group might reflect in some part anger that the group was ending—a type of fight/flight response. The fact that his butt was showing brings up images of mooning the group —perhaps hostility towards the group as a whole.

Brad: This continues to show the "regulation" component of executive functioning. This is especially interesting to see this approach to neuropsychology in the context of functioning in a large group.

Sixteenth Group:

This group was comprised of 24 members, eight male, sixteen female. Two male consultants and one female consultant were in the group as were two student observers. One of the students had a dog and had been using the dog in pet facilitated psychotherapy at the institution. There had not been a group for some six weeks.

The group started with M stating that she felt very alone and not included and that her mother did not feed her enough. The other members of the group responded to this with talk of keeping a positive attitude and looking on the bright side of things. After a short while the dog padded across the room and rubbed against M who responded by petting the dog. A consultant mentioned that the dog seemed to respond to feelings in the group more than did the humans.

At this a male member opened up and stated that he had lost 12 people who were dear to him in the past year. He was devastated by this loss. Other members joined him in their litany of losses and their responses to it. All of the aspects of grief were touched upon—sadness, depression, despair, emptiness, pointlessness, relief, guilt, anger—each member adding to the facets of this complex experience. This was simply pointed to by one of the consultants and the sharing continued. Many members got in touch with a deep sense of loss. There was also a good deal of reaching out to each other and offering of company and companionship.

Eventually one member stated that it was difficult to develop skills if one did not persist. This seemed to cue the group into a series of attempts of flight from grief—shopping, going to Starbucks, hobbies and so on. Since this seemed to leave many members of the group awash in their feelings, a consultant pointed out that there seemed to be a wish to quickly make the grief go away, but perhaps this did not work since hearts that are broken seem to want to mend in their own sweet time. This seemed to be on target and the group resumed its sharing of sorrowful losses. In addition, one member who had Tay-Sachs disease shared that often people died a psychological death before they died an actual physical death. This was not responded to but seemed quite telling. Throughout all of this, the dog, which was on a long leash was making rounds of members and they petted him in turn.

About one minute from the end, a member said, "It is like Phantom of the Opera!" She then got quite afraid, asking, "Did I say something wrong?" A consultant replied that no, she had not said anything wrong, that, in fact, she might have said something quite helpful. It was just that we needed a few more sentences so we could connect what she had said to the group as it was operating in the here and now. The member shared and a few connections were initiated—connections about, death, love, masks and beauty that seemed to have potential meaning for the group process. At this the group ended.

Comments on Group 16:

Clive: This group demonstrates being well-attuned to the emotional life of the group. The group seemed mostly to function as a "grief group," with members sharing and, for the most part, listening to the sorrowful experiences of others. This did seem to have tremendous utility for the group although it was hard at times for the consultants to bear. It also seemed hard for the group to bear as demonstrated by their attempted "flight" from the painful feelings. However, even one consultation was enough to get them back to what seemed to be deeper work of sharing and coping with the feelings of loss. It is important to note that two members of the institution had died in the last two weeks.

Di: It does seem like the extreme losses that members have experienced are frequently mentioned in the group experience and that the group does serve as a container for processing these feelings. At the same time the frequent talk of loss may underlie some unconscious fear that the group might end. The group serves as a mother, parent, friend, place of refuge. "What if it might disappear?" This relates back to the fear of the institution closing due to spending cuts. The woman who complained that her mother didn't feed her enough at the beginning of the group might speak to the fear that the group might not provide a good enough feed during this session.

Seventeenth Group:

This group took place one week after Father's Day. A new member who was an Egyptian Coptic had been admitted to the institution. J had been hospitalized the previous week and had been under-prescribed medications. It seemed the doctors had forgotten to take into account his weight.

The group started with one of the students resonating a Tibetan singing bowl. There were 18 members; 6 male, 12 female. Membership fluctuated throughout with many departures and arrivals.

P, who was a new member of the group, asked at the outset, "What is the theme?" He was informed that it was an open discussion, we could talk about whatever we wanted.

G, who often takes the lead asked if anyone had summer goals they wished to achieve. The group then discussed food, family meetings and the Fall elections. There was a long discussion of different types of food, especially Chinese food. People said they missed different foods.

The consultation to this was that the new members in the group offered a smorgasbord, and that in addition there was a mixture of excitement and anxiety at the changes. This anxiety had something to do with sadness and relief at the loss of the old.

The group responded to this by continuing to talk about food, about the merits of different restaurants. Someone outside of the circle, but in the room, was talking loudly and it made it difficult to focus on the group's conversation. A consultant mentioned this, linking this difficulty in connecting thoughts to the anxiety of change. Perhaps there were inner voices that also interfered with keeping on track.

C took up his usual role of offering something of a sermon and it had its usual calming and somewhat numbing effect on the group. It was something of a relief to hear his measured tones. The sermon was on the importance of hope. People listened attentively.

Then P, the new member, offered to share his knowledge on chants stating that they could be used to calm oneself down and help focus. He demonstrated one and then asked others to join him. He started chanting--"EEEEEWWWW".

In response to this one member asked if these chants came from a cult. Another member brought up the topic of the KKK. Another member mentioned that she used her rosary to calm herself down. The atmosphere in the room felt a tad paranoid. The consultation to this was, "Someone has just brought something quite different into the room. They themselves are a new member and the group is anxious and unsure how to deal with this difference. How does one introduce new ideas into this group?"

The group then spoke about terrorism. A member repeated the story of her struggles with alcoholism and the problems it had created for her. The group then moved on to talk of the tornadoes that had hit the area in recent weeks. The consultation was made that while there had been physical tornadoes in the outside world, there had been psychological, psychosocial, emotional tornadoes in this room.

At this the group ended. The pitch of anxiety in the room was moderately high.

Comments on Group 17:

Di: The presence of both the Coptic Christian and the new member who did the unusual chanting may have contributed to the paranoia in the room. Simultaneously the group may have been experimenting with ways to calm itself down (chanting and Tibetan bowl).

Brad: I would also say that while most individuals' brains might see this introduction of a new person and activity as "novel and curious," this group mentality with its background and traumatic history, viewed it more as a threat due to deeper "wirings" and programs in the brain.

Eighteenth Group:

This group was comprised of 18 members, 10 female and 8 male. There was one student observer and three consultants, two male, one female. Significant in the adaptive context of this group is the fact that there had not been a meeting for three months. This was due to work overload, vacations and job changes amongst the consultant team.

A female member stated that she had some contact with her son but that she missed him and was concerned since was in the military. To this another member stated, "At least you have some family."

This was followed by G speaking to his feeling of well-being in this group and the institution. It gave him the opportunity to help others and to entertain in the shows that they put on. This sentiment was echoed by another member. This was consulted to as referring to the three month break in the meetings of this group. It was nice to be close to one's family, but if they were not available then one relied on this group more and the satisfactions it might have to offer.

At this a member turned to Consultant H and said, "Yes, where were you Dr. H?" And then he very quickly helped out by saying, "It's OK. I know people need to take a break." It felt as though there was an emotion of resentment and hurt that was immediately patched over by understanding.

However, the group continued on the theme of gratitude for the group, even citing C's frequent reference to "We need each other" in his perorations. This was consulted to with, "It is as though the group did have some feelings about the gap in the meetings but that the consultant has been forgiven for leaving, even welcomed back."

This led to a series of stories. G said, "Oh don't worry, Dr. H. We have managed to get rid of some bad people." Then there was a series of stories of bad people--nurses, administrators, psychiatrists--who had been mean and who had left, often with the feeling that the group had something to do with their departure.

This was not consulted to. However, it was followed by a series of members sharing very sad and painful stories of disruptions in their lives extending often over decades. These involved being forced from homes and placed in various institutions--some very bad, some not so bad and ending up in this one which they experienced as good.

This was consulted to as relating to the groups' concerns about continuity and breaks in the continuity of one's relationships and the resulting sense of instability, of insecurity.

At this, an older male suffering from Parkinson's Disease mumbled incoherently. The student leaned forward to hear what was said and translated. "He said, 'Thank you for coming.'" This led to a few more comments on gratitude for the group and the institution. Then the group, in the midst of these feelings, ended.

Comments on Group 18:

Di: The group experienced gratitude that the large group had once again assembled. Talk of getting rid of bad people may have resonated with the fact that after three months the "good" group was held—fantasies that it could have been gotten rid of may have been floating in the group's unconscious. But the group had not been terminated and that was good for the members.

Nineteenth Group:

The group was comprised of 18 members, 10 female and 8 male. There were three consultants; Brad, Maureen(an intern) and Dr H. There was a volunteer, Mr. B, also present. Significantly, this was the first group where Dr. Di was absent.

C commenced, as is so often the case with something of a "sermon" on the importance of trust. He linked this with the changes in the staff at the home recently and how this was difficult to adjust to.

This was followed by M, again as she often does, expressing gratitude for the home. She had been other places and this was by far better than any of them. As this was going on, the intercom "spoke" summoning members of the institution to social services. Everybody stopped and listened to this list as if they might be called from the group. Then there was an announcement that the church group would be shortly meeting in the very room we were occupying.

This was consulted to in a reflective way by stating that there seemed to be a good deal of anxiety in the group about the staff changes and that this might, perhaps, be linked to hope as trust and hope were often intertwined. Also the two intercom interruptions were addressed as boundary violations and that this was disruptive to thought and contacting one another. This was met with C mentioning that they now had to wait a lot longer for coffee than before, and felt somewhat ignored by the new staff.

And how the announcements made it difficult to connect one's thoughts together and make contact with one another. This was frustrating.

Another member mentioned that she had been told that she would have to attend certain groups and that she did not have a choice and that if she did not attend the groups she would be ejected from the home. This was stated with a good deal of anger. Someone also mentioned that there seemed to be fewer groups in the home than before. This was consulted to that these comments might relate to the fact that it had been some five months since the last meeting. Also it was consulted to that not being able to string one's thoughts together and not being able to make contact with others was not only frustrating, it was also frightening.

The members then mentioned that there was the possibility that people you trusted could let you down and leave you in the lurch, and this was very painful. At this a member asked "Where is Dr. Di? What is she doing?" Someone else wondered if it was true that Dr. Di was leaving the home. This led to a good deal of consternation, with someone uttering, "What are you talking about?" This was reflected back as the group having to cope with the change in staff, the gap in the groups and feelings and fantasies about the departure of Dr. Di, upon whom there was a considerable dependence.

At this M reiterated her story of struggling with alcoholism and her gratitude for the home. There was continuing talk of concern for Dr. Di and this moved on to a concern for the longevity of the home. This led to a discussion of terrorism and the fears they had of this. This was consulted to as being a reference to the dislocation and anxiety they felt in the home—the change of staff, anxieties about its funding, Dr. Di—and that terrorism resulted from such dislocations. They were not terrorists but they felt some of the dislocations terrorists feel. This was not accepted and there was a disavowal of their own terroristic sentiments. Instead there was a terror in them and a fear of being attacked, perhaps persecuted. This was consulted to as the group almost pleading for safety from the terrorists, "Please do not let them come near here!"

This consultation was accepted. Then a member who had not spoken up until that point mentioned the movie "Billy Jack." She had mentioned it in a group and had not expected the new, younger staff to know about it, but they did and she was gratified by this. This was consulted to as containing a lot of the themes of the group—being "Native American" and looked down upon, being penned up in a reservation, overcoming the odds—

At this, the group ended.

Comments on Group 19:

Clive: This group has some very obvious themes—the reaction to the adaptive context of the missed months and the linkage of this with the change in staff and the uncertainties of Dr. Di and the future of the home. It is also linked perhaps to the primary elections going on at the time in the country which are quite heated and "symptomatic." The theme of "residential insecurity," deterritorialization or refugee status is in this group and is of a global concern. It is also related to the theme of terrorism.

Also of interest is the apparent utility of the model of community found in Hazell and Kiel (2016) regarding the co-ordination of the spheres of the political, managerial and community. A large group meeting such as this can facilitate such a co-ordination.

Di: Group members have histories of being let down. The theme of worries about the longevity of the home, and perhaps the group, bled into the groups unconscious. They would be let down again this time by the group. Perhaps the fantasy that Dr. Di had been taken down by a "terrorist group," or that a terrorist existed in the group who had taken her down floated in the unconscious of the group.

Brad: These events could have triggered, consciously and unconsciously autobiographical and episodic memories that may have occurred in very early life, that is, pre-verbally.

Twentieth Group:

This group was comprised of 19 members, 9 male and 10 female. There were two male consultants and one student observer.

The group started on a familiar theme, that of gratitude for the institution in which it was housed. This was followed by statements regarding the nurse assistants who were sometimes not as attentive as they ought to be. This was followed by statements to the effect that, on balance, the home was a good place to be, much better than others with which some members were familiar. At this point one male member abruptly and forcefully said, "I want to get out of here." Others were curious as to what he meant and he clarified that he wanted to have the freedoms of the outside world. This was countered by several members stating that they felt very anxious about the outside world and did not think they would be able to cope there.

This was consulted to (rather abstractly) with the idea that the group was dealing with boundaries, boundaries between staff and residents and boundaries between residents and the outside world. In addition, the consultants and the staff went back and forth over this boundary, inhabiting both the institution and the outside world.

At this some members spoke about the practical difficulties encountered in trying to bridge between the world inside the institution and the outside world. They needed a van with a lift for people in wheelchairs and the state regulators had placed limitations on what staff were able to do in the way of taking residents out to, say, a coffee house. Two members stated that they sorely missed their work and they felt especially limited in their action-space. In addition, it was noted that Dr Di could not take people out on spontaneous trips any more. This led into the voicing of anxieties over the future of the institution itself. This was consulted to quite straightforwardly that the special regard for Dr. Di coupled with the limitations she seemed to be placed under led to deep feelings of vulnerability.

This was followed by the group expressing deep feelings of gratitude towards Dr. Di. Suddenly, someone asked, "Where is she now?" This was followed by a flurry of side conversations in the group and anxiety in the group seemed to peak at this point. This was consulted to with the recognition of the spike in the anxiety and the consultant wondering if the group felt that perhaps the demands they had placed on Dr. Di had done something to her. There was some confirmation of this idea as members expressed concern over Dr. Di's well-being. Then the conversation shifted back to the need to work and the problems in engaging in something like work in the institution.

A consultant then said that Freud had said that life was all about love and work and that there were many different types of work, even what was going on in the group right now was a sort of work. In addition there appeared to be realistic practical problems to be addressed in the question of how to get to work?

The group then started to discuss general issues and problems in getting along with other people and the consultant remarked that this too was a type of work, problem solving about relationships.

Comments on Group 20:

Clive: This group is interesting in that the issue of the outside world and related topics, e.g. work and transport, has not come up before so explicitly. In addition there was a distinctly "practical" feel to a lot of these concerns. One felt as though some managers should be present at several points throughout the meeting. One could conceptualize the group concern as a dialectic between "Work/expansion and Retreat/contraction."

Of additional interest is the reparative concern regarding what might have befallen Dr. Di. Had she been damaged by the "greed" of the members? This has a distinctly Kleinian/ reparative feel to it. As such, it could be a positive sign, especially since the group seemed to cope with these feelings quite well.

Di: The group had a distinct flavor of paranoia. Fears of

not being recognized. Fears that Dr. Di might have crossed the boundary between the home and the outside world and only to leave permanently.

Twenty-First Group :

The group consisted of 19 members, 5 males and 14 females. There were three consultants, 2 male and 1 female. Also present was one male volunteer in an observer role.

The group started talking about the presidential election. G emphasized that it was important that members vote for the pro-mental health candidate. This lead to a discussion centered on one female member who was a resident alien who could not vote and others who might not be registered to vote.

This led to the consultation that perhaps members were concerned about the legitimacy of their voice in the group. "Will my voice be registered?" In addition it was pointed out that the word "suffrage" was derived from the word "shard" or "chip" of pottery with which the vote was cast. Perhaps people were concerned about how to "chip in." This was followed by a discussion about who one could vote for. "Who would speak for you? Who would represent you?" The consensus seemed to be that nobody was perfect.

This was consulted to as being an interesting discussion about the problems of representation in groups. The group was asking, "Who could represent me?" To this was added the question, "How can I even represent myself?"

This was followed by a concerned discussion of wars—most of the wars of the twentieth and early twenty-first century were touched upon. Several members made references to friends and family members who had been hurt or killed by the wars. This was consulted to with a comment pointing out that perhaps members of this group had "been through the wars."

This consultation was followed by a discussion of the various traumas that members had been through—loss of relatives, poverty and the trauma of warfare.

This led to the consultation that the group had perhaps drawn links in this discussion between politics and trauma, perhaps through inter-generational trauma.

This was followed by a discussion of all the bad things happening in the world and this evolved into a discussion of Hitler. A member pointed out with some vehemence that Hitler was not German, but Austrian. To this was offered the consultation that it was as if the group wanted to locate the badness somewhere else, outside the group, perhaps in Austria.

This led to a good deal of anxiety in the group with several conversations going on at the same time. Eventually, M gained the attention of all as she divulged that her father was a member of the Hitler Youth. This was followed by a consultation that it appeared that the group was struggling with the complexity of things. There were even very complex mixtures of people in this group, people with very complex inter-generational histories.

To this there followed a comment from X, who had been silent up until this point. He stated that he would like the group to be goal oriented, more like a business meeting in future. At this, a member started to offer the Lord's Prayer and this felt like a plea for protection from evil. The group ended at this point.

Comments on Group 21:

Clive: It is interesting in this group how there is such a focus on the outside world of politics. This leads to a discussion of the problems of representation and this in turn leads to a discussion of trauma. This, in turn leads back to a discussion of political evil and terror. These connections are tantalizing indeed.

Di: The notion that one might not have a vote my link to the fact that so many of the members of the group have not been heard—had a voice. And while the greater political arena is important the idea that one would have a vote/voice in the community of the group seems to play out. The speaking of the Lord's Prayer at the end of the group speaks to the groups fear that the group along cannot protect them. True protection must come from an outside godlike force.

Brad: This experience also stimulated the clients neurocognitively by connecting positive emotions and memory which were eventually attributed to the overall group experience rendering more rewarding and reinforcing memories of the group.

IX

Conclusion

The Tavistock method's capacity to be applied to a group of severely mentally ill institutionalized individuals seems remarkable. The fact that this can be done in a large group format speaks to the resilience of the members to maintain a work group even though the pressures of the basic assumption dimension of group interaction might easily seep through the minds of individuals with compromised egos and at times overtly operating psychotic processes. And yet, these individuals seemed to thrive on the group process showing great gratitude for the community spirit these groups appeared to foster. It is possible that the psychotic core of many of these individuals allows them to view the world with a more binocular perspective than the an individual not identified as severely mentally ill who might tend towards a more "myopic" view.This allows them to be more open and willing to take in the highly metaphorical quality of the "group as a whole" interpretations. Results support those obtained by Czochara, Hazell, Semmelhack & Ende (2017) that in the large group format members appeared to show reduced anxiety regarding participating in the large group. The group was well attended by a core group of people. Also, a relatively stable set of growth promoting norms such as listening and openness to experience were understood and experienced by group members.

References

Adorno, T. (1983). *The Authoritarian Personality*, New York, W.W. Norton.

_____, (2001). *The Culture Industry: Selected Essays on Mass Culture*, London, Routledge.

_____, (2006) *Minima Moralia*, London, Verso.

Agamben, G. (1993). *The Coming Community*, Minneapolis, University of Minnesota Press.

Agazarian, Y and Peters, R. (1995). *The Visible and Invisible Group*, London, Karnac.

AI (2001) Motion Picture, Dir. Steven Speilberg, Amblin Entertainment, USA.

Ainsworth, M. (2015) *Patterns of Attachment*, London, Routledge.

Alford, C. (2002). *Whistleblowers: Broken Lives and Organizational Power*, Cornell University Press.

Althusser, L. (2014) *On the Reproduction of Capitalism: Ideology and Ideological State Apparatuses*, London, Verso.

Allport, G. (1955) *Becoming, Basic Considerations for a Psychology of Personality*, New Haven, CT, Yale.

Analyze That, 2002, Village Roadshow Pictures, Warner Brothers, Directed by Harold Ramis, United States

Argyris, C. and Schon, D. (1995). *Organizational Learning II: Theory, Method and Practice*. Upper Saddle River, NJ, FT Press.

Astruc, R. (2015) *Nous? L'aspiration a la communaute et les arts: post-scriptum par Jean-Luc Nancy*, RKI Publications, Berlin.

Atwood, M. (1989) *The Handmaid's Tale*, New York, Fawcett Crest.

Aulagnier, P. (2001) *The Violence of Interpretation*, London, Routledge.

Austin, J. (1953). "How to Talk—some simple ways," *Proceedings of the Aristotelian Society*, 53: 227–246.

Baburoglu, O. (1988) "Vortical Environment The Fifth in the Emery Trist Levels of Organizational Environment " *Human Relations* also in the 3rd volume of Tavistock Anthology, (1997 Eds.: E.Trist, et.al.).

Bachmann-Medick, D. (2016) *Cultural Turns*, Berlin, de Gruyter.

Bacon, F. (2000) *Francis Bacon: The New Organon*, Cambridge, Cambridge University Press.

Badiou, A. (2013). *Being and Event, London*, Bloomsbury Academic.

Bahktin, M. (1982). *The Dialogic Imagination: Four Essays*, Austin, TX, University of Texas Press.

Balint, M. (1955) Friendly Expanses, Horrid Empty Places, *International Journal of Psychoanalysis*, 36: 225-241.

_____ (1979) *The Basic Fault:Therapeutic Aspects of Regression*, New York, Brunner /Mazel.

Barkham, M., Guthrie, E., Hardy, G. and Margison, F. (2017) *Psychodynamic Interpersonal Therapy,*Singapore, Sage.

Baron-Cohen, S. (2012). *The Science of Evil: On Empathy and the Origins of Cruelty*, New York, Basic Books.

Baron-Cohen, S. 2015, January 30th (Video File) *"Harvard Commencement 2004"* https://youtu.be/GUCy75CA3Aw

Bataille, G. (1991). *The Accursed Share: an Essay on General Economy, Vol1: Consumption*, Cambridge, MA, Zone Books.

Baudrillard, J. (1994) *Simulacra and Simulation (The Body in Theory: Histories of Cultural Materialism)*, Ann Arbor, MI. University of Michigan Press.

Becker, E. (1997). *The Denial of Death*, New York, Free Press.

Beckett, S. (1982). *Waiting for Godot: A Tragicomedy in Two Acts*, New York, Grove Press.

Benjamin, W. (2008) *The Work of Art in an Age of Mechanical Reproduction*, Penguin, London.

Berger, P. and Luckman, T. (1967) *The Social Construction of Reality: A Treatise on the Sociology of Knowledge*, New York, Anchor.

Berman, M. (1988). *All That is Solid Melts into Air: The Experience of Modernity*, New York, Penguin.

Berne, E. (1996). *Games People Play: The Basic Handbook of Transactional Analysis*, New York, Ballantine Books.

Bertalanffy, L. (1969). *General System Theory: Foundation, Development, Application*, New York, Braziller.

Betjeman, J. (1937) "Slough", in *Continual Dew*, J. Murray, London.

Bicentennial Man (1999) Motion Picture, Dir. Chris Colombus, Touchstone Pictures, USA.

Bion, W.R. (1959). "Attacks on Linking," *Second Thoughts*, London, Heinemann.

_____, (1961). *Experiences in Groups*, London, Tavistock.

_____ (1978). *Seven Servants: Four Works*, New York, Jason Aronson.

_____(1997). *Taming Wild Thoughts*, London, Karnac Books.

Birdwhistell, R. (1970). *Kinesics and Context*, Philadelphia, PA, University of Pennsylvania Press.

Blade Runner, (1982) (Motion Picture, Directed by Ridley Scott, Warner Bros. USA.

Blake, W. (1997) *Jerusalem (The Illuminated Books of William Blake)*,Princeton, New Jersey, Princeton University Press.

Blaikie, P. (2003) *At Risk: Natural Hazards, People's Vulnerability and Disasters*, London, Routledge.

_____, (2018) *The Political Economy of Soil Erosion in Developing Countries*,London, Routledge.

Blanchot, M. (1988). *The Unavowable Community*, Barrytown, NY, Station Hill Press.

_____, (1998). *Death Sentence*, Barrytown, NY, Station Hill Books.

Bourdieu, P. (1994) *The Field of Cultural Production*, New York, Columbia University Press.

Bowlby, J. (1952). *Maternal care and mental health : a report prepared on behalf of the World Health Organization as a contribution to the United Nations programme for the welfare of homeless children.* Geneva: World Health Organization.

_____, (1976) *Separation: Anxiety and Anger, Volume Two*, New York, Basic Books

_____, (1982) *Loss: Sadness and Depression, Volume Three*, New York, Basic Books..

_____(1983) *Attachment: Attachment and Loss Volume One*, New York, Basic Books.

Brand, S. (1971) *The Last Whole Earth Catalog*, New York, Random House.

Breuer, J. and Freud, S. (2000/1885). *Studies on Hysteria*, New York, Basic Books. (reissue edition).

Briggs-Myers, I. (1995) *Gifts Differing*, Sunnyvale, CA. CPP.

Bristow, D. (2018) *Joyce and Lacan*, London, Routledge.

Brown, Q. (1967) *At the Winter Sea ice Camp* (Documentary Video) Netsilik Eskimo Series, Dir. Quentin Brown, Documentary Educational Resources, USA

Buber, M. (1958) *I and Thou*, Scribners, New York.

Burke, K. (1945). *A Grammar of Motives.*University of California Press.

Cannon, W. B. (1942). "Voodoo Death", *American Anthropologist,* 44. 1942. 169-181.

Carlin, G. (2008) *American bullshit truth politics,* Youtube Video, 2008.

Cervantes, M. (2018) *Don Quixote,* New York, Penguin.

Chapman, L. (2014). Neurobiologically Informed Trauma Therapy with Children and Adolescents, New York, Norton.

Chasseguet-Smirgel, J. (1985). *The Ego Ideal: A Psychoanalytic Essay on the Malady of the Ideal,* London, Free Association Books.

Chernobyl (2019) T.V. Series, Directed by Johan Renck, Warner Bros. USA.

The China Syndrome, (1979) Moving Picture, Directed by James Bridges, Columbia Pictures, USA.

Chodorow, N. (1991) *Feminism and Psychoanalytic Theory,* Hartford, CT. Yale University Press.

Clare, John. (2003) *I am,* New York, Farrar, Strauss and Giroux.

Clark, K. and Clark, M. (1947). *Racial identification and preference among negro children. Readings in Social Psychology.* New York: Holt, Rinehart, and Winston.

Clemens, J. and Grigg, R. (2006). Jacques Lacan and the Other Side of Psychoanalysis, Durham and London.

Clynes, M. (1989). *Sentics: The Touch of the Emotions,* New York, Prism Press Ltd.

Collingwood, R. G. (2014) *The Idea of History*, Eastford, CT, Martino Fine Books.

Colman, A. and Geller, W. (eds) (1985). *Group Relations Reader 2*, Washington, DC. A.K. Rice Institute.

Corvo-Lopez, R. (1999) *Self-Envy*, New York, Jason Aronson.

Csikszentmihalyi, M. (2008) *Flow: The Psychology of Optimal Experience*, New York, Harper.

Czochara, B., Semmelhack,D. and Hazell, C. (2016). "We Need Each Other," Adapting the Tavistock Method for Large Group Therapy for Adults with Severe Mental Illness, *International Journal of Psychosocial Rehabilitation*, Vol. 20.

Dabrowski, K., Kawczak, A., Piechowski, M. (1970) *Mental Growth through Positive Disintegration*, Gryf, London.

Dabrowski, K, Piechowski, M. (1977) *Theory of Emotional Development*, Dabor, Oceanside, New York.

Daruna, J. (2004). *Introduction to Psychoneuroimmunology*, Elsevier, Burlington, MA.

Debord, G. (2002) *The Society of the Spectacle*, Detroit, MI. Black and Red Books.

De Certeau, M. ((2011) *The Practice of Everyday Life*, Berkely, University of Claifornia Press.

Deleuze, G. and Guatttari, F. (1986) *Kafka: Toward a Minor Literature*, Minneapolis, University of Minnesota Press.

_____, (1987) *A Thousand Plateaus: Capitalism and Schizophrenia,* Minneapolis, University of Minnesota Press.

_____, (2009) *Anti-Oedipus: Capitalism and Schizophrenia,* London, Penguin.

De Loach, S. (2009). *The Institutional System Event (ISE): Design and management.* Unpublished Manuscript.

De Mare, P. (2011). From Hate through Dialogue to Culture in the Larger Group, Karnac.

Derrida, J. (1985) *Margins of Philosophy,* Chicago, University of Chicago Press

Devereux, G. (1951) *Reality and Dream: Psychotherapy of a Plains Indian,* New York, IUP.

_____,(1961) *Mojave Ethnopsychiatry and Suicide,* Washington, DC, US Government Printing Office.

_____, (1980) *Basic Problems of Ethnopsychiatry,* Chicago, University of Chicago Press.

Dewey, J. (1997). *Experience and Education,* New York, Free Press.

Diamond, J. (2011) *Collapse: How Societies Choose to Fail or Succeed,* New York, Penguin.

Dick, P. (2009) *The Philip K. Dick Collection: A Library of America Boxed Set,* New York, Library of America.

Donnay, D. (1997) E. K. Strong's Legacy and Beyond: 70 Years of the Strong Interest Inventory, *Career Development Quaterly,* 46: 12-22.

Down the Tracks, The Economist, (October 12th-18th, 2019) Vol. 433, No. 9164, London, U.K.

Dostoyevsky, F. (2002) *The Brothers Karamazov*, Farrar, Strauss and Giroux, New York.

DSM V, Diagnostic and Statistical Manual of Mental Disorders, 5th Edition, Washington, DC, American Psychiatric Association.

Eagleton, T. (2008). *Literary Theory: An Introduction*, Minneapolis, MN, University of Minnesota Press.

Edelson, M. (1970). *Sociotherapy and Psychotherapy*, Chicago, University of Chicago Press.

Ellenberger, H. (1981). *The Discovery of the Unconscious*, New York, Basic Books.

Ellul, J. (1967). *The Technological Society*, New York, Vintage Books.

Emery, F. and Trist, E. (1965), The Causal Texture of Organizational Environments, *Human Relations*, 18: 21-32.

Empson, W. (1966). *Seven Types of Ambiguity*, New York, New Directions.

Ende, L., Semmelhack, D., Hazell, C., Freeman, A. et al (2015) *The Interactive World of Severe Mental Illness: Case Histories of the U.S. Mental Health System*, New York, Routledge.

Endurance, (1998). Motion Picture, Dir. Leslie Woodhead, Walt Disney Pictures, USA.

Erikson, E. (1977) *Toys and Reasons*, New York, Norton.

_____, (1993a). *Childhood and Society*, New York, W.W. Norton and Company.

_____, (1993b). *Young Man Luther*, New York, W.W. Norton and Company.

_____, (1993c) *Ghandi's Truth*, New York, W.W. Norton and Company.

Evers, J. 2010, May 6th *"Excerpt from 'Lacan Parle' by Francoise Wolff"* (Video File) https://youtu.be/6aqGYYBwKbQ

Fairbairn, W.R.D. (1952). *Psychoanalytic Studies of the Personality*, London, Routledge.

Ferenczi, S. (1995). *The Clinical Diary of Sandor Ferenczi*, Cambridge, MA, Harvard University Press.

Feuerbach, L. (2013). *The Fiery Brook*, New York, Verso.

Fisher, J. *Body Oriented Trauma Therapy*, (video), Nevada City, CA. Cavalcade Productions Inc.

Fraser, J. (1958) *The Golden Bough: A Study in Magic and Religion*, New York, Macmillan.

French, J. and Raven, J. (1954) The Bases of Social Power, in *Studies in Social Power*, ed. Cartwright, D. pp 150-167, Michigan Institute for Social Research, Ann Arbor, MI.

Freud, A. (1965). *Normality and Pathology in Childhood*. New York: International Univ. Press.

_____, (1993) *The Ego and the Mechanisms of Defence*, London, Routledge.

Freud, S. (1900). *The Interpretation of Dreams, Standard Edition*, 4-5.

_____, (1901). *The Psychopathology of Everyday Life, Standard Edition*, 6.

_____, (1905). *Jokes and Their Relation to the Unconscious*, Standard Edition, 8.

_____, (1911). *Psychoanalytic notes on an Autobiographical Account of a case of Paranoia (Dementia Paranoides), Standard Edition. 12, 3.*

_____, (1912-13). *Totem and Taboo, Standard Edition, 13,1.*

_____, (1916-17). *Introductory Lectures on Psychoanalysis, Standard Edition, 15-16.*

_____, (1919). *The Uncanny,* Standard Edition, 17, 217-256.

_____, (1920) *Beyond the Pleasure Principle,* Standard Edition, VolXVII.

_____, (1921). *Group Psychology and the Analysis of the Ego, Standard Edition, 18.*

_____, (1925). *A Note upon the "Mystic Writing Pad".* Standard Edition, 19.

_____, (1927). *The Ego and the Id, Standard Edition, 19,3.*

_____, (1928). *The Future of an Illusion, Standard Edition, 21, 3.*

Foucault, M. (1980). *History of Sexuality, Volume 1,* Vintage

_____, (1995) *Discipline and Punish: The Birth of the Prison* .New York, Vintage.

Franzen, T. (2005). *Godel's Theorem, An Incomplete Guide to its Use and Abuse*, A.K. Peters, Wellesley, MA.

Fukuyama, F. F. (2006). *The End of History and the Last Man*, New York, Free Press

Fuller, B. (2008) *Operating Manual for Spaceship Earth*, Zurich, Lars Muller.

Ganzerain, R. (1989). *Object Relations Group Psychotherapy: Group as an Object, a Tool, and a Training Base*, New York, Guilford Press.

Gattaca, 1997, (Motion Picture) Directed by Andrew Niccol, Columbia Pictures, USA.

Gedo, J. and Goldberg, A. (1976). *Models of the Mind*, Chicago and London, University of Chicago Press.

Gell-Mann, M. (1995) *The Quark and the Jaguar*, Griffin, Chicago, IL.

Gervais, R. (2010) *Ricky Gervais at the Golden Globes, 2020*, Fire Films, Youtube Video, Pub. January 9th, 2020.

Gilligan, C. (2016) *In a Different Voice*, Cambridge, MA. Harvard University Press.

Gleick, J. (1987). *Chaos: Making a New Science*. Viking Publishing.

The Godfather (1972) Motion Picture, Dir. F.F. Coppola, Paramount, USA.

The Godfather 2 (1990) Motion Picture, Dir. F.F. Coppola, Paramount, USA.

Golding, W. (1972) *"Envoy Extraordinary"* in *"The Scorpion God"* New York, Harcourt, Brace and Jovanovitch,

_____, (2013) *Lord of the Flies*, Leesburg, VA. A and A Publishers.

Gordon, W. (1969). *Synectics: The Development of Creative Capacity*, New York, Collier-Macmillan.

Gould, L. (ed) (2006). *The Systems Psychodynamics of Organizations: Integrating the Group Relations Approach and Organizational Systems Perspective*, London, Karnac.

The Great Dictator, 1940, Charles Chaplin Film Corporation, Directed by Charlie Chaplin, USA.

Greenacre, P. (1971) *Emotional Growth*, New York, IUP.

Gregor, T. (1987) *Anxious Pleasures: The Sexual Lives of an Amazonian People*, Chicago, IL. University of Chicago Press.

Grossmann, D. (2009) *On Killing: The Psychological Cost of Learning to Kill in War and Society*, New York, Back Bay Books.

Grotstein, J. (1977). *Splitting and Projective Identification*, New York, Jason Aronson.

Guntrip, H. (1992). *Schizoid Phenomena, Object Relations and the Self*, London, Karnac.

Harmon-Jones, E. and Winkielman,P. (2007) *Social Neuroscience: Integrating Biological and Psychological Explanations of Social Behavior*, Guilford Press, New York.

Harrison, E. F. (1998). *The Managerial Decision-Making Process*, Cincinnati, OH, South Western College Pub.

Harrison, O. (2008). *Open Space Technology: A User's Guide, (3rd ed.)* Oakland, CA, Berret Kohler.

Harrison, T. (2000). *Bion, Rickman, Foulkes and the Northfield Experiments*, London, Jessica Kingsley.

Harvey, O.J., Hunt, D and Schroder, H. (1961) *Conceptual Systems and Personality Organization*, Wiley, New York.

Hazell, C. (1984). "Experienced Levels of Emptiness and Existential Concern with different Levels of Emotional Development and Profile of Values." *Psychological Reports*, 55, 967-76.

_____, (2003). *The Experience of Emptiness*, Bloomington, IN. AuthorHouse.

_____, (2005). *Imaginary Groups*, Bloomington, IN. Authorhouse.

_____, (2006). *Family Systems Activity Book*, Bloomington, IN. Authorhouse.

_____, (2009). *Alterity: The Experience of the Other*, Bloomington, IN. Authorhouse.

Hazell, C. and Perez, R. (2011). What Happens When You Touch the Body?: The Psychology of Body-Work. Bloomington, IN. Authorhouse.

Hazell, C. and Kiel, M. (2017) *The Tavistock Learning Group:Exploration Outside the Traditional Frame*, London, Routledge.

Hegel, G.W.F. (1977). *The Phenomenology of Spirit*, Oxford University Press.

Heidegger, M. (1994). *Hegel's Phenomenology of Spirit*, Bloomington and Indianapolis, Indiana University Press.

_____, (2008). *Being and Time*, New York, Harper Perennial.

_____, (2013). *The Question Concerning Technology and Other Essays*, New York, Harper.

Herman, J. (2015). *Trauma and Recovery*, New York, Basic Books.

Hersey, P. (2012) *Management of Organizational Behavior*, London, Pearson.

Hesse, H. (1949) *Magister Ludi (The Glass Bead Game)* Holt, Rinehart and Winston, New York.

Hoeller, S. (2012). The Gnostic Jung and the Seven Sermons to the Dead, Wheaton, IL, Quest Books.

Hofstede, G. (2010). *Cultures and Organizations*, New York, McGraw-Hill.

Hopper, E. (2003). *Traumatic Experience in the Unconscious Life of Groups: The Fourth Basic Assumption: Incohesion: Aggregation/ Massification or BaI:A/M*, London, Jessica Kingsley.

Horne, G. (2016) *The Counter Revolution of 1776: Slave Resistance and the Origins of the United States of America.* New York, NYU Press.

Hill, W. F. (1965). *Hill Interaction Matrix*, University of Southern California, Youth Study Center.

Hirschorn, L. (1990). *The Workplace Within*, Cambridge, MA, MIT Press.

Huizinga, J. (2014) *Homo Ludens:A Study of the Play-Element in Culture*, Eastford, CT. Martino Fine Books.

Huntington, S. (1996) *The Clash of Civilizations and the Remaking of World Order*, Simon and Schuster, New York.

Husserl, E. (2014) *Ideas for a pure phenomenology and phenomenological philosophy: First Book*. Indianapolis, Hackett.

Huxley, A. (2002) *Island*, New York, Harper Perrenial.

_____, (2006) *Brave New World*, New York, Harper Perrenial.

Hyde, S. 2013, October 5th, *"2070 Paradigm Shift"* (Video File) https://youtu.be/ 9cflCyyEA21

Jameson, F. (1981) *The Political Unconscious: Narrative as a Socially Symbolic Act*, Cornell University Press, Ithaca, NY.

Janet, P. (1889/1973). L'automatisme Psychologique: essai de psychologie experimentale sur les formes inferieures de l'activite humaine, Paris, Felix Alcan, 1889. Societe Pierre Janet/Payot, 1973.

Jason, L. (2013). *Principles of Social Change*. Oxford University Press.

Johnson, S. (2001). *Emergence: The Connected Lives of Ants, Brains, Software, Cities and Software*. Scribner.

Jones, M. (1968). *Beyond the Therapeutic Community*, London, Yale University Press.

_____(1976). *Maturation of the Therapeutic Community*, New York, Human Sciences Press.

Jourard, S. (1965) *The Transparent Self; Self-Disclosure and Well-Being*, New York, Van Nostrand.

_____,(1971) *Self-Disclosure: An Experimental Ana;lysis of the Transparent Self,* New York, Wiley Interscience.

Joy Luck Club, 1993, Hollywood Pictures, Directed by Wayne Wang, United States.

Joyce, J. (1999). *Finnegan's Wake,* New York, Penguin Classics.

Jung, C. G. (1970). Analytical Psychology: Its Theory and Practice (The Tavistock Lectures), Vintage.

_____, (1977). *Mysterium Coniunctionis,* Princeton, NJ, Princeton University Press.

Kafka, F. (1926a). *Das Schloss,* Munchen, Kurt Wolff Verlag.

_____, (1926b). *Der Prozess,* Berlin, Verlag die Schmeide.

_____, (1995) *The Complete Stories,* New York, Schocken.

_____, (2019) *Amerika,* New York, Penguin.

Kaplan, R (2012) *Revenge of Geography,* Random House, New York.

Kardiner, A. (1939) *The Individual and his Society,* New York, Columbia University Press.

Kant, E. (2008) *Critique of Pure Reason,*New York, Penguin.

Keats, J. (1899). The *Complete Poetical Works and Letters of John Keats,* Cambridge Edition, Boston, MA, Houghton, Mifflin and Company.

Kernberg, O. (1994). *Internal World and External Reality,* New York, Jason Aronson.

Khan, M. (1996). *The Privacy of the Self,* London, Maresfield Library, Karnac.

Kierkegaard, S. (1970). *Fear and Trembling.* Princeton University Press.

Klein, M. (1975). *Envy and Gratitude and Other Works 1946-1963,* New York, The Free Press.

Koestler, A. (1945). *Darkness at Noon,* New York, Macmillan.

_____, (1967). The Act of Creation, a Study of the Conscious and the Unconscious in Science and Art, New York, Dell.

Kohut, H. (1971). *The Analysis of the Self,* Chicago and London, University of Chicago Press.

_____, (1977). *The Restoration of the Self,* New York, IUP.

Kojeve, A. (1980). *Introduction to the Reading of Hegel: Lectures on the Phenomenology of Spirit,* Ithaca, NY, Cornell University Press

Kreeger, L. (ed) (1975). *The Large Group: Dynamics and Therapy,* London, Constable.

Kristeva, J. (1984). *Revolution in Poetic Language,* New York, Columbia University Press.

Kuhn, T. (1962) *The Structure of Scientific Revolutions, Chicago, University of Chicago Press.*

Lacan, J. (1981). *The Four Fundamental Concepts of Psychoanalysis,* New York, W.W. Norton and Company.

_____, (1997). *The Seminar of Jacques Lacan: The Psychoses,* New York, W.W. Norton and Company.

_____, (2007a). *The Seminar of Jacques Lacan: The Other Side of Psychoanalysis,* New York, W.W. Norton and Company.

_____, (2007b). *Ecrits: The First Complete Edition in English,* New York, W.W. Norton.

_____, (2018) *The Sinthome: The Seminar of Jacques Lacan, Book XXIII,* Cambridge, UK. Polity Press.

Laing, R.D. (1965). *The Divided Self: An Existential Study in Sanity and Madness,* London, Penguin.

Land of the Lost (2009) Motion Picture, Dir. Brad Siberling, Universal Pictures, USA.

Langs, R. (1979). *The Listening Process,* New York, Jason Aronson

Lansing, S. (2007) *Priests and Programmers:Technologies of Power in the Engineered Landscape of Bali,* Princeton, Princeton University Press.

Laplanche, J. (1999) *Essays on Otherness,* London, Routledge.

Laszlo, E. (1969) *System, Structure and Experience,* London, Routledge.

Lawrence, W.G. (2003). *Experiences in Social Dreaming,* London, Karnac.

LeBon, G. (2002). *The Crowd: A Study of the Popular Mind,* Mineola, NY, Dover Publications.

Lecky, P. (1969). *Self-Consistency: A Theory of Personality,* New York, Anchor Books.

Levinas, E. (1969). *Totality and Infinity*, Pittsburgh, PA, Duquesne University Press.

_____, (2005). *Humanism of the Other*, Champaign, IL, University of Illinois Press.

Levine, P. *Resolving Trauma in Psychotherapy: A Somatic Approach.* (video) Mill Valley, CA, Psychotherapy.net

_____, (2010). *In an Unspoken Voice: How the Body Releases Trauma and Restores Goodness*, Berkeley, CA, North Atlantic.

Levinson, H. (1972) *Organizational Diagnosis*, Cambridge, MA., Harvard University Press.

Liddick, G. (2011). *Oxford Handbook of Group Counseling.* Oxford University Press.

Lieberman, M. (2013). *Social: Why Our Brains are Wired to Connect,* New York, Random House.

Lilly, J (1968) *Programming and Metaprogramming in the Human Biocomputer,* Juklian Press, New York.

Lipgar, R. and Pines, M. (2002). *Building on Bion: Branches,* London, Jessica Kingsley.

Lorraine Schroeder, J. (2008). *The Four Lacanian Discourses Or Turning the Law Inside Out,* Abingdon, Oxon, UK, Birkbeck Law Press.

Lowen, A. (1972). *Depression and the Body,* New York, Penguin.

_____, (2003). *Fear of Life,* Alachua, FL, Bioenergetics Press.

_____, (2005). *Betrayal of the Body*, Alachua, FL, Bioenergetics Press.

_____, (2012). *The Language of the Body*, New York, The Alexander Lowen Foundation.

Machiavelli, N. (2015) *The Prince*, New York, Penguin.

Machin, A. and Dunbar, R. (2011) The Brain Opioid Theory of Social Attachment; a Review of the Evidence, *Behavior*, Vol148, No. 9/10 (2011) pp. 985-1025.

Madigan, S. (2010). *Narrative Therapy*, Washington, DC, American Psychological Association.

Mahler, M. (1975). The Psychological Birth of the Human Infant, New York, Basic Books.

Mamet, D. (1978) *The Water Engine and Mr. Happiness*, New York, Grove Press.

Marcuse, H. (1991). *One Dimensional Man: Studies in Ideology of Advanced Industrial Society*, Boston, MA, Beacon Press.

Masefield, J. (1944) "Cargoes" in Salt-Water Poems and Ballads, New York, Macmillan.

Marshall, T. (2015) *Prisoners of Geography*, Scribner, New York.

Marx, K. (1965)(Bottomore, T.B. and Fromm, E. eds.). *Marx's Concept of Man; Marx's Economic and Philosophic Manuscripts*, New York, Frederick Ungar.

_____, (1993) *Capital*, New York, Penguin.

M.A.S.H. (1972-1983) Television Series, Developed by Gelbart, L., Reynolds, G. and Metcalfe, B., 20th Television, USA.

Maslow, A. (2013). *A Theory of Human Motivation*, Eastford, CT, Martino Fine Books.

MaTeOWaN, 2018, April 30th "Tony Clifton Letterman 02/18/1982" (Video File) https://youtu.be/MOFzOXNTQFw

Matte-Blanco, I. (1981) *The Unconscious as Infinite Sets: An Essay in Bi-logic*, London, Routledge.

The Matrix (1999) Moving Picture, Directed by: The Wachowskis, Warner Bros. USA.

Mauss, M. (2000) *The Gift*, W.W. Norton, New York.

McGinn, R.E. (1990). *Science, Technology and Society*, New York, Pearson.

Mcluhan, M, Berkeley (1994). *Understanding Media: The Extensions of Man*, Berkeley, CA. Gingko Press.

_____, . (2001) *The Medium is the Massage*, Berkely, CA. Gingko Press.

_____, (2011) *The Gutenberg Galaxy*, Toronto, University of Toronto Press.

Meltzer, D, (1973). *Sexual States of Mind*, Perthshire, The Clunie Press.

Menzies-Lyth, I. (1960). "A Case in the functioning of Social Systems as a defense against anxiety: a report of a study of a nursing service in a general hospital." *Human Relations*, 13, 95-121.

Miller, G. (2011) *Rendez-vous chez Lacan*, Television Movie (*A Story from Lacan's Practice*, Lacan Online, Video File)

Minuchin, S. (1978). *Psychosomatic Families: Anorexia Nervosa in Context*, Cambridge, MA, Harvard University Press.

Mitchell, M. (1936) *Gone with the Wind*, Macmillan, New York.

Modern Times (1936) Moving Picture, Directed by Charlie Chaplin, United Artists, USA.

Monty Python's Flying Circus (1969-1974) T.V. Series, Directed by Ian McNaughten and John Howard-Davies, BBC, UK.

Morris, D. (1999) *The Naked Ape: A Zoologist's Study of the Human Animal*, New York, Dell

My Big Fat Greek Wedding, 2002, Gold Circle Films, Directed by Joel Zwick, Canada, USA.

Nancy, J-L, (1991). *Inoperative Community*, Minneapolis, MN, University of Minnesota Press.

Obholzer, R., Roberts, A.V. (1994). *The Unconscious at Work*, New York, Routledge.

The Office (2001-2003) T.V. Series, Created by Ricky Gervais and Stephen Merchant, BBC, UK.

Ogden, T. (1993) *The Matrix of the Mind*, New York, Jason Aronson.

Orwell, G. (1950) *1984*, New York, Signet Classics.

_____, (2009), *All Art is Propaganda: Critical Essays*, Ware, Hertfordshire, UK. Wordsworth Publishing.

Owen, W. (2018) *The War Poems of Wilfred Owen*, London, Random House UK.

Parsons, T. (1971). *System of Modern Societies*, Upper Saddle River, NJ, Prentice Hall.

Peanuts (October 2nd, 1950 – February 13th, 2000) Syndicated Comic Strip, Author: Charles M. Schultz, United Feature Syndicate, USA.

Perls, F. (1965). *Gestalt Therapy Verbatim*, Lafayette, CA., Real People Press.

_____, (1973). *The Gestalt Approach and Eyewitness to Therapy*, New York, Bantam.

Perry, W. (1981). "Cognitive and Ethical Growth: The Making of Meaning", in *Arthur W. Chickering and Associates, The Modern American College*, San Francisco, Jossey Bass: 76-116.

Piaget, J., Inhelder, B. (1969). *The Psychology of the Child*, New York, Basic Books.

Piechowski, M. Silverman, L. Cunningham, K. and Falk, R. (1982) *A Comparison of Intellectually Gifted and Artists on Five Dimensions of Mental Functioning*, Paper presented at the American Education Research Association meeting, March 1982, New York.

Polanyi, M. (1974) *Personal Knowledge: Towards a Post-Critical Philosophy*, Chicago and London, University of Chicago Press.

Popper, K. (2013) *The Open Society and its Enemies*, Princeton, Princeton University Press.

Porges, S. (2011) *The Polyvagal Theory:Neurophysiological Foundations of Emotions, Attachment, Communication, and Self-Regulation*,New York, Norton.

Pye, C. (1986) An Ethnography of Mayan Speech to Children, *Working Papers in Child Language*, 30-58, The Child Language Program, University of Kansas.

Quine, W. V. (1970) *The Web of Belief*, New York, Random House.

Rank. O. (1954, 2014). *The Trauma of Birth*, London, Routledge.

Redl, F. (1967). *When We Deal With Children: Selected Writings*, New York, The Free Press.

Reich, W. (1980a). *The Mass Psychology of Fascism*, Farrar, Strauss and Giroux.

_____, (1980b). *Character Analysis*, New York, Farrar, Strauss and Giroux.

Reik, T. (1948) *Listening with the Third Ear: The Inner Experience of a Psychiatrist*, New York, Grove Press.

The Ren and Stimpy Show, 1991-1995, Nickelodeon, Created by John Kricfalusi, USA.

Rice, A.K. (2013). *Learning for Leadership*, London, Routledge.

Rogers, C. (2003) *Client-Centered Therapy,London, Constable and Robinson.*

Roheim, G. (1971) *The Origin and Function of Culture*, New York, Doubleday.

_____, (1974) *Children of the Desert*, New York, Basic Books.

_____, (2010) *Magic and Schizophrenia*, Whitefish, Montana, Kessinger Publishing.

Romanyshyn, R. (1989) *Technology as Symptom and Dream*, London, Routledge.

Rorty, R. (2000). *Philosophy and Social Hope*, New York, Penguin.

_____, (2009). *Philosophy and the Mirror of Nature*, Princeton, NJ, Princeton.

Rosenfeld, H. (1985). *Psychotic States: A Psychoanalytic Approach* (Maresfield Library), London, Karnac.

_____, (1987). *Impasse and Interpretation: Therapeutic and Antitherapeutic Factors in the Psychoanalytic Treatment of Psychotic, Borderline and Neurotic Patients* (The New Library of Psychoanalysis), London, Routledge.

Saha,S. Chant, D. Welham, J. McGrath, J. (2005) A Systematic Review of the Prevalence of Schizophrenia, *PLoS Med.* 2005;2:e141.

Sartre, J.P. (1993). *Being and Nothingness*, New York, Washington Square Press.

_____, (2004). *Critique of Dialectical Reason*, London, Verso.

Scarface, (1983) Universal Pictures, Directed by Brian de Palma, USA.

Shumacher, E. F. (1973) *Small is Beautiful*, Blond and Briggs, London, UK.

Seinfeld (1984-1998) T.V. Series, Created by Larry David and Jerry Seinfeld, Sony Pictures Television, USA.

Searles, H. (1960) *The Non-Human Environment in Normal Development and Schizophrenia*, International Universities Press, New York.

_____, (1979) *Countertransference and Related Subjects,* International Universities Press, New York.

_____, (1986) *Collected Papers on Schizophrenia and Related Subjects,* Routledge, London.

Seligman, M. (1992). *Helplessness: On Depression, Development, and Death* (Series of Books in Psychology), New York, W. H. Freeman and Company.

Sellars, W. and Yeatman, R. (2010) *1066 and All That,* North Yorkshire, Methuen and Co.

Selye, H. (1978). *The Stress of Life,* New York, McGraw Hill.

Seikkula, J. and Arnkil, T. (2006). *Dialogical Meetings in Social Networks,* London, Karnac.

Self, Will ((2017) *Psychogeography,* London, Bloomsbury Publishing.

Semmelhack, D., Ende, L., Hazell, C. (2013). *Group Therapy for Adults with Severe Mental Illness: Adapting the Tavistock Method,* Routledge, New York.

Semmelhack, D., Ende, L., Hazell, C.G., and Freeman, A. (2015). *The Interactive World of Severe Mental Illness: Case Studies in the U.S. Mental Health System,* New York, Routledge.

Seuss, Dr. (1954). *Horton Hears a Who,* New York, Random House Books.

Schumacher, E.F. (2010) *Small is Beautiful: Economics as if People Mattered,* New York, Harper Perennial.

Silkwood, (1983) Moving Picture, Directed by Mike Nichols, ABC Motion Pictures, USA.

The Simpsons, 1989- Present, 20th Century Fox, Created by Matt Groening, USA.

The Sopranos, (1997-2007) HBO Cable Network, Created by David Chase, USA.

Soja, E. (2011) *Postmodern Geographies: The Reassertion of Space In Critical Social Theory*, London, Verso.

2001: A Space Odyssey (1968) Moving Picture, Directed by Stanley Kubrick, Metro-Goldwyn-Mayer, USA.

This is Spinal Tap (1984) Moving Picture, Directed by: Rob Reiner, Embassy Pictures, USA.

Spitz, R. (1965) *The First Year of Life: A Psychoanalytic Study of Normal and Deviant Development of Object Relations*, New York, IUP.

Stern, D. (2000). *The Interpersonal World of the Infant: A View From Psychoanalysis and Developmental Psychology*, New York, Basic Books.

Stevenson, R. L. (1886) *The Strange case of Dr. Jekyll and Mr. Hyde*, Longmans Green and Co. London.

Strathearn, L. (2011) Maternal Neglect: Oxytocin, Dopamine and the Neurobiology of Attachment, *Journal of Neuroendocrinology*, Nov. 23 (11) 1054-1065.

Sullivan, H. (1953). *The Interpersonal Theory of Psychiatry*. Norton Publishing, New York.

Tally, R (2013) *Spatiality*, Routledge, London.

Taylor, F. W. (2016) *The Principles of Scientific Management*, Createspace Publishing, Virginia Beach, VA.

The Terminator (1984) Motion Picture, Dir. James Cameron, Hemdale, USA.

Tesla, N. (2018) *My Inventions: The Autobiography of Nikola Tesla*, Eastford, CT. Martino Fine Books.

Tillich, P. (1952). *The Courage to Be*, New Haven, CT. Yale.

Toffler, A. (1984) *The Third Wave*, New York, Bantam.

Tompkins, S. (1962) *Affect, Imagery, Consciousness, Volume 1*, New York, Springer.

_____ (1963) *Affect, Imagery, Consciousness, Volume 2*, New York, Springer.

_____ (2000) *Affect, Imagery, Consciousness, Volume 3*, New York, Springer.

Trist, E. & Bamforth, K. (1951). *Some social and psychological consequences of the longwall method of coal getting*, in: Human Relations, 4, pp.3-38. p.14.

Trudeau, R. (1993) *Introduction to Graph Theory*, Dover, New York.

Tuckman, B. (1965). Developmental sequence in small groups. *Psychological Bulletin*, Vol 63(6), Jun 1965, 384-399.

Tustin, F. (1972). *Autism and Childhood Psychoses*, London, Hogarth.

Unamuno, M. de (2015). *Tragic Sense of Life*, Hamburg, Tradition.

Vaillant, G. (1998) *Adaptation to Life*, Cambridge, MA. Harvard University Press.

Van der Kolk, B. (2015). *The Body Keeps the Score*, New York, Penguin.

Veblen, T. (2009) *The Theory of the Leisure Class*, Oxford, Oxford University Press.

Volkan, V. (2014). *Psychoanalysis, International Relations, and Diplomacy: A Sourcebook on Large-Group Psychology*, London, Karnac.

Volosinov, V. ((2013) *Freudianism: A Marxist Critique*. London, Verso.

Wampold, B. (2001). *The Great Psychotherapy Debate*. Lawrence Earbaum Associates, Inc.

Watzlawick, P., Bavelas, J. and Jackson, D. (1967*). Pragmatics of Human Communication: A Study of Interactional Patterns, Pathologies, and Paradoxes*, New York, W.W. Norton.

Wells, L. (1985) "The group-as-a-whole perspective and its theoretical roots," in Colman, A.D. and Geller, M.H. (eds) *Group Relations Reader 2*, Washington, DC: A.K. Rice Institute, 109-126

What About Bob? (1991) Motion Picture, Dir. Frank Oz, Touchstone Pictures, USA.

"What Women Want." (2000), Paramount Pictures.

Wings of Desire (1987) Motion Picture, Dir. Wim Wenders, Road Movies, USA.

Winnicott, D. W. (1965). *The Maturational Processes and the Facilitating Environment*, New York, International Universities Press.

_____, (1992) *The Child, the Family and the Outside World*, New York, Perseus.

Woolf, V. (1978). *The Waves*, Arlington Heights, IL, Harvest Books.

_____, (1990). *Mrs Dalloway*, New York, Mariner Books.

Yalom, I. and Leszcz, M. (2005). *The Theory and Practice of Group Psychotherapy*, New York, Basic Books.

Yeats, W. B. (1989) "The Second Coming" in *Collected Poems of W. B. Yeats*,Finneran, R. J.(ed) Macmillan, New York.

Zizek, S. (1993). *Tarrying with the Negative: Kant, Hegel and the Critique of Ideology* (Post Contemporary Interventions), Duke University Press.

_____, (2012). *Enjoy Your Symptom! Jacques Lacan In Hollywood and Out*, New York, Routledge

Printed in the United States
by Baker & Taylor Publisher Services